אם תשאל לשמי למולדתי ולמדינתי ואיזה משפחתי אשיכן תרעמנו

‏ ‏ ‏ ‏

**TOBIAS COHN**

1652-1759

FROM THE FRONTISPIECE OF HIS MA'ASEH TOBIAH

# THE HASKALAH
## Movement in Russia

### JACOB S. RAISIN, Ph.D., D.D.

GENIZAH
EDITIONS
2001

First published by The Jewish Publication Society of America, 1914. This paperback edition released by Genizah Editions, 2001

ISBN 1-59021-155-3
Manufactured in the United States of America

GENIZAH EDITIONS
102 Heritage Avenue
Maple Shade, NJ 08052
genizaheditions@aol.com

Genizah Editions is a registered imprint of Lethe Press

## TO AARON S. RAISIN

*Your name, dear father, will not be found in the following pages, for, like "the waters of the Siloam that run softly," you ever preferred to pursue your useful course in unassuming silence. Yet, as it is your life, devoted entirely to meditating, learning, and teaching, that inspired me in my effort, I dedicate this book to you; and I am happy to know that I thus not only dedicate it to one of the noblest of Maskilim, but at the same time offer you some slight token of the esteem and affection felt for you by*

*Your Son,*

*JACOB S. RAISIN*

# CONTENTS

PAGE

PREFACE ............................................. 11

CHAPTER I. THE PRE-HASKALAH PERIOD ................. 17

CHAPTER II. THE PERIOD OF TRANSITION ................. 53

CHAPTER III. THE DAWN OF HASKALAH ................. 110

CHAPTER IV. CONFLICTS AND CONQUESTS ................. 162

CHAPTER V. RUSSIFICATION, REFORMATION, AND ASSIMILA-

TION ............................................. 222

CHAPTER VI. THE AWAKENING ......................... 268

NOTES ............................................. 305

BIBLIOGRAPHY ......................................... 331

INDEX ............................................. 339

# LIST OF ILLUSTRATIONS

TOBIAS COHN (1652-1759) ............... .......... Frontispiece

ISAAC BÄR LEVINSOHN (1788-1860) ............ facing page 64

MAX LILIENTHAL (1815-1882) ................... " " 120

ALEXANDER ZEDERBAUM (1816-1893) .......... " " 175

PEREZ BEN MOSHEH SMOLENSKIN (1842-1885)... " " 220

MOSES LÖB LILIENBLUM (1843-1910)........... " " 280

# PREFACE

To the lover of mankind the history of the Russo-Jewish renaissance is an encouraging and inspiring phenomenon. Seldom has a people made such rapid strides forward as the Russian Jews. From the melancholy regularity that marked their existence a little more than two generations ago, from the darkness of the Middle Ages in which they were steeped until the time of Alexander II, they emerged suddenly into the life and light of the West, and some of the most intrepid devotees of latter-day culture, both in Europe and in America, have come from among them. Destitute of everything that makes for enlightenment, and under the dominion of a Government which sought to extinguish the few rushlights that scattered the shadows around them, they nevertheless snatched victory from defeat, sloughed off medieval superstition, and, disregarding the Dejanira shirt of modern disabilities, compelled their countrymen to admit more than once that

> Tho' I've belted you and flayed you,
> By the livin' Gawd that made you,
> You're a better man than I am!

Similar movements were started in Germany during the latter part of the eighteenth century, and in Austria, notably Galicia, at the beginning of the nineteenth, but none stirred the mind of the Jews to the same degree as the Haskalah movement in Russia during the last fifty years. In the former, the removal of restrictions soon rendered attempts toward self-emancipation unnecessary on the part of Jews, and the few Maskilim among them, satisfied with the present, devoted themselves to investigating and elucidating the past of their people's history. In Russia the past was all but forgotten on account of the immediate duties of the present. The energy and acquisitiveness that made the Jews of happier and more prosperous lands prominent in every sphere of practical life, were directed toward the realm of thought, and the merciless severity with which the Government excluded them from the enjoyment of things material only increased their ardor for things spiritual and intellectual.

In its wide sense Haskalah denotes enlightenment. Those who strove to enlighten their benighted coreligionists or disseminate European culture among them, were called Maskilim. A careful perusal of this work will reveal the exact ideals these terms embody. For Haskalah was not only

12

progressive, it was also aggressive, militant, sometimes destructive. From the days of Mordecai Günzburg to the time of Asher Ginzberg (Ahad Ha-'Am), it changed its tendencies and motives more than once. Levinsohn, " the father of the Maskilim," was satisfied with removing the ban from secular learning; Gordon wished to see his brethren " Jews at home and men abroad "; Smolenskin dreamed of the rehabilitation of Jews in Palestine; and Ahad Ha-'Am hopes for the spiritual regeneration of his beloved people. Others advocated the levelling of all distinctions between Jews and Gentiles, or the upliftment of mankind in general and Russia in particular. To each of them Haskalah implied different ideals, and through each it promulgated diverse doctrines. To trace these varying phases from an indistinct glimmering in the eighteenth century to the glorious effulgence of the beginning of the twentieth, is the main object of this book.

In pursuance of my end, I have paid particular attention to the causes that retarded or accelerated Russo-Jewish cultural advance. As these causes originate in the social, economic, and political status of the Russian Jew, I frequently portray political events as well as the state of knowledge, belief, art, and morals of the periods under consideration. For this reason also I have marked the boundaries of the Haskalah epochs in correspondence to the dates of the reigns of the several czars, though the correspondence is not always exact.

Essays have been published, on some of the topics treated in these pages, by writers in different languages: in Russian, by Bramson, Klausner, and Morgulis; in Hebrew, by Izgur, Katz, and Klausner; in German, by Maimon, Lilienthal, Wengeroff, and Weissberg; in English, by Lilienthal and Wiener; and in French, by Slouschz. The subject as a whole, however, has not been treated. Should this work stimulate further research, I shall feel amply rewarded. Without prejudice and without partiality, by an honest presentation of facts drawn from what I regard as reliable sources, I have tried to unfold the story of the struggle of five millions of human beings for right living and rational thinking, in the hope of throwing light on the ideals and aspirations and the real character of the largely prejudged and misunderstood Russian Jew.

In conclusion, I wish to express my gratitude and indebtedness to those who encouraged me to proceed with my work after some specimens of it had been published in several Jewish periodicals. espe-

cially to Doctor Solomon Schechter, Rabbi Max
Heller, and Mr. A. S. Freidus, for their courtesy
and assistance while the work was being written.

JACOB S. RAISIN.

E. Las Vegas, N. Mex.,
Thanksgiving Day, 1909.

## CHAPTER I

# THE PRE-HASKALAH PERIOD

## ?-1648

" There is but one key to the present," says Max Müller, " and that is the past." To understand fully the growth and historical development of a people's mind, one must be familiar with the conditions that have shaped its present form. It would seem necessary, therefore, to introduce a description of the Haskalah movement with a rapid survey of the history of the Russo-Polish Jews from the time of their emergence from obscurity up to the middle of the seventeenth century.

Among those who laid the foundations for the study of this almost unexplored department of Jewish history, the settlement of Jews in Russia and their vicissitudes during the dark ages, the most prominent are perhaps Isaac Bär Levinsohn, Abraham Harkavy, and Simon Dubnow. There is much to be said of each of these as writers, scholars, and men. Here they concern us as Russio-Jewish historians. What Linnaeus, Agassiz, and Cuvier did in the field of natural philosophy, they accomplished in their chosen province of Jewish history.[1] Levinsohn was the first to express the opinion that the Russian Jews hailed, not from Germany, as is commonly supposed, but from the banks of the Volga. This hypothesis, corroborated by tradition, Harkavy established as a fact. Originally the vernacular of the Jews of Volhynia, Podolia, and Kiev was Russian and Polish, or, rather, the two being closely allied, Palaeo-Slavonic. The havoc wrought by the Crusades in the Jewish communities of Western Europe caused a constant stream of German Jewish immigrants to pour, since 1090, into the comparatively free countries of the Slavonians. Russo-Poland became the America of the Old World. The Jewish settlers from abroad soon outnumbered the native Jews, and they spread a new language and new customs wherever they established themselves.[2]

Whether the Jews of Russia were originally pagans from the shores of the Black and Caspian Seas, converted to Judaism under the Khazars during the eighth century, or Palestinian exiles subjugated by their Slavonian conquerors and assimilated with them, it is indisputable that they inhabited what we know to-day as Russia long before the

18

Varangian prince Rurik came, at the invitation of
Scythian and Sarmatian savages, to lay the foundation of the Muscovite empire. In Feodosia there is
a synagogue at least a thousand years old. The
Greek inscription on a marble slab, dating back to
80-81 B. C. E., preserved in the Imperial Hermitage
in St. Petersburg, makes it certain that they flourished in the Crimea before the destruction of the
Temple. In a communication to the Russian Geographical Society, M. Pogodin makes the statement,
that there still exist a synagogue and a cemetery in
the Crimea that belong to the pre-Christian era.
Some of the tombstones, bearing Jewish names, and
decorated with the seven-branched Menorah, date
back to 157 B. C. E.; while Chufut-Kale, also known
as the Rock of the Jews (Sela' ha-Yehudim), from
the fortress supposed to have been built there by the
Jews, would prove Jewish settlements to have been
made there during the Babylonian or Persian
captivity.[3]

Though the same antiquity cannot be established
for other Jewish settlements, we know that Kiev,
"the mother of Russian cities," had many Jews
long before the eighth century, who thus antedated
the Russians as citizens. According to Joseph Hakohen they came there from Persia in 690, accord-

ing to Malishevsky in 776. It is certain that their influence was felt as early as the latter part of the tenth century. The Russian Chronicles ascribed to Nestor relate that they endeavored, in 986, to induce Grand Duke Vladimir to accept their religion. They did not succeed as they had succeeded two centuries before with the khan of the Khazars.' Yet the grand duke, who had the greatest influence in introducing and spreading Greek Catholicism, and who is now worshipped as a saint, was always favorably disposed toward them.

There were other places that were inhabited early by Jews. There are traditions to the effect that Jews lived in Poland as early as the ninth century, and under the Boreslavs (992-1278) they are said to have enjoyed considerable privileges, carried on a lively trade, and spread as far as Kiev. Chernigov in Little Russia (the Ukraine), Baku in South Russia (Transcaucasia), Kalisz and Warsaw, Brest and Grodno, in West Russia (Russian Poland), all possess Jewish communities of considerable antiquity. In the townlet Eishishki, near Vilna, a tombstone set in 1171 was still in existence at the end of the last century, and Khelm, Government Kovno, has a synagogue to which tradition ascribes an age of eight hundred years.'

The Jewish population in all these communities was prosperous and respected. Jews were in favor with the Government, enjoyed equal rights with their Gentile neighbors, and were especially prominent as traders and farmers of taxes. Their monoxyla, or one-oared canoes, loaded with silks, furs, and precious metals, issued from the Borysthanes, traversed the Baltic and the Euxine, the Oder and the Bosphorus, the Danube and the Black Sea, and carried on the commerce between the Turks and the Slavonians. They were granted the honorable and lucrative privilege of directing and controlling the mints, and that of putting Hebrew as well as Slavonic inscriptions on their coins.° In the Lithuanian Magna Charta, granted by Vitold in 1388, the Jews of Brest were given many rights, and about a year later those of Grodno were permitted to engage in all pursuits and occupations, and exempted from paying taxes on synagogues and cemeteries. They possessed full jurisdiction in their own affairs. Some were raised to the nobility, notably the Josephovich brothers, Abraham and Michael. Under King Alexander Jagellon, Abraham was assessor of Kovno, alderman of Smolensk, and prefect of Minsk; he was called " sir " (jastrzhembets), was presented with the estates of Voi-

dung, Grinkov, and Troki (1509), and appointed
Secretary of the Treasury in Lithuania (1510).
The other brother, Michael, was made " fiscal agent
to the king." In the eighteenth century, Andrey
Abramovich, of the same family but not of the
Jewish faith, was senator and castellan of Brest-
Litovsk.' They were not unique exceptions. Abraham Shmoilovich of Turisk is spoken of as " honorable sir " in leases of large estates. Affras Rachmailovich and Judah Bogdanovich figure among the
merchant princes of Livonia and Lithuania; and
Francisco Molo, who settled later in Amsterdam,
was financial agent of John III of Poland in 1679.
The influence of the last-named was so great with
the Dutch States-General that the Treaty of Ryswick was concluded with Louis XIV, in 1697,
through his mediation.'

That Russo-Poland should have elected a Jewish
king on two occasions, a certain Abraham Prochovnik in 842 and the famous Saul Wahl' in the
sixteenth century, sounds legendary; but that there
was a Jewish queen, called Esterka, is probable,
and that some Jews attained to political eminence is
beyond reasonable doubt." Records have been discovered concerning two envoys, Saul and Joseph,
who served the Slavonic czar about 960, and an

interesting story is told of two Jewish soldiers, Ephraim Moisievich and Anbal the Jassin, who won the confidence of Prince Andrey Bogolyubsky of Kiev, and afterwards became leaders in a conspiracy against him (1174).[11] Henry, Duke of Anjou, the successor of Sigismud August on the throne of Poland and Lithuania, owed his election mainly to the efforts of Solomon Ashkenazi. Ivan Vassilyevich, too, had many and important relations with Jews, and his favorable attitude towards them is amply proved by the fact that his family physician was the Jew Leo (1490). Throughout his reign he maintained an uninterrupted friendship with Chozi Kokos, a Jew of the Crimea, and he did not hesitate to offer hospitality and protection to Zacharias de Guizolfi, though the latter was not in a position to reciprocate such favors.[12]

In addition there are less prominent individuals who received honors at the hands of their non-Jewish countrymen. Meïr Ashkenazi of Kaffa, in the Crimea, who was slain by pirates on a trip from " Gava to Dakhel," was envoy of the khan of the Tatars to the king of Poland in the sixteenth century. Mention is made of " Jewish Cossacks," who distinguished themselves on the field of battle, and were elevated to the rank of major and colonel.[13]

While the common opinion regarding Jews expressed itself in merry England in such ballads as " The Jewish Dochter," and " Gernutus, the Jew of Venice," many a Little Russian song had the bravery of a Jewish soldier as its burden. In everything save religion the Jews were hardly distinguishable from their neighbors.

There are—writes Cardinal Commendoni, an eye-witness—a great many Jews in these provinces, including Lithuania, who are not, as in other places, regarded with disrespect. They do not maintain themselves miserably by base profits; they are landed proprietors, are engaged in business, and even devote themselves to the study of literature and, above all, to medicine and astronomy; they hold almost everywhere the commission of levying customs duties, are classed among the most honest people, wear no outward mark to distinguish them from the Christians, and are permitted to carry swords and walk about with their arms. In a word they have equal rights with the other citizens.

A similar statement is made by Joseph Delmedigo, who spent many years in Livonia and Lithuania as physician to Prince Radziwill.⁴

In his inimitable manner Gibbon describes the fierce struggle the Greek Catholic Church had to wage before she obtained a foothold in Russia, but he neglects to mention the fact that Judaism no less than paganism was among her formidable oppon-

ents. The contest lasted several centuries, and in
many places it is undecided to this day.[15] The
Khazars, who had become proselytes in the eighth
century, were constantly encroaching upon Russian
Christianity. Buoyant as both were with the vigor
of youth, missionary zeal was at its height among
the two contending religions. Each made war upon
the other. We read that Photius of Constantinople
sent a message of thanks to Archbishop Anthony
of Kertch (858-859) for his efforts to convert the
Jews; that the first Bishop of the Established
Church (1035) was "Lukas, the little Jew" (Luka
Zhidyata), who was appointed to his office by
Yaroslav; and that St. Feodosi Pechersky was fond
of conversing with learned Jews on matters of theology.[16] On the other hand, the efforts of the Jews
were not without success. The baptism of the pious
Olga marks an era in Russian Christianity, the beginning of the " Judaizing heresy," which centuries
of persecution only strengthened. In 1425, Zacharias of Kiev, who is reputed to have " studied
astrology, necromancy, and various other magic
arts," converted the priest Dionis, the Archbishop
Aleksey, and, through the latter, many more clergy-
men of Novgorod, Moscow, and Pskov. Aleksey
became a devout Jew. He called himself Abraham

and his wife Sarah. Yet, strange to say, he retained the favor of the Grand Duke Ivan Vassilyevich, even after the latter's daughter-in-law, Princess Helena, his secretary Theodore Kuritzin, the Archimandrite Sosima, the monk Zacharias, and other persons of note had entered the fold of Judaism through his influence.

The "heresy" spread over many parts of the empire, and the number of its adherents constantly grew. Archbishop Nikk complains that in the very monastery of Moscow there were presumably converted Jews, " who had again begun to practice their old Jewish religion and demoralize the young monks." In Poland, too, proselytism was of frequent occurrence, especially in the fifteenth and sixteenth centuries. The religious tolerance of Casimir IV ( 1434-1502 ) and his immediate successors, and the new doctrines preached by Huss and Luther, which permeated the upper classes of society, rendered the Poles more liberal on the one hand, and on the other the Jews more assertive. We hear of a certain nobleman, George Morschtyn, who married a Jewess, Magdalen, and had his daughter raised in the religion of her mother. In fact, at a time when Jews in Spain assumed the mask of Christianity to escape persecution, Russian and

Polish Christians by birth could choose, with little fear of danger, to lead the Jewish life. It was not till about the eighteenth century that the Government began to resort to the usual methods of eradicating heresy. Katharina Weigel, a lady famous 'for her beauty, who embraced Judaism, was decapitated in Cracow at the instigation of Bishop Peter Gamrat. On the deposition of his wife, Captain Vosnitzin of the Polish navy was put to death by auto-da-fé (July 15, 1738). The eminent " Ger Zedek," Count Valentine Pototzki, less fortunate than his comrade and fellow-convert Zaremba, was burnt at the stake in Vilna (May 24, 1749), and his teacher in the Jewish doctrines, Menahem Mann, was tortured and executed a few months later, at the age of seventy. But these measures proved of little avail. According to Martin Bielski, the noted historian, Jews saved their proselytes from the impending doom by transporting them to Turkey. Many of them sought refuge in Amsterdam. For those who remained behind their new coreligionists provided through collections made for that purpose in Russia and in Germany. To this day these Russian and Polish proselytes adhere steadfastly to their faith, and whether they migrate to America or Palestine to escape the persecution of their countrymen, they seldom, if ever, indulge in the latitudinarianism into which many of longer Jewish lineage fall so readily when removed from old moorings."

That the Russian Jews of the day were not altogether unenlightened, that they not only practiced the Law devoutly, but also studied it diligently, and cultivated the learning of the time as well, we may safely infer from researches recently made. Cyril, or Constantine, " the philosopher," the apostle to the Slavonians, acquired a knowledge of Hebrew while at Kherson, and was probably aided by Jews in his translation of the Bible into Slavonic. Manuscripts of Russo-Jewish commentaries to the Scriptures, written as early as 1094 and 1124, are still preserved in the Vatican and Bodleian libraries, and copyists were doing fairly good work at Azov in 1274.

Jewish scholars frequented celebrated seats of learning in foreign lands. Before the end of the twelfth century traces of them are to be found in France, Italy, and Spain. That in the eleventh century Judah Halevi of Toledo and Nathan of Rome should have been familiar with Russian words cannot but be attributed to their contact with Russian Jews. However, in the case of these two scholars, it may possibly be ascribed to their great erudition or extensive travels. But the many Slavonic expressions occurring in the commentaries of Rashi (1040-1105), and employed by Joseph Caro (ab. 1140), Benjamin of Tudela (ab. 1160), and Isaac of Vienna (ab. 1250), lend color to Harkavy's contention, that Russian was once the vernacular of the Russian Jews, and they also argue in favor of our contention, that these natives of the " land of Canaan "—as the country of the Slavs was then called in Hebrew—came into personal touch with the " lights and leaders " of other Jewish communities. Indeed, Rabbi Moses of Kiev is mentioned as one of the pupils of Jacob Tam, the Tosafist of France (d. 1170), and Asheri, or Rosh, of Spain is reported to have had among his pupils Rabbi Asher and Master (Bahur) Jonathan from Russia. From these peripatetic scholars perhaps came the martyrs of 1270, referred to in the *Memorbuch* of Mayence. It was Rabbi Moses who, while still in Russia, corresponded with Samuel ben Ali, head of the Babylonian Academy, and called the attention of Western scholars to certain Gaonic decisions. Another rabbi, Isaac, or Itshke, of Chernigov, was probably the first Talmudist in England, and his decisions were regarded as authoritative on certain occasions. These and others like them wrote super-commentaries on the commentaries of Rashi and Ibn Ezra, the most popular and profound scholars medieval Jewry produced, and made copies of the works of other authors.[18]

Soon the Russo-Polish Jews established at home what they had been compelled to seek abroad. Hearing of the advantages offered in the great North-East, German Jews flocked thither in such numbers as to dominate and absorb the original Russians and Poles. A new element asserted itself. Names like Ashkenazi, Heilperin, Hurwitz, Landau, Luria, Margolis, Schapiro, Weil, Zarfati, etc., variously spelled, took the place, through intermarriage and by adoption, of the ancient Slavonic nomenclature. The language, manners, modes of thought, and, to a certain extent, even the physiognomy of the earlier settlers, underwent a more or less radical change. In some provinces the conflict lasted longer than in others. To this day not a few Russian Jews would seem to be of Slavonic rather than Semitic extraction. As late as the sixteenth century there was still a demand in certain places for a Russian translation of the Hebrew Book of Common Prayer, and in 1635 Rabbi Meïr Ashkenazi, who came from Frankfort-on-the-Main to study in Lublin, and was retained as rabbi in Mohilev-on-the-Dnieper, had cause to exclaim, " Would to God that our coreligionists all spoke the same language—German." [19] Even Maimon, in the latter half of the eighteenth century, mentions one, by no means an exception, who did not " understand the Jewish language, and made use, therefore, of the Russian." [20] But by the middle of the seventeenth century the amalgamation was almost complete. It resulted in a product entirely new. As the invasion of England by the Normans produced the Anglo-Saxon, so the inundation of Russia by the Germans produced the Slav-Teuton. This is the clue to the study of the Haskalah, as will appear from what follows.

Russo-Poland gradually became the cynosure of the Talmudic world, the " Aksanye shel Torah," the asylum of the Law, whence " enlargement and deliverance " arose for the traditions which the Jews carried with them, through fire and water, during the dreary centuries of their dispersion. It became to Jews what Athens was to ancient Greece, Rome to medieval Christendom, New England to our early colonies. With the invention and importation of the printing-press, the publication and acquisition of the Bible, the Talmud, and most of the important rabbinic works were facilitated. As a consequence, yeshibot, or colleges, for the study of Jewish literature, were founded in almost every community. Their fame reached distant lands. It became a popular saying that " from Kiev shall go forth the Law, and the word of God from Starodub." Horodno, the vulgar pronunciation of Grodno, was construed to mean Har Adonaï, " the Mount of the Lord." A pious rabbi did not hesitate to write to a colleague, " Be it known to the high honor of your glory that is is preferable by far to dwell in the land of the Russ and promote the study of the Torah in Israel than in the land of Israel." ²¹ Especially the part of Poland ultimately swallowed up by Russia was the new Palestine of the Diaspora. Thither flocked all desirous of becoming adepts in the dialectics of the rabbis, " of learning how to swim in the sea of the Talmud." It was there that the voluminous works of Hebrew literature were studied, literally " by day and by night," and the subtleties of the Talmudists were developed to a degree unprecedented in Jewish history. Thither was sent, from the distant Netherlands, the youngest son of Manasseh ben Israel, and he " became mighty in the Talmud and master of four languages." Thither came, from Prague, the after-

wards famous Cabbalist, author, and rabbi, Isaiah
Horowitz (ab. 1555-1630), and there he chose to
remain the rest of his days. Thither also went,
from Frankfort, the above-mentioned Meïr Ashkenazi, who, according to some, was the first author
of note in White Russia.

From everywhere they came " to pour water on
the hands and sit at the feet " of the great ones of
the second Palestine.[22]

For Jewish solidarity was more than a word in
those days. " Sefardim " had not yet learned to
boast of aristocratic lineage, nor " Ashkenazim " to
look down contemptuously upon their Slavonic coreligionists. It was before the removal of civil disabilities from one portion of the Jewish people had
sowed the seed of arrogance toward the other less
favored portion. Honor was accorded to whom it
was due, regardless of the locality in which he happened to have been born. Glückel von Hameln
states in her *Memoirs* that preference was sometimes given to the decisions of the " great ones of
Poland," and mentions with pride that her brother
Shmuel married the daughter of the great Reb
Shulem of Lemberg.[23] With open arms, Amsterdam, Frankfort, Fürth, Königsberg, Metz, Prague,
and other communities renowned for wealth and

learning, welcomed the acute Talmudists of Brest, Grodno, Kovno, Lublin, Minsk, and Vilna, whenever they were willing or compelled to consider a call. The practice of summoning Russo-Polish rabbis to German posts was carried so far that it aroused the displeasure of the Western scholars, and they complained of being slighted.[24]

The reverence for Slavonic learning was strikingly illustrated during the years following the Cossack massacres, when many Russo-Polish rabbis fled for safety to foreign lands. Frankfort, Fürth, Prague, and Vienna successively elected the fugitive Shabbataï Horowitz of Ostrog as their religious guide. David Taz of Vladimir became rabbi of Steinitz in Moravia; Ephraim Hakohen was called to Trebitsch in Moravia and to Ofen in Hungary; David of Lyda, to Mayence and Amsterdam, and Naphtali Kohen, to Frankfort-on-the-Main in 1704, and later to Breslau. No less personages than Isaac Aboab and Saul Morteira welcomed the merchant-Talmudist Moses Rivkes of Vilna when he sought refuge in Amsterdam, and they entrusted to him the task of editing the *Shulhan 'Aruk*, his marginal notes to which, the *Beër ha-Golah*, have ever since been printed with the text. In addition to rabbis, Lithuania and other provinces furnished teachers for the young, melammedim, who exerted considerable influence upon the people among whom they lived. Their opinions, we are told, were highly valued in the choice of rabbis.[25]

It must not be supposed that supremacy in the Talmud was secured at the cost of secular knowledge, or what was then regarded as such. Their familiarity with other branches of study was not inferior to that of the Jews in better-known lands. Not a few of the prominent men united piety with philosophy, and thorough knowledge of the Talmud with mastery of one or more of the sciences of the time. Data on this phase of the subject might have been much more abundant, had not the storm of persecution suddenly swept over the communities, destroying them and their records. What we still possess indicates what may have been lost. The Ukraine was famous for its scholars. Among them was Jehiel Michael of Nemirov, reputed to have been " versed in all the sciences of the world." [26] Several of them were poets and grammarians. Poems of a liturgical character are still extant in which they bemoan their plight or assert their faith hopefully. Such were the poems of Ephraim of Khelm, Joseph of Kobrin, Solomon of Zamoscz, and Shabbataï Kohen. The last, eminent as a Tal-

35

mudist, the author of commentaries on the *Shulhan
'Aruk* approved by the leading rabbis of his generation, is also known as a very trustworthy historian.
His *Megillah 'Afah,* written in classic Hebrew, is
a valuable source of information on the critical
period in which he lived. He won the esteem of the
Polish nobility by his secular attainments. To judge
from his correspondence, he must have been on intimate terms with Vidrich of Leipsic.[27] Of the grammarians, Jacob Zaslaver wrote on the Massorah,
and Shabbataï Sofer was the author of annotations
and treatises.[28] Our taste in poetry and grammar
is no longer the same, but the polemic and apologetic writings of those days, called forth by the
discussions between Rabbanites and Karaites and
by the constant attacks of Christianity, are still
of uncommon interest. Specimens of the former
kind are the polemics of Moses of Shavli, which
caused consternation in the camp of the Karaites.
Of the apologetic writings should be mentioned the
reply, in Polish, of Jacob Nahman of Belzyc to
Martin Chekhovic (Lublin, 1581), and the *Hizzuk
Emunah* of the Karaite Isaac ben Abraham of
Troki. In the latter the weakness of Christianity
and the strength of Judaism are pointed out with
trenchancy never before reached. The work stirred

36

up heated discussions among the various Christian sects, with the tenets of which the author was intimately acquainted. It was translated into Latin (1681, 1705), Yiddish (1717), English (1851), and German (1865, 1873). Voltaire says that all the arguments used by free-thinkers against Christianity were drawn from it.[29]

In philosophy, mathematics, and medicine, the three main branches of medieval knowledge, many Slavonian Jews attained eminence. Devout Karaites as well as diligent Talmudists found secular learning a diversion and a delight. For the lovers of enlightenment Italy, especially Padua, was the centre of attraction, as France and Spain had been before, and Germany, particularly Berlin, became afterwards.[30] Towards the middle of the sixteenth century we find young Delacrut at the University of Bologna, the philosopher and Cabbalist, known for his commentaries to Gikatilla's *Sha'are Orah* (Cracow, 1600) and Ben Avigdor's *Mar'eh ha-Ofanim* (1720), and his translation of Gossuin's *L'image du monde* (Amsterdam, 1733). His famous disciple Mordecai Jaffe (Lebushim) spent ten years in the study of astronomy and mathematics before he occupied the rabbinate of Grodno (1572)[31] At the request of Yom-Tob Lipman Heller, Joseph

37

ben Isaac Levi wrote a commentary on Maimuni's *Moreh Nebukim,* which was published with the former's annotations, *Gibe'at ha-Moreh* (Prague, 1611). Deservedly or not, Eliezer Mann was called " the Hebrew Socrates " ; and many a Maskil in his study of mathematics turned for guidance to Manoah Handel of Brzeszticzka, Volhynia, author and translator of several scientific works, who rendered seven Euclidean propositions into Hebrew.[32]

Polyglots they were compelled to be by force of circumstances. When the exotic Judeo-German finally asserted itself as the vernacular, the language in which they wrote and prayed was still the ancient Hebrew, with which every one was familiar, and commercial intercourse with their Gentile neighbors was hardly feasible without at least a smattering of the local Slavonic dialect. " Look at our brethren in Poland," exclaims Wessely many years later in his address to his countrymen. " They converse with their neighbors in good Polish. . . . What excuse have we for our brogue and jargon ? " He might have had still better cause for complaint, had he been aware that the Yiddish of the Russo-Polish Jews, despite its considerable Slavonic admixture, was purer German than that of his contemporaries in Germany, even as the English of our New England colonies was superior to the Grub Street style prevalent in Dr. Johnson's England, and the Spanish of our Mexican annexations to the Castilian spoken at the time of Coronado. But we are here concerned with their knowledge of foreign languages. We shall refer only to the Hebrew-German-Italian-Latin-French dictionary *Safah Berurah* (Prague, 1660; Amsterdam, 1701) by the eminent Talmudist Nathan Hannover.[33]

In medicine Jews were pre-eminent in the Slavonic countries, as they were everywhere else. They were in great demand as court physicians, though several had to pay with their lives " for having failed to effect cures." Doctor Leo, who was at the court of Moscow in 1490, was mentioned above. Jacob Isaac, the " nobleman of Jerusalem " (Yerosalimska shlyakhta), was attached to the court of Sigismund, where he was held in high esteem. Prince Radziwill's physician was Itshe Nisanovich, and among those in attendance on John Sobieski were Jonas Casal and Abraham Troki, the latter the author of several works on medicine and natural philosophy.[34]

Medieval Jewish physicians were prone to travel, and those of Russo-Poland were no exception. We find them in almost every part of the civilized world, and their number increases with the disappearance of prejudice. Some were noted Talmudists, such as Solomon Luria and Samuel ben Mattathias. Abraham Ashkenazi Apotheker was not only a compounder of herbs but a healer of souls, for the edification of which he wrote his *Elixir of Life* (*Sam Hayyim*, Prague, 1590). To the same class belong Moses Katzenellenbogen and his son Hayyim, who was styled Gaon. In 1657 Hayyim visited Italy. He was welcomed by the prominent Jews of Mantua, Modena, Venice, and Verona, but he preferred to continue the practice of his profession in his home town Lublin.[35] Nor may we omit the names of Stephen von Gaden and Moses Coën, because of their high standing among their colleagues and the honors conferred upon them for their statesmanship. Stephen von Gaden, who with Samuel Collins was physician-in-ordinary to Czar Aleksey Mikhailovich, was instrumental in removing many disabilities from the Jews of Moscow and in the interior of Russia. Moses Coën, in consequence of the Cossack uprising, escaped to Moldavia, and was made court physician by the hospodar Vassile Lupu. But for Coën, Lupu would have been dethroned by those who conspired against him. To his loyalty may probably be attributed the

40

kind treatmentMoldavian Jews later enjoyed at the hands of the prince. Coën also exposed the secret alliance between Russia and Sweden against Turkey, and his advice was sought by the doge of Venice.[36]

The personage who typifies best the enlightened Slavonic Jew of the pre-Haskalah period is Tobias Cohn (1652-1729). He was the son and grandson of physicians, who practiced at Kamenetz-Podolsk and Byelsk, and after 1648 went to Metz. After their father's death, he and his older brother returned to Poland, whence Tobias, in turn, emigrated first to Italy and then to Turkey. In Adrianople he was physician-in-ordinary to five successive sultans. In the history of medicine he is remembered as the discoverer of the *plica polonica,* and as the publisher of a Materia Medica in three languages. To the student of Haskalah he is interesting, because he marks the close of the old and the beginning of the new era. Like the Maskilim of a century or two centuries later, he compiled and edited an encyclopedia in Hebrew, that " knowledge be increased among his coreligionists." His acquaintance with learned works in several ancient and modern languages of which he was master, enabled him to write his magnum opus, *Ma'aseh*

41

*Tobiah,* with tolerable ease. This work is divided into eight parts, devoted respectively to theology, astronomy, pharmacy, hygiene, venereal diseases, botany, cosmography, and chemistry. It is illustrated with several plates, among them the picture of an astrolabe and one of the human body treated as a house. From the numerous editions through which it passed (Venice, 1707, 1715, 1728, 1769), we may conclude that it met with marked success.[37]

To understand the *raison d'être* of the Haskalah movement, it may not be superfluous to cast a glance at the inner social and religious life of the Slavonic Jews during pre-Haskalah times. The labors of the farmer are crowned with success only when nature lends him a helping hand. His soil must be fertile, and blessed with frequent showers. Nor would the Maskilim have accomplished their aim, had the material they found at hand been different from what it was.

The Jews in the land of the Slavonians were fortunate in being regarded as aliens in a country which, as we have seen, they inhabited long before those who claimed to be its possessors by divine right of conquest. If their position was precarious, their sufferings were those of a conquered nation.

42

As the whim and fancy of the reigning prince, knyaz, varied, they were induced one day to settle in the country by the offer of the most flattering privileges, and the next day they were expelled, only to be requested to return again. Now their synagogues and cemeteries were exempt from taxation, now an additional poll-tax or land-tax was levied on every Jew (serebshizna); one day they were allowed to live unhampered by restrictions, then they were prohibited to wear certain garments and ornaments, and commanded to use yellow caps and kerchiefs to distinguish them from the Gentiles (1566).

But all this was the consequence of political subjugation. Judged by the standard of the times, they were veritable freemen, freer than the Huguenots of France and the Puritans of England. They were left unmolested in the administration of their internal affairs, and were permitted to appoint their own judges, enforce their own laws, and support their own institutions. Forming a state within a state, they developed a civilization contrasting strongly with that round about them, and comparing favorably with some of the features of ours of to-day. Slavonic Jewry was divided into four districts, consisting of the more important communities (kahals), to which a number of smaller ones (pri-kahalki) were subservient. These, known as the Jewish Assemblies (zbori zhidovskiye), met at stated intervals. As in our federal Government, the administrative, executive, and legislative departments were kept distinct, and those who presided over them (roshim) were elected annually by ballot. These roshim, or elders, served by turns for periods of one month each. The rabbi of each community was the chief judge, and was assisted by several inferior judges (dayyanim). For matters of importance there were courts of appeal established in Ostrog and Lemberg, the former having jurisdiction over Volhynia and the Ukraine, the latter over the rest of Jewish Russo-Poland. For inter-kahal litigation, there was a supreme court, the Wa'ad Arba' ha-Arazot (the Synod of the Four Countries), which held its sessions during the Lublin fair in winter and the Yaroslav fair in summer. In cases affecting Jews and Gentiles, a decision was given by the *judex Judaeorum*, who held his office by official appointment of the grand duke.

So far their system of self-government appears almost a prototype of our own. The same is true of their municipal administration. The rabbi, who had the deciding vote in case of a dead-lock, stood

44

in the same relation to them as the mayor holds to us, only that his term of office, nominally limited to three years, was actually for life or during good behavior. Yet the power vested in him was only delegated power. A number of selectmen, or aldermen, guarded the rights of the community with the utmost jealousy, and tolerated no innovation, unless previously sanctioned by them. There were also several honorary offices, with a one-year tenure, which none could fill who had not had experience in an inferior position. The chief duties attached to these offices were to appraise the amount of taxation, pay the salaries of the rabbi, his dayyanim, and the teachers of the public schools, provide for the poor, and, above all, intercede with the Government.[38]

Still more interesting and, for our purpose, more important were their public and private institutions of learning. Jews have always been noted for the solicitous care they exercise in the education of the young. The Slavonic Jews surpassed their brethren of other countries in this respect. At times they wrenched the tender bond of parental love in their ardor for knowledge. With a republican form of government they created an aristocracy, not of wealth or of blood, but of intellect. The education

45

of girls was, indeed, neglected. To be able to read her prayers in Hebrew and to write Yiddish was all that was expected of a mother in Israel. It was otherwise with the boys. Every Jew deemed himself in duty bound to educate his son. " Learning is the best merchandise "—*Torah iz die beste sehorah*—was the lesson inculcated from cradle to manhood, the precept followed from manhood to old age. All the lullabies transmitted to us from earliest times indicate the pursuit of knowledge as the highest ambition cherished by mothers for their sons:

Patsché, patsché, little tootsies,
We shall buy us little bootsies;
Little bootsies we shall buy,
To run to heder we shall try;
Torah we'll learn and all good ma'alot (qualities),
On our wedding eve we shall solve sha'alot (ritual problems).[39]

To have a scholarly son or son-in-law was the best passport to the highest circles, a means of rising from the lowliest to the loftiest station in life.

It is no wonder, then, that schools abounded in every community. At the early age of four the child was usually sent to the heder (school; literally, room), where he studied until he was ready for the yeshibah, the higher " seat " of learning.

46

The melammedim, teachers, were graded according to their ability, and the school year consisted of two terms, zemannim, from the first Sabbath after the Holy Days to Passover and from after Passover to Rosh ha-Shanah. The boy's intellectual capacities were steadily, if not systematically, cultivated, sometimes at the expense of his bodily development. It was not unusual for a child of seven or eight to handle a difficult problem in the Talmud, a precocity characteristic to this day of the children hailing from Slavonic countries. Their 'illuyim (prodigies) might furnish ample material for more than one volume of *les enfants célèbres*.

Nor were the children of the poor left to grow up in ignorance. Learning was free, to be had for the asking. More than this, stringent measures were taken that no child be without instruction. Talmud Torahs were founded even in the smallest kehillot (communities), and the students were supplied, not only with books, but also with the necessaries of life. Communal and individual benefactors furnished clothes, and every member (ba'al ha-bayit) had to provide food and lodging for an indigent pupil at least one day of each week. The " Freitisch " (free board) was an inseparable adjunct to every school. Poor young men were not regarded as " beggar students." They were looked upon as earning their living by study, even as teachers by instructing. To pray for the dead or the living in return for their support is a recent innovation, and mostly among other than Slavonic Jews. It is a custom adopted from medieval Christianity, and practiced in England by the poor student, who, in the words of Chaucer,

> Busily 'gan for the souls to pray
> On them that gave him wherewith to scolay.

For a faithful and vivid description of the yeshibot we cannot do better than transcribe the account given in the pages of the little pamphlet *Yeven Mezulah,* in which Nathan Hannover, mentioned above, has left us a reliable history of the Cossack uprisings and the Kulturgeschichte of his own time.

I need bring no proof for the statement that nowhere was the study of the Law so universal as in Russo-Poland. In every community there was a well-paid dean (rosh yeshibah), who, exempt from worry about a livelihood, devoted himself exclusively to teaching and studying by day and by night. In every kahal, many youths, maintained liberally, studied under the guidance of the dean. In turn, they instructed the less advanced, who were also supported by the community. A kahal of fifty [families] had to provide for at least thirty such. They boarded and lodged in the homes of their patrons, and frequently received pocket-money in addition. Thus there was hardly a house in which the Torah was not studied, either by the master of the house, a son, a son-in-law, or a student stranger. They always bore in mind the dictum of Rabba, "He who loves scholars will have scholarly sons; he who welcomes scholars will have scholarly sons-in-law; he who admires scholars will become learned himself." No wonder, then, that every community swarmed with scholars, that out of every fifty of its members at least twenty were far advanced, and had the morenu (*i. e.* bachelor) degree.

The dean was vested with absolute authority. He could punish an offender, whether rich or poor. Everybody respected him, and he often received gifts of money or valuables. In all religious processions he came first. Then followed the students, then the learned, and the rest of the congregation brought up the rear. This veneration for the dean prompted many a youth to imitate his example, and thus our country was rendered full of the knowledge of the Law.

What became of the students when they were graduated? Let us turn once more to Hannover's interesting narrative. The "fairs" of those days were much more than opportunities for barter; they afforded favorable and attractive occasions for other objects. Zaslav and Yaroslav during the summer, Lemberg and Lublin in the winter, were "filled with hundreds of deans and thousands of students," and one who had a marriageable daughter had but to resort thither to have his worries allayed. Therefore, "Jews and Jewesses attended these bazaars in magnificent attire, and [each sea-son] several hundred, sometimes as many as a thousand, alliances were consummated."

That the rabbi, living in a strange land and recalling a glorious past, should have indulged in a bit of exaggeration in his sorrowful retrospect, is not more than natural; and that his picture on the whole is true is proved by similar schools which existed in Russia till recently. The descriptions of these institutions by Smolenskin as well as writers of less repute are graphic and intensely interesting. They constituted a unique world, in which the Jewish youth lived and moved until he reached man's estate. In later years, when Russian Jewry became infected, so to speak, with the Aufklärungs-bacilli, they became the nurseries of the new learning. But in the earlier time, too, a spirit of enlightenment pervaded them. The study of the Talmud fostered in them was regarded both as a religious duty and as a means to an end, the rabbinate. Even in the Middle Ages Aristotle was a favorite with the older students, and Solomon Luria complained that in the prayer books of many of them he had noticed the prayer of Aristotle, for which he blamed the liberal views of Moses Isserles! [40]

Another typically, though not exclusively, Slavonic Jewish institution was the study-hall, or bet ha-midrash. As the synagogues gradually became Schulen (schools), so, by a contrary process, the bet ha-midrash assumed the function of a house of prayer. Its uniqueness it has retained to this day. It was at once a library, a reading-room, and a class-room; yet those who frequented it were bound by the rigorous laws of none of the three. There were no restrictions as to when, or what, or how one should study. It was a place in which originality was admired and research encouraged. As at a Spartan feast, youth and age commingled, men of all ages and diverse attainments exchanged views, and all benefited by mutual contact.

Those whose position precluded devotion to study availed themselves at least of the means for mutual improvement at their disposal. They organized societies for the study of certain branches of Jewish lore, and for the meetings of these societies the busiest spared time and the poorest put aside his work. It was a people composed of scholars and those who maintained scholars, and the schol-ars, in dress and appearance, represented the aris-tocracy, an aristocracy of the intellect."

Such was the pre-Haskalah period. From the meagre data at our disposal we are justified in con-cluding, that, left undisturbed, the Slavonic Jews would have evolved a civilization rivalling, if not surpassing, that of the golden era of the Spanish Jews. But this was not to be. Their onward march met a sudden and terrific check. Hetman Chmielnicki at the head of his savage hordes of Russians and Tatars conquered the Poles, and Jews and Catholics were subjected to the most inhuman treatment. The descendants of those who, in 1090, had escaped the Crusaders fell victims in 1648 to the more cruel Cossacks. About half a million Jews, it is estimated, lost their lives in Chmielnicki's horrible massacres. The few communities remaining were utterly demoralized. The education of the young was neglected, both sacred and secular branches of study were abandoned. And when the storm calmed down, they found themselves deprived of the accumulations of centuries, forced, like Noah after the deluge, but without his means, to start again from the very beginning. Indeed, as Levinsohn remarks, the wonder is that, despite the fiendish persecution they endured, these unfortunates should have preserved a spark of love of knowledge. Yet a little later it was to burst into flame again and bring light and warmth to hearts crushed by " man's inhumanity to man."

[Notes, pp. 305-310.]

## CHAPTER II

# THE PERIOD OF TRANSITION

## 1648-1794

The storm of persecution that had been brewing in the sixteenth century, and which burst in all its fury by the middle of the seventeenth century, was allayed but little by the rivers of blood that streamed over the length and breadth of the Slavonic land. Half a million Jewish victims were not sufficient to satisfy the followers of a religion of love. They only whetted their insatiable appetite. The anarchy among the Gentiles increased the misery of the Jews. The towns fell into the hands of the Lithuanians, Poles, Russians, and Tatars successively, and it was upon the Jews that the hounds of war were let loose at each defeat or conquest. Determined to exterminate each other, they joined forces in exterminating the Jews. When Bratzlav, for instance, was destroyed by the Tatars, in 1479, more than four hundred of its six hundred Jewish citizens were slain. When the city was attacked by the Cos-

sacks in 1569, the greater number of the plundered
and murdered were Jews. The same happened
when Chmielnicki gained the upper hand in Bratzlav in 1648, again when the Russians slaughtered
all the inhabitants in 1664, and when the Tatars
plotted against their victorious enemy, Peter the
Great.[1] Swedish attacks without and popular uprisings within rendered the Polish pan (dubbed among
Jews poriz, rowdy or ruffian) as reckless as he was
irresponsible. The Jew became for him a sponge
to be squeezed for money, and a clown to contribute
to his brutal amusements. The subtle and baneful
influence of the Jesuits succeeded, besides, in introducing religion into politics and making the Jew the
scapegoat for the evils of both. The *Judaeus
infidelis* was the target of abuse and persecution.
It was only the fear that the Government's ex-
chequer might suffer that prevented his being turned
into a veritable slave. His condition, indeed, was
worse than slavery; his life was worth less than a
beast's. It was frequently taken for the mere fun of
it, and with impunity. An overseer once ordered
all Jewish mothers living on the estate to climb to
the tree-tops and leave their little ones below. He
then fired at the children, and when the women fell
from the trees at the horrible sight, he presented

each with a piece of money, and thanked them for the pleasure they had afforded him.[2]

In the cities, though the pan's excesses were bound to be somewhat bridled there, the lot of the Jews was equally gloomy. They were treated like outlaws, were forbidden to engage in all but a few branches of trade or handicraft, or to live with Christians, or employ them as servants. In 1720 they were prohibited to build new synagogues or even repair the old ones. Sometimes the synagogues were locked " by order of . . . " until a stipulated amount of money bought permission to reopen them. We of to-day can hardly imagine what pain a Jew of that time experienced when he hastened to the house of God on one of the great Holy Days only to find its doors closed by the police!

Their status was no better in Lithuania and Great Russia. The accession of Ivan IV, the Terrible (1533-1584), dealt their former comparative prosperity a blow from which it has not recovered to this day. As if to remove the impression of liberalism made by his predecessor and obliterate from memory his amicable relations with Doctor Leo, de Guizolfi, and Chozi Kolos, this monster czar, with the fiendishness of a Caligula, but lacking the accomplishments of his heathen prototype, delighted to invent tortures for inoffensive Jews. He expelled them from Moscow, and deprived them of the right of travel from place to place. During his occupancy of Polotsk he ordered all Jews residing there either to become converts to Greek Catholicism or choose between being drowned in the Dwina and burnt at the stake.

But even the removal of the terrible czar and the dawn of the century of reason and humanitarianism failed to effect a change for the better in the condition of the Slavonic Jews. For a while it appeared as if the Zeitgeist might penetrate even into Russo-Poland, and the Renaissance and the Reformation would not pass over the eastern portion of Europe without beneficent results. In Lithuania Calvinism threatened to oust Catholicism, science and culture began to be pursued, and Jewish and Gentile children attended the same schools. The successors of Ivan IV were men of better breeding, and the praiseworthy attempts of Peter the Great to introduce Western civilization are known to all.[2] But Slavonic soil has never been susceptible to the elevating influences that have transformed the rest of Europe. Every reformatory effort was nipped in the bud. The lot of the Jews accordingly grew from bad to worse. In 1727 they were expelled from the Ukraine and other provinces, and they were recalled, " for the benefit of the citizens," only at the instance of Apostol, the hetman of the very Cossacks that had massacred them in 1648. Baruch Leibov was burned alive in St. Petersburg, in 1738, for having dared " insult the Christian religion by building a synagogue in the village of Zvyerovichi," an offence that was aggravated by the suspicion that he had converted the Russian Captain Vosnitzin to Judaism. The same fate was, in 1783, meted out to Moses, a Jewish tailor, for refusing to accept Christianity, and in 1790 a Jew was quartered in Grodno, though the king had declined to sign his death warrant. In some places Jews had to contribute towards the maintenance of churches, and in Slutsk the law, enacted there in 1766, remains unrevoked to this day. Elizabeta Petrovna did not imitate Ivan III. When she discovered that Sanchez, her physician, was of the Jewish persuasion, she discharged him without notice, after eighteen years of faithful service. Similarly, when the Livonian merchants remonstrated, maintaining that the exclusion of Jews from their fairs was fraught with disastrous consequences to the commerce of the country, she is reported to have replied, " From the enemies of Christ I will not receive even a benefit." '

But worse things were yet to come, the worst since Chmielnicki's massacres. The bitterness of both Poles and Russians against the Jews grew especially intense as the days of the rozbior, the Partition of Poland, drew near (1794). The Poles, forgetting the many examples of loyalty and self-sacrifice shown by Jews in times of peace and war, suspected them of being treacherous and unreliable; while the Russians, though denying the patriotism of their own Jews, persisted in the accusation that Polish Jews spent money lavishly in fomenting rebellion and anarchy. The pupils of the Jesuits found great delight in attacks upon the Jews, which frequently culminated in riot and bloodshed and the payment of money by Jews to Catholic institutions. " What appalling spectacles," exclaims a Christian writer, " must we witness in the capital [Warsaw] on solemn holidays. Students and even adults in noisy mobs assault the Jews, and sometimes beat them with sticks. We have seen a gang waylay a Jew, stop his horses, and strike him till he fell from the wagon. How can we look with indifference on such a survival of barbarism? " The commonest manifestations of hatred and superstition, however, were, as in other countries, the charge that Jews were magicians, using the black art to avenge themselves on their persecutors, and that they used Christian blood for their observance of the Passover. The latter crime, the imputing of which was sternly prohibited by an edict of the liberal Bathòry, in 1576, was so frequently laid at their door, that in the short period of sixty years (1700-1760) not less than twenty such accusations were brought against them, ending each time in the massacre of Jews by infuriated mobs. Even more shocking, if possible, was the frequent extermination of whole communities by the brigand bands known as Haidamacks. They added the " Massacre of Uman " (1768) to the Jewish calendar of misfortunes, the most terrible slaughter, equalled, perhaps, only by that of Nemirov in 1648.[s]

That all this should have left a marked impression on the mentality and intellectuality of the Jews, is little to be wondered at. The marvel is that they should have maintained their superiority over their surroundings, and continued to be a law-abiding and God-fearing people. While among the Russians and Poles the nobles who learned to read or write formed a rare exception, there was hardly one among the Jews, the very lowliest of them, who could not read Hebrew, and even translate it into the vernacular. Maimon tells us that in his early youth he became the family tutor of " a miserable farmer in a still more miserable village," who yet was ambitious of giving his children an education of some kind.

Fortunately for the Jews of those times—says a writer—their civilization was by far superior to that of the Christians. The rabbi, though in no way inferior to the priest mentally, was immeasurably above him morally. The students of the yeshibot, despite their exclusive devotion to the study of the Talmud, yet were better equipped for intellectual work, were of broader minds and better manners, than the pupils of the Jesuits. And the Jewish ba'ale battim, with an education as good as that of the Gentile shlyakhta, had a more ennobling and elevating object in life.[5]

It is remarkable how quickly they recuperated from the blows they received. In 1648 thousands of people were killed, whole communities exterminated, Volhynia, Podolia, and a great part of Lithuania utterly ruined. In 1660, in those very places, we hear again of Jewish settlements, with synagogues and schools and a system of education of the kind described in the preceding chapter, and we hear of the Council of Lithuania struggling to re-establish and cement the shattered foundation of their self-government. Yet all their efforts improved the demoralized condition of the country but little. As always in national crises, the individual was sacrificed to the community, and deprived of the few rights remaining to him. The kehillot became brutally oppressive. There were no longer men of the stamp of Abraham Rapoport, Solomon Luria, Mordecai Jaffe, and Meïr Katz, to put their feet on the neck of tyranny. Without special permission no one could buy or sell, or move from one place to another, or learn a trade or practice a profession. Rabbinism became synonymous with rigorism, the coercion of untold customs became unbearable, and the spirit of Judaism was lost in a heap of innumerable rites. The Jew's every act had to be sanctioned by religion. He knew of the outward world only from the heavy taxes he paid in order to be allowed to exist, and from the bloody riots with which his people was frequently visited.

What could result from such a state of affairs but poverty, material and spiritual, with all the suffering it engenders? Those at the head of the kehillot, being responsible solely to the Government, often had to deliver the full tale of bricks like the Jewish overseers in Egypt, though no straw was given to them. On one occasion Rabbi Mikel of Shkud was arrested because the kahal could not pay the thousand gulden it owed. In 1767, the whole kahal of

Vilna went to Warsaw to protest against intolerable taxation. Such protests were usually of little avail. On the other hand, a few powerful families throve at the expense of their oppressed coreligionists. This aroused a spirit of animosity and a clamor for the abolition of the kahal institution. Jewish autonomy was more and more encroached upon. Rabbinates were bought and sold, and the aid of the Government was invoked in religious controversies. A question regarding the preferable form of prayer was submitted to the decision of Paul I. In 1777, Prince Radziwill decided who should officiate as rabbi in so important a centre of Judaism as Vilna,' and in 1804 the Government issued a " regulation " depriving the kahal of its judicial functions altogether.

What was even more disastrous was the spiritual poverty of the masses. Seldom have the awful warnings of the great lawgiver been fulfilled so literally as during the eighteenth century:

And upon them that remain of you, I will send a faintness into their hearts in the land of their enemies; and the sound of a shaken leaf shall chase them; and they shall flee as fleeing from a sword; and they shall fall, when none pursueth. And they shall fall one upon another, as it were before a sword, when none pursueth: and ye shall have no power to stand before your enemies (Lev. 26: 36-37).

But the Lord shall give thee there a trembling heart, and failing of eyes, and sorrow of mind. And thy life shall hang in doubt before thee; and thou shalt fear day and night, and thou shalt have none assurance of thy life (Deut. 29: 65-66).

Having learned from sad experience that there was no crime their foes were incapable of perpetrating, they gave credence to every rumor as to an established fact. A report that boys and girls were to be prohibited from marrying before a certain age resulted in behalot (panics), during which children of the tenderest ages were united as husband and wife (1754, 1764, 1793). Mysticism became rampant. "Messiah" after "Messiah" "revealed" himself as the one promised to redeem Israel from all his troubles. Love of God began to be tinged with fear of the devil, and incantations to take the place of religious belief. The *Zohar* and works full of superstition, such as the *Kab ha-Yashar, Midrash Talpiyot,* and *Nishmat Hayyim,* the first studied by men, the others by both sexes, but mostly by women, prepared their minds for all sorts of mongrel beliefs. "In no land," says Tobias Cohn, "is the practice of summoning up devils and spirits by means of the Cabbalistic

63

abracadabra so prevalent, and the belief in dreams
and visions so strong, as in Poland." ' All this,
though it strengthened religious fervor in some,
undermined it in others. Sects came into being,
struggled, and, having brought added misery upon
their followers, disappeared. Jewish criminals escaped justice by invoking the power of the Catholic
priesthood and promising to become converted to
Christianity.' And now and then even Talmudists
left the fold, as, for instance, Carl Anton, the Courland pupil of Eybeschütz, who became professor of
Hebrew at Hamsted, and wrote numerous works
on Judaism. Others hoped to win the favor of the
Gentiles by preaching a mixture of Judaism and
Catholicism. In many places, especially in the
Ukraine, the seat of learning that had suffered most
from the ravages of the Cossacks, the state of
morals sank very low, owing to the teaching of
Jacob Querido, the self-proclaimed son of the
pseudo-Messiah Shabbataï Zebi, " that the sinful-
ness of the world can be overcome only by a super-
abundance of sin." This paved the way for the last
of the long list of Messiahs, Jacob (Yankev Leibovich) Frank of Podolia. His experiences, adven-
tures, and hairbreadth escapes, his entire career,
beginning with his return from his travels in Tur-

ISAAC BÄR LEVINSOHN
1788-1860

key, through his conversion to Catholicism (1759), to the day of his death as " Baron von Offenbach," would furnish material for a stirring drama. As if to counteract this demoralizing tendency, a new sect, known as Hasidim, originating in Lithuania and headed by Judah Hasid of Dubno and Hayyim Malak, taught its devotees to hasten the advent of the Messiah by doing penance for the sins of Israel. They were so firmly convinced of the efficacy of fasts and prayers that they went to Jerusalem by hundreds to witness the impending redemption (ab. 1706). But the ascetic Hasidim and the epicurean Frankists were alike doomed to disappear or to be swallowed up by a new Hasidism, combining the teachings and aspirations of both, the sect founded by Israel Baal Shem, or Besht (ab. 1698-1759), and fully developed by Bär of Meseritz and Jacob Joseph of Polonnoy.

Time was when all writers on the subject, usually Maskilim, thought it their duty to cast a stone at Hasidism. They described it as a Chinese wall shutting the Jews in and shutting the world out. It is becoming more and more plainly recognized and admitted, that it was, in reality, an attempt at reform rendered imperative by the tyranny of the kahal, the rigorism of the rabbis, the superciliousness of the learned classes, and the superstition of the masses. Its aim was to bring about a deep psychologic improvement, to change not so much the belief as the believer. It insisted on purity rather than profundity of thought. Unable to remove the galling yoke, it gave strength to its wearers by prohibiting sadness and asceticism, and emphasizing joy and fellowship as important elements in the fabric of its theology.

Hasidism was thus a plant the seeds of which had been sown by the various sects. Like the former Hasidim, or even the Assideans of nearly two thousand years before, their latter-day namesakes rigidly adhered to the laws of Levitical purification, and, to a certain extent, led a communistic life. In addition they accepted, in a modified form, certain customs and beliefs of the Catholic church that had been adopted by the followers of Frank. The prayers to the saints (zaddikim), the conception of faith as the fountain of salvation, even the belief in a trinity consisting of the Godhead, the Shekinah, and the Holy Ghost, these and other exotic doctrines introduced by the Cabbala took root and grew in the vineyard of Hasidism.[10]

The founder of the sect has an interesting history. In his childhood he gave no evidence of future greatness. His education was of a low order, but his feeling heart and sympathetic soul won him the esteem of all that knew him. The woods possessed the same charm for him as for Wordsworth or Whitman. With the latter especially he seems to have much in common. While a child, he absented himself frequently from the narrow and noisy heder, and spent the day in the quiet of the neighboring woods. When he grew up, he accepted the menial position of a school usher. His office was to go from house to house, arouse the sleeping children, dress them, and bring them to heder. But the time soon came when humble and obscure Israel " revealed " himself to the world. Owing to his tact and knowledge of human nature, combined with the conditions of the times, his teachings spread rapidly. He was speedily crowned with the glory of a " good name " (Baal Shem Tob), and in the end he was immortalized.

From such a man we can expect only originality, not profundity. Indeed, his whole life was a protest against the subtleties of the Talmudists and the ceremonies, meaningless to him, which they introduced into Judaism. His object was to remove the petrified rabbinical restrictions (gezerot) and develop the emotional side of the Jew in their stead.

He was primarily a man of action, and had little love for the rabbis, their passivity, world-weariness, and pride of intellect. It is said that when he " overheard the sounds of eager, loud discussions issuing from a rabbinical college, closing his ears with his hands, [he] declared that it was such disputants who delayed the redemption of Israel from captivity." Men like these, who study the Law for the sake of knowing, not of feeling, cannot claim any merit for it. They deserve to be called " Jewish devils." Only he is worthy of reward who is virtuous rather than innocent, who does what he is afraid to do, who, as Jacob Joseph of Polonnoy puts it, " acquires evil thoughts and converts them into holy ones." No asceticism for him. All kinds of human feelings deserve our respect, for it is not the body that feels but the soul, and the soul, " being a part of God on high, cannot possibly have an absolutely bad tendency." Men may not be heresy-hunters and fault-finders, for none is free from heresy and faults himself : the face he brings to the mirror, he finds reflected in it. Yea, even the followers of Abraham possess evil propensities, and noble qualities frequently belong to the disciples of Balaam himself."

These democratic principles put the most igno-

rant Jew in Russia on an equality with the erudite
Lithuanian. No wonder that they obtained such
strong hold on the people of the Ukraine, the province shorn of all its glory. Hasidism invaded
Podolia and Volhynia, swept over Galicia and Hungary, and found adherents even in many a large
community in Western Russia and Prussia. It
brought cheer and happiness in its wake, and rendered the unfortunate Jew forgetful of his misery.
Gottlober maintains that the inspiring melodies of
the Hasidic hymns were largely responsible for the
spread of the movement, even as Moody attributed
the success of his revivals to the singing of Sankey.
For, as Doctor Schechter has it, " the Besht was a
religious revivalist in the best sense, full of burning
faith in his God and his cause; convinced of the
value of his teaching and his truth." [12]

One province there was to which the Besht could
not penetrate, at least not without a long siege and
great losses. In Lithuania the inroads of Hasidism
were strenuously opposed, and its advance disputed
step by step. The Lithuanian Jews, to whom the
Talmud was as dear as ever, could not countenance
a movement sprung, as they believed, from the seed
sown by Shabbataï Zebi, an opponent of the Talmud, and by Jacob Frank, at whose instigation the

69

Bishop of Kamenetz ordered the Talmud to be publicly burnt.[13]

The opponents (Mitnaggedim) of Hasidism were headed by a leader who was as typical an exponent of the cause he espoused as the Besht was of his. Among the students of Jewish literature since the close of the Talmud, few have surpassed, or even equalled, Elijah of Vilna (1720-1797). Not inappropriately he was called Gaon and Hasid, for in mental and moral attainments he was unique in his generation. As the Besht was noted in his early life for dulness and indifference, so Elijah was remarkable for diligence and versatility. His life, like the Besht's, became the nucleus of many wonderful tales, which his biographer narrates with painstaking exactness. They present the picture of a man diametrically different from Israel Baal Shem Tob. Every year, we are told, added to the marvellous development of the young intellectual giant. When he was six years old, none but Rabbi Moses Margolioth, the renowned Talmudist and author, was competent enough to teach him. At seven, he worsted the chief rabbi of his native city in a Talmudic discussion. At nine, there was nothing in Jewish literature with which he was not familiar, and he turned to other studies to satisfy his craving for knowledge. And at thirteen, he was acknowledged by his fellows as the greatest of Talmudists.[14] He had neither guide nor teacher. All unaided he discovered the path of truth. He held neither a rabbinical nor any other public office. He was as retiring as the Besht was aggressive. Nevertheless his word was law, and his influence immense. The centenary of his death (1897) was celebrated among all classes with the solemnity which the memories of " men of God " inspire.[15]

Now, this Gaon of Vilna, or Hagra, was perhaps no less dissatisfied with prevailing conditions than the Besht, but his remedy for them was as different as the two personalities were unlike. He did not desire to abolish the Talmud, but rather to render it more attractive, by making its acquisition easier and putting its study on a scientific basis. Even in Lithuania, the citadel of the Talmud, the development of Talmudic learning had been hampered. In accordance with a Talmudic principle, mankind is continually degenerating, not only physically, but morally and mentally as well. It holds that if " the ancients were angels, we are mere men; if they were but men, we are asses." This high regard for antiquity produced a belief in the infallibility of the rabbis on the part of the

71

Mitnaggedim, similar to that in their zaddikim by the Hasidim. No scholar of a later generation dared disagree with the statement of a rabbi of a previous generation. But as authorities sometimes conflict with each other, the Talmudists regarded it their duty to reconcile them or to prove, in the words of the ancient sages, that " these as well as those are the words of the living God." Similarly, the popes declared that, despite their contradictions, the Biblical translations of Sixtus V and Clement VIII were both correct.

It is true that Lithuanian Talmudists were not always the slaves of authority which they ultimately became. A study of the works of the early Slavonian rabbis, before and after Rabbi Polack, shows that they were free from unhealthy awe of their predecessors, and sometimes were audaciously independent. Neither Solomon Luria (Maharshal), Samuel Edels (Maharsha), or Meïr Lublin (Maharam) refrained from criticising and amending whenever they deemed it necessary. But in the course of time the casuistic method, originally a mere pastime, became the approved method of study, and produced what is known as pilpul. Scholars wasted days and nights in heaping Ossa upon Pelion, in reconciling difficulties which no logic could harmonize. Here the Gaon found the first and most urgent need for reform. The Talmudists, he declared, were not infallible. Every one may interpret the Mishnah in accordance with reason, even if the interpretation be not in keeping with the traditional meaning as construed by the Amoraim.[16]

His views on religion were equally liberal. The same process of reasoning which, spun out to its logical conclusion, led to pilpul in the schools, produced, when turned into the channel of religion, the over-piety culminating in the *Shulhan 'Aruk*. This remarkable book, with the euphonious name *The Ready Table*, prescribed enough regulations to keep one busy from early morning till late at night. The Jews found themselves bound hand and foot by ceremonial trammels and weighted down by a burden of innumerable customs. The spirit of freedom that had animated Slavonian Judaism during the Middle Ages had fled. The breadth of view that had marked the decision of many of its rabbis was gone.[17] Judaism was a mere mummy of its former self. Here, too, the Gaon came to the rescue. Rightly or wrongly, he " established the importance of Minhagim [religious ceremonies] according to their antiquity or primitivism, regarding

those which have originated since the codification of
the *Shulhan 'Aruk* as not binding at all; those which
have been adopted since the Talmudic period to be
subject to change by common consent; while those
of the Bible and in the Talmud were to him funda-
mental and unalterable." [18]

But the Gaon's influence on the Haskalah movement by far surpassed his influence on the study of
the Talmud or on the ceremonials of the synagogue.
Many, in point of fact, regard him as the originator
of the movement. As he was the first to oppose the
authority of the Talmudists, so he was the first to
inveigh against the educational system among the
Jews of his day and country. The mania for distinction in rabbinical learning plunged the child
into the mazes of Talmudic casuistry as soon as he
could read; frequently he had not read the Bible or
studied the rudiments of grammar. The Gaon
insisted that every one should first master the
twenty-four books of the Bible, their etymology,
prosody, and syntax, then the six divisions of the
Mishnah with the important commentaries and the
suggested emendations, and finally the Talmud in
general, without wasting much time on pilpul, which
brings no practical result. " These few lines," says
a writer, " contain a more thorough course of study

than Wessely suggested in his *Words of Peace and Truth*. Though they did not entirely change the system in vogue—for great is the power of habit—they produced a wholesome effect, which was visible in a short time among the people." Furthermore, the Gaon exhorted the Talmudists to study secular science, since, "if one is ignorant of the other sciences, one is a hundredfold more ignorant of the sciences of the Torah, for the two are inseparably connected." He set the example by writing, not only on the most important Hebrew books, Biblical, Talmudic, and Cabbalistic, but also on algebra, geometry, trigonometry, astronomy, and grammar." And his example served as an impetus and encouragement to the Maskilim in spreading knowledge among their coreligionists.

Such was the man who led the crusade against the converts to Hasidism. But even he could not stem the current. In their despair, the Lithuanian Jews turned to their coreligionists in Germany, and implored their assistance in eradicating, or at least suppressing, the threatened invasion. The great learning and literary ability of the " divine philosopher, Rabbi Moses ben Menahem " (Mendelssohn, 1729-1786), were appealed to for help. Not a stone was left unturned to crush the new sect (kat), so called. Volumes of the *Toledot Ya'akob Yosef,* in which Rabbi Jacob Joseph of Polonnoy set forth the principles of the Besht, were burnt in the market-place in Vilna. Intermarriage, social intercourse of any kind, was prohibited between Hasidim and Mitnaggedim. In Vilna, Grodno, Brest, Slutsk, Minsk, Pinsk, etc., the ban was hurled against the dissenters by the most prominent rabbis. Israel was divided into two hostile camps.[20] But soon everything was changed. Hasidim and Mitnaggedim discovered that while they were fighting each other, a common enemy was undermining the ground on which they stood. The Haskalah was steadily drawing recruits from both, and it threatened ultimately to become more dangerous to both than they were to each other.

From the South had come the impulse of religious revivalism through the followers of the Besht, and the North was showing signs of awakening through the reforms of the Gaon. At the same time a ray of enlightenment from the West pierced through the night. To make the regeneration of Slavonic Judaism complete, the element of estheticism had to be added to emotionalism and reason. From the warm South came Besht, from the studious North Hagra, and Rambman (Mendelssohn)

76

made his appearance from the enlightened West. The triumvirate was complete.

Not that Mendelssohn ever visited or resided in Russo-Poland. But the gentle, cultured little savant of Berlin, with whose lips, Carlyle tells us, Socrates spoke like Socrates in German as in no other modern language, " for his own character was Socratic," was at no period of his life wholly cut off from influencing Slavonic Jews and from being influenced by them. As a lad Mendelssohn was instructed by Israel Moses Halevi of Zamoscz (ab. 1700-1772). This teacher of his, who is credited with several inventions, and of whom Lessing says, in a letter to Mendelssohn, that he was " one of the first to arouse a love for science in the hearts of Jews," imbued him with love for philosophy. When Mendelssohn emerged from obscurity, and, despite ill-health and ignorance, attained culture and breeding, his associate, who was with him the most important factor in German Haskalah, was the renowned Naphtali, or Hartwig, Wessely, whose grandfather Joseph Reis had been among the fugitives from the Cossack massacres in 1648. And when he became famous, and took his place among the greatest of his age, he still sought diversion and instruction among the Slavonian Jews, and boasted of being a descendant of one of them, Moses Isserles of Cracow. As formerly with the Talmud, the Haskalah seemed, at the time of Mendelssohn, to be moving from the East westward, through the agency of the Slavonic Jews pouring perennially into Germany. Positions, from the lowly melammed's to the honorable chief rabbi's in prominent communities, were filled almost exclusively by them. The cause of Judaism seems to have been entrusted to them. Ezekiel Landau, whose tactful intercession helped greatly to establish peace between the Emden-Eybeschütz factions, was rabbi of Prague for almost forty years (1755-1793); the equally prominent, but at first somewhat less liberal Phinehas Horowitz was rabbi and dean in Frankfort-on-the-Main for over thirty years (1771-1805); his brother Shmelke, regarded as a saint, was chief rabbi of Moravia (1775). Another Horwitz, Aaron Halevi, was rabbi of Berlin, one of those who favored Mendelssohn's translation of the Pentateuch; while the cultured and profound Tadmudist Raphael Hakohen, whose grandson, Gabriel Riesser, became the greatest champion of Jewish emancipation Germany has yet produced, was offered the rabbinate of Berlin (1771). He declined the post, and finally became chief rabbi

78

(1776-1803) of the united congregations of Altona, Hamburg, and Wandsbeck. It is also re-
corded that Samuel ben Avigdor, the last rabbi of
Vilna, held the rabbinate of Königsberg,[21] and there
certainly must have been many more who, because
of their inferior positions, cannot be so easily traced.
Besides, Germany, as we have seen, was the common fatherland of the greater part of both Slavonic
and Teutonic Jews. It never remained a *terra
incognita* to the former for any length of time. Its
proximity to Russia, the business relations between
the Jews of the two countries, intermarriage, and,
with a few insignificant exceptions, the identity of
language, made the Jews of both countries come
into closer contact than was possible with any other
Jews. For the studious, Germany possessed the
attraction which the " land of universities " exerts
upon seekers after knowledge the world over. To
whom, indeed, could the profound and abstruse
speculations of Leibnitz and Kant make a stronger
appeal than to the Jew who had been initiated into
metaphysical abstractions from his very childhood?
It is no wonder, then, that immigration from Russo-
Poland into Germany was constantly on the increase, until, under Alexander II, the advancement
of Russian civilization put a stop in a measure to

these roamings, to be resumed under Alexander III and Nicholas II.

The Russo-Polish youth, therefore, found himself quite at home in the country of Mendelssohn, and thither, in case of necessity, he would go. In the eleventh century Jews had gone from Germany to Poland. In the eighteenth they retraced their steps from Poland to Germany. Outnumbering by far those who went there from choice or by invitation, were those compelled to go in search of a livelihood. " When I reached the age of twenty, peaceful and comfortable in my father's house, I began to hope that henceforth I should pursue my studies uninterrupted. But all at once my father lost his fortune, and I was forced to go somewhere to provide for myself. So I became a melammed in Berlin." This piece of autobiography in the preface to a Talmudic treatise by Reuben of Zamoscz might have been written by many others, too. But there were also the goodly number led thither by thirst for knowledge, whose remarkable abilities attracted the admiration of Jew and Gentile alike. Wessely the poet and Linda the mathematician more than once expressed surprise at the amount of learning many of the poor immigrants were found to possess.[22]

Among these immigrants were two who may justly be regarded as the conducting medium through which the Haskalah currents were transmitted from Germany to Russo-Poland: Solomon Dubno, the indefatigable laborer in the province of Jewish science, and Solomon Maimon, the brilliant but unfortunate philosopher, both of them teachers in the house of Mendelssohn.

Solomon Dubno (1738-1813) was all his life a bee in search of flowers, to turn their sweetness into honey. Having exhausted the knowledge of his Volhynian instructors, he went to Galicia, where he became proficient in Hebrew grammar and Biblical exegesis. Thence, attracted by its rich collection of books, he left for Amsterdam, where he spent five years in study and research. Finally he settled in Berlin, and earned a livelihood by teaching among others the children of Mendelssohn. The gentle disposition and profound learning of the Polish emigrant made a favorable impression on the Berlin sage, who invited him to participate in his translation of the Bible, which revolutionized the Judaism of the nineteenth century more than the Septuagint that of the first century. The result was the *Biur* (commentary), which he, together with his countryman, Aaron Yaroslav, also a

6                      81

teacher, wrote on several books of the Bible. Comparatively few of Dubno's works have been published, but judging from such as are known we may safely pronounce him a master of the Massorah and a scholar of unusual attainments. Of his poems Delitzsch says that they are " in the truest sense Hebrew in expression, Biblical in imagery and subject-matter, medieval in rhyme and rhythm, and in general genuinely Jewish in manner of treatment," —laudation which this exacting critic bestowed on no other Hebrew poet of his time. It was mainly through the endeavors of Dubno that Mendelssohn's Pentateuch, later regarded with suspicion, was everywhere bought and studied eagerly.[23]

One better known to the outside world than Dubno, and who has engraved his name forever on the history of theology and philosophy, was Solomon Maimon (Nieszvicz, Lithuania, 1754—Niedersiegersdorf, Silesia, 1800). In his famous autobiography is mirrored the lot of hundreds of his countrymen who, like him, left their homes and hearths, their nearest and dearest, and led a wretched and miserable existence, all because they were anxious to be *ma'amike be-hakmah* ("delvers in knowledge"), as he himself might have said, and avail themselves of the opportunities for acquiring the truth and wisdom unattainable in their own land.

But Maimon was doomed to suffer abroad even more than at home. He was one of those unfortunates whose sufferings are regarded as well-deserved. His exceptional ability was never to develop to its fullest capacity. Great injustice has been done to him, not only by the rabid orthodox, who denied him a grave in their cemetery, but even by the enlightened historian Graetz. Fortunately he left behind him his *Lebensgeschichte,* among the best of its kind in German literature, in which, with the frankness of a Rousseau, he described the events of his short and checkered career.[24]

From this admirable work, in which he neither hides his follies nor flaunts his talents, we learn that Maimon possessed rare virtues. His sympathy for the poor, his ready helpfulness even at the sacrifice of himself, rendered him as uncommon in moral action as in philosophic speculation. To the English reader a striking parallelism suggests itself between him and his contemporary Oliver Goldsmith. Both were afflicted with generosity above their fortunes; both had a " knack at hoping," which led frequently to their undoing; neither could subscribe easily to the " decent formalities of rigid virtue "; and, as of the latter we may also say of the former, in the language of a reviewer, " He had lights and shadows, virtues and foibles—vices you cannot call them, be you never so unkind."

As Goldsmith came to London, so came Maimon to Berlin, " without friends, recommendation, money, or impudence." His only luggage was two manuscripts: a commentary on the works of Maimuni, whose name he had adopted, and to whom he paid divine reverence; and a treatise in which he attempted to rationalize the recondite doctrines of the Cabbala, and which he always kept by him " as a monument of the struggle of the human mind after perfection in spite of all hindrances which were put in its way." The little bundle, which, to the zealot Jewish elders of that community, seemed sufficient indication that Maimon was tainted with heresy, and that his intentions were to devote himself to the study of science and philosophy, proved a great impediment to entering Berlin; and when, after a long, incredible struggle, he was finally admitted, he found himself incapable of earning a livelihood. In his childlike naïveté he was betrayed by the very persons upon whom he relied most. All this could not deaden his love for knowledge and truth. By chance he obtained Wolff's *Meta-*

*physics,* and this marked a new epoch in his life. " Not only the sublime science in itself," says he, " but also the order and mathematical method of the celebrated author, the precision of his explanations, the exactness of his reasoning, and the scientific arrangement of his expositions—all this kindled a new light in my mind."

So profound a thinker could not for long be a mere pupil. Wolff's argument *a posteriori* for the existence of God, in accordance with his philosophic hobby, the " principle of sufficient reason," displeased him wholly. A Hebrew letter to Mendelssohn, in which he shook the foundation of the *Metaphysics* by means of his irrefutable ontology, won him the admiration of the Berlin sage, who invited him to become his daily guest.

Maimon's intellect unfolded from day to day, until, some time afterwards, he astonished the philosophic world by his great work, *Die Transcendentale Philosophie* (Berlin, 1790), in reference to which Kant wrote to his beloved disciple Marcus Herz: " A mere glance at it enabled me to recognize its merits, and showed me, that not only had none of my opponents understood me and the main problem so well, but very few could claim so much penetration as Herr Maimon in profound inquiries

85

of this sort." He demolished the prevalent Leib-
nitzo-Wolffian system in it, and proved that even the
Kantian theory, though irrefutable from a dog-
matic point of view, is exposed to severe attacks
from the skeptic's point of view.

Thenceforth he became a leading figure in philosophic controversy. In 1793 he published *Ueber
die Progresse der Philosophie;* in 1794, *Versuch
einer neuen Logik,* and *Die Kategorien des Aris-
toteles,* and, three years later, *Kritische Untersuch-
ungen über den menschlichen Geist* (Berlin, 1797),
wherein he originated a speculative, monistic ideal-
ism, which pervaded not only philosophy, but all
sciences during the first half of the nineteenth century, the system by which Fichte, Schelling, and
Hegel were influenced. According to Bernfeld,
he was the greatest Jewish philosopher since the
time of Spinoza, with whose depth of reasoning he
combined an ease and straightforwardness of illustration characteristic of Benjamin Franklin.[25]

With all this he remained an ardent lover of the
Talmud to the last. In fact, his philosophy is dis-
tinctively Jewish. Like Spinoza, he exhibited the
effects of the Cabbala and of rabbinic speculation,
with which he had been familiar from childhood.
The honor of the Talmudic sages was always dear

to him, and he never mentioned them without expressing profound respect. Persecuted though he was by his German coreligionists, he never bore them a grudge. As a man he loved them as brothers, but as a philosopher he could not subscribe to their views implicitly. But for friends and benefactors his affection was unusually strong. With what love he talks of Mendelssohn in the chapter dedicated to him in his autobiography, even though " he could not explain the persistency of Mendelssohn and the Wolffians generally in adhering to their system, except as a political dodge, and a piece of hypocrisy, by which they studiously endeavored to descend to the mode of thinking common to the popular mind! " His devotion to his wife was not diminished even after he had been compelled to divorce her because of his supposed heretical proclivities. " When the subject [of his divorce] came up in conversation, it was easy," says his biographer,[26] " to read in his face the deep sorrow he felt: his liveliness then faded away sensibly. By and by he would become perfectly silent, was incapable of further entertainment, and went home earlier than usual." Of his Russo-Polish brethren he speaks in the highest terms. He cannot bestow too much praise on their care for the poor and the sick, and he always hoped once more to see his native land, to whose king he dedicated his *Transcendental Philosophy.* " For," says he, " the Polish Jews are, indeed, for the most part not enlightened by science; their manners and way of life are still rude, but they are loyal to the religion of their fathers and to the laws of their country." [27]

It is because I regard him as the greatest Maskil of his time that I have dwelt on Maimon at such length. Mendelssohn's philosophy, if he had an original system, has long since passed into oblivion; Maimon's will be studied as long as Spinoza, Leibnitz, and Kant are in vogue. His importance to us does not lie in the circumstance that his autobiography—" that wonderful bit of Autobiography," as George Eliot speaks of it, or " that curious and rare book," as Dean Milman calls it—and the pictures drawn of him by Berthold Auerbach and Israel Zangwill [28] have made him the hero of some of the world's best biographies and novels. Over and above this, he is the prototype of his unfortunate countrymen during the days of transition. He embodied the aspiration, courage, and disappointments of them all, and if, as Carlyle said, " the history of the world is the history of its great men," Maimon's life should be studied by all interested in the Kulturkampf of the Russo-Polish and of the German Jews in the eighteenth century.

What could he not have accomplished, he to whom Kant and Goethe, Schiller and Körner paid tributes of unstinted praise, had he not been doomed to suffer and to starve. Only at the last moment, before he was silenced forever, was he able to say, *Ich bin ruhig* ("I am at peace"). Yet, in spite of the difficulties and impediments besetting him at every step, his promise of greatness and usefulness was not belied. In the Introduction to his commentary on Maimuni's *Guide to the Perplexed* (*Gibe'at ha-Moreh*), in which he attempted to reconcile his master's system with that of modern philosophy— even as the master had tried to reconcile Judaism with Aristotelianism—he gave a brief sketch of the development of modern thought. This part of his work was assiduously studied by his compatriots. Among his unpublished writings was found a work on mathematical physics, *Ta'alumot Hokmah,* and in his Talmudic treatise, *Heshek Shelomoh,* he inserted a dissertation, *Ma'aseh Hosheb,* on arithmetic, like a skilful physician putting a healing, though to some it may appear a repelling, balm into a delicious, attractive capsule.

89

The story of Maimon, as I have said, is the story
of many of the peripatetic apostles of Haskalah,
and his experience was more or less also theirs.
Issachar Falkensohn Behr (or Bär Falkensohn,
1746-1796?), without funds, friends, or rudimentary knowledge of the subjects necessary for
admission into a public school, left his native city
of Zamoscz with the determination to enter the
university of "Little Berlin," as Königsberg was
called. Too poor to carry out his plan, he tramped
to Berlin. Through the influence of his relatives
and countrymen, Israel Moses Halevi and Daniel
Jaffe, he was introduced to Mendelssohn, and was
enabled to devote himself systematically to the
study of German, the alphabet of which he had
learned from Wolff's treatise on mathematics, and
to French, Latin, physics, philosophy, and medicine.
In a very short time he mastered them all, especially German. His *Gedichte eines polnischen
Juden* (Mitau and Leipsic, 1772) caused no little
stir among the poets. Lessing and Goethe, close
observers of symptoms of enlightenment among the
Jews, expressed themselves differently as to the real
merit of the collection; but both concurred with
Boie, who, writing to Knebel, the friend of Goethe,
remarked concerning them, " You are right; the

Jewish nation promises much after it is once awakened." [29]

For one reason or another we find that some Slavonic Jewish youths preferred other places to Berlin for the pursuit of their studies. Such were Benjamin Wolf Günzberg and Jacob Liboschüts. The former was probably the only Jew at the Göttingen University. It was from there that he inquired of Jacob Emden " whether it was permissible to dissect on the Sabbath," and his thesis for the doctor's degree was *De medica ex Talmudicis illustrata* (Göttingen, 1743). [30] Liboschüts studied at the University of Halle. After graduation, finding that as a Jew he could not settle in St. Petersburg, he established himself in Vilna, where he became celebrated as a diplomat, philanthropist, and, more especially, expert physician. When Professor Frank was asked who would take care of the public health in his absence, he is reported to have said, *Deus et Judaeus,* " God and the Jew " [Liboschüts]!

In their deep-rooted love for learning, they sometimes ventured even beyond the German boundaries, into countries whose language and customs had little in common with theirs. Padua continued to be the resort of Russo-Polish Jews that it had been before 1648. Moses Hayyim Luzzatto found an ardent admirer and zealous propagandist of his principles in the young medical student Jekuthiel Gordon (ab. 1729), who wrote concerning his master to friends in Vienna and Vilna.<sup>31</sup> Judah Halevi Hurwitz (d. 1797), whose work *Ammude Bet Yehudah* (Amsterdam, 1765) was highly recommended by Mendelssohn and Wessely, was a graduate of the same famous institution. In addition to his medical and philosophic attainments, he wrote a number of poems, and he was among the first to translate fables from German into Hebrew.<sup>32</sup>

The story of Zalkind Hurwitz (1740-1812), " le fameux," as he was called by a French writer, is interesting. Starting, as usual, by going to Berlin, and succeeding, as usual, in gaining the friendship of Mendelssohn, he then visited Nancy, Metz, and Strasburg, and finally settled in Paris. Like Doctor Behr, he had to resort to peddling as a means for a livelihood. The rudiments of French he acquired from any book he chanced to obtain. Nevertheless, he soon became proficient in the language of his adopted country, and wrote his excellent *Apologie des juifs*, which, crowned by the Academy of Metz and quoted by Mirabeau, was largely instrumental in removing the disabilities of the Jews in France.

Clermont-Tonnerre, the advocate of Jewish emancipation, said of him, *Le juif polonais seul avait parlé en philosophe.* He was suggested as a member of the Sanhedrin convoked by Napoleon in 1807. Though for some reason he never enjoyed the honor of membership in it, he was, nevertheless, the ruling spirit in the august assembly, and later generations have paid him the homage he deserves.[33]

Where Hurwitz failed, another of his countrymen was to succeed. Judah Litvack (1776-1836) removed from Berlin to Amsterdam, became prominent among the Dutch mathematicians, and wrote a Dutch work, *Verhandeling over de Profgetallen Gen. ii* (Amsterdam, 1817), which appeared in a second edition four years after the first. The author was elected a member of the Mathesis Artium Genetrix Society, and appointed one of the deputation sent to the Sanhedrin (February 12, 1807), before which he delivered a discourse in the German language.

The " distant isles of the sea," the British Islands, Russo-Polish Jews seem to have frequented ever since the Restoration, probably contemporaneously with the settlement of the Spanish Jews. The famous mystic Hayyim Samuel Jacob Falk, one of the many Baal-Shems who flourished in

Podolia at the beginning of the eighteenth century, settled in London before 1750, and became the subject of many wonder stories. Sussman Shesnovzi, apparently a countryman of his, describes him, in a letter to Jacob Emden, as " standing alone in his generation by reason of his knowledge of holy mysteries." That this was the opinion of many and prominent personages may be inferred from the fact that among his callers were such distinguished visitors as the Marchese de Crona, Baron de Neuhoff, Prince Czartorisky, and the Duke of Orleans. The confidence of such as these brought Falk a considerable fortune, a large part of which he bequeathed to a charity fund, the interest of which the overseers of the United Synagogue still distribute annually among the poor.[34] Shortly before " Doctor " Falk's death (1782), there settled in London Phinehas Phillips of Krotoschin, the founder of the Phillips family, which has furnished two Lord Mayors to the city of London.

It was not merely because of its business facilities that England appealed to the Slavonic Jews. Baruch Shklover, or Schick (1740-1812), went thither to study medicine, and it was from English literature that he selected the material for his *Keneh ha-Middah* (Prague, 1784; Shklov, 1793), on trigonometry. It would appear that the first Hebrew book, *Toledot Ya'akob*, printed for a Jew in England, was, as the name of the author, Eisenstadt, suggests, that of a Slavonic Jew. Although a silversmith by profession, Israel Lyons (d. 1770) was appointed teacher of Hebrew at the University of Cambridge. He acquired repute as a Hebrew scholar, and published, in 1757, the *Scholar's Instructor, or Hebrew Grammar* (4th ed., 1823), and in 1768 a treatise printed by the Cambridge Press, *Observations and Inquiries Relating to Various Parts of Scripture History.* In the same chosen field labored Hyman Hurwitz (1770-1844), the friend of Coleridge, who founded the Highgate Academy (1799), and wrote an *Introduction to Hebrew Grammar, Vindica Hebraica,* and *Hebrew Tales,* which were translated into various languages. He finally became professor of Hebrew in University College, London.

A younger contemporary of Abrahamson, the Jewish German medallist, was Solomon (Yom Tob) Bennett (1780-1841), the engraver of Polotsk, who spent a number of years at Copenhagen and Berlin in perfecting himself in his art. Among his works is a highly praised bas-relief of Frederick II, which was much admired by the professors of

the Academy. An ardent lover of liberty, of which
there was little more in Germany at that time than
in Russia, he left for England, where he spent the
remaining years of his life, in Bristol. Besides
being an artist and an engraver he was a profound
theologian, anxious to defend the cause of Judaism
against enemies within and without. The enemy
within he attacked in his cutting criticism of Solomon Cohen's *Rudiments of Religion,* and the enemy
outside, in his other work, *The Constancy of Israel*
(*Nezah Yisraël,* London, 1809). He also wrote
expositions on many important Biblical topics, such
as sacrifices (1815) and the Temple (1824). Having pointed out the defects of the Authorized Version (1834), he was ambitious of publishing a complete revised translation of the Bible. Specimens
appeared in 1841. Death intervened and frustrated his plans. As Schick was the first Jew to
translate from English into Hebrew, so Bennett
was the first after Manasseh ben Israel to write in
English in behalf of his people.[35]

If the contributions of Slavonic Jews to Latin,
German, French, Dutch, and English literature
were not less considerable at that time than those
of the Jews residing in the countries where these
languages were respectively used as media, they

excelled them in Hebrew literature. In the renaissance of the holy tongue, they played the most
important part from the first. The striving for
knowledge, not for the purpose of obtaining a coveted privilege, but for its own sake, became an
irresistible passion, and it was accompanied by an
unquenchable desire to disseminate knowledge
among the masses, to make learning and wisdom
common property. The Hebrew language being
the best vehicle for the purpose, it was soon impressed into the service of Haskalah. The pioneer
Maskilim learned to handle it with ease and clear-
ness that would do credit to a modern writer in a
much more developed European language.

From the middle of the fifteenth to the latter
part of the eighteenth century, Hebrew literature
consisted, if a few scattered books on philosophy,
mostly translations from the Arabic, are excepted,
mainly of Talmudic disquisitions, written in the
rabbinic dialect and in a euphuistic style. Besides
the great Maimuni, there were few able or willing
to write Hebrew " as she should be spoke." The
early German Maskilim, in trying to escape the
Scylla of Rabbinism, fell victims to the Charybdis
of Germanism. They possessed originality neither
of style nor of sentiment, neither of rhyme nor of

reason. Hebrew poetry was an adaptation of current German poetry. The very best the period produced, the *Mosaïde* of Wessely, was influenced by and largely an imitation of Klopstock and others. Like English classic poetry, it is pretty in form but poor in spirit. The element of nationality, or distinctiveness, the life-giving and soul-uplifting element in all poetry, as Delitzsch justly maintains it to be, was lacking in the German Maskilim, anxious for naturalization as they were. It was the Slavonic Maskilim who mastered Hebrew in its purity, as it had not been mastered since the day of Judah Halevi. In those days of transition the diligent student can find, in germ, what was later to develop into the resplendent poetical flowers produced by the Lebensohns, the Gordons, Dolitzky, Schapiro, Mane, and Bialik.

The Slavonic contributors to the Meassef, the first Hebrew literary periodical (1784-1811), were not conspicuous in number, but if quality can compensate for quantity, they made up for it by the value of their articles. Dubno and Maimon enriched the early issues, the one with poetry, the other with philosophy; and when it began to struggle for its existence, and was on the point of giving up the ghost, Shalom Cohen (1772-1845) came to the rescue, and, as editor, prolonged its existence by a few years. Among the best articles in the Meassef are those of Isaac Halevi Satanov (1733-1805). This "conglomeration of contrasts," whom Delitzsch regards as the restorer of Hebrew poetry to its primitive beauty and purity, was the embodiment of the period in which he lived. "He was," we are told, "a thorough master of Jewish traditional lore, and at the same time a most advanced thinker, a profound physicist, and an inspired poet; a master of the old school and at the same time the founder of the new school, the national-classical, of Hebrew poetry." His pure and precise style, his good-natured, Horace-like, delicate, yet unmistakable, humor, he showed in a series of books bearing the name of Asaf, which still must be counted among the gems of Hebrew literature.[36]

Satanov was greatly in favor of expanding the Hebrew language, but the first to borrow expressions from the Talmud literature or coin words of his own was Mendel Levin, also of Satanov, Podolia (1741-1819), the friend of Mendelssohn while in Berlin, the inspirer of Perl and Krochmal while in Brody, the companion of Zeitlin and Schick while in Mohilev. The Meassefim, the

name generally applied to all who participated in
the publication of the Meassef, were shocked by
what they regarded a profanation of the sacred
tongue. Their idea was that Hebrew was to be
utilized as a means of introducing Western civilization. Afterwards it was to be relegated once more
to the holy Ark. To Levin Hebrew had a far
higher significance. Not only should Western civilization be introduced into Jewry through its means,
but Hebrew itself should be so perfected as to
take a place by the side of the more modern and
cultivated languages. It should find adequate expressions for the new thoughts and ideas which the
new learning would introduce into it directly or
indirectly. The medieval translations from the
Arabic should be retranslated into the new Hebrew,
he held, and he furnished an example by recasting
the first part of Maimuni's *Moreh Nebukim*. His
modernized version, lucid and fluent, printed along-
side of Ibn Tibbon's, presents a striking contrast to
the stiffness and obscurity of the Provençal scholar's.
Levin was also the first to write in the Yiddish,
or Judeo-German, dialect, for the instruction of
the masses, which made him the butt of more
than one satire. But what was generally regarded
as a degrading task was fraught with the greatest

consequences to the Haskalah. To this day Yiddish has continued an important medium for disseminating culture among Russian Jews, both in the Old World and in the New."

The century remarkable among other things for encyclopedia enterprises,—*Chambers' Encyclopedia* in England, the *Universal Lexicon* in Germany, and that wonderful and monumental work, the *Encyclopédie* in France—saw, before its close, a similar attempt, in miniature, in Hebrew and by a Slavonic Maskil. Whether the Hebrew encyclopedist was influenced by the example of Dr. Tobias Cohn's *Ma'aseh Tobiah,* mentioned above, or was unconsciously imbued with the prevailing tendency of the times, it is impossible to tell. In any event, he resorted to the same means, and presented the Jewish world with a volume containing a little of every science known, under the innocent name *The Book of the Covenant (Sefer ha-Berit,* Brünn, 1797).

The book appeared anonymously. This, the author assures us, was due not to humbleness of spirit, but to a vow. His diligence and constant application had greatly impaired his eyes. He vowed that if God restored his sight, and enabled him to finish his task, he would publish the book without disclosing his authorship. God hearkened unto his prayers, and the work was soon completed. But an unforeseen trouble arose. His book was ascribed " by some to the sage of Berlin, by others to the Gaon of Vilna, and by many to the united efforts of a coterie of scholars, for it could not be believed that so many and diverse sciences could be mastered by one person." Moreover, the author was censured for being afraid to come out openly and boldly as a champion of Haskalah.[38] In spite of obstacles and strictures, the book met with success surpassing the author's expectations. It found its way not only into Russia, Poland, and Germany, but even into France, Italy, England, Holland, and Palestine. An edition of two thousand copies was entirely exhausted, unusual at a time when books were costly and money was scarce, and another edition was issued. What Phinehas Elijah (Hurwitz) of Vilna had sown in tears, he lived to reap in joy.

There was a crying need in Russia for a work of the sort. In Germany the very Government encouraged organizations and publications aiming at enlightenment. Accordingly, a Society for the Promotion of the Good and the Noble was started, and the Meassef was published. In Russo-Poland not even a Hebrew printing-press was permitted, and certainly no periodical publications would have been tolerated. Phinehas Elijah, therefore, grasped the opportunity, and showed himself equal to it. His aim was, like that of the French encyclopedists, to lead his readers " through nature to God." He gives an account of the various sciences, natural and philosophical, as a prolegomenon to the study of theology, even of the mystic teachings of Vital's *Gates of Holiness*. Withal he evinces a sound intellect and refined, if rudimentary, taste. He decries the " ancestor worship " that rendered the Jew of his day a fossil specimen of an extinct species. The present is superior to the past, " a dwarf on a giant's shoulder seeth farther than doth the giant himself." He ridicules the base and degrading habit of dedicating books to " benefactors, friends, lovers, parents, men, or women." His work was written for the glory of God, and he dedicates it to eternal, all-conquering truth.[39]

All these Maskilim, so many hands reaching out into the light, were both the cause and the consequence of the longing for enlightenment characteristic at all times of the Slavonic Jew. Graetz and his followers among the latter-day Maskilim delighted in calling them " they that walk in darkness." Facts, however, prove that at no time before Nicholas I was education per se regarded with the least suspicion, though the Talmud was given the preference. As in the pre-Haskalah period, the greatest Talmudists deemed it a sacred duty to perfect themselves in some branch of secular science. When, in 1710, a terrible plague broke out in his native town, Rabbi Jonathan of Risenci (Grodno) vowed that, "if he were spared, he would disseminate a knowledge of astronomy among his countrymen." To fulfil the vow he went to Germany (1725), where, though blind, he devoted himself assiduously first to the acquisition of astronomy, then to writing on it.[40] Baruch Yavan of Volhynia, who more than any one exposed the impostures of Jacob Frank, "spoke and wrote Hebrew, Polish, German, and probably French," and his accomplishments and address won him the admiration of Count Brühl, the virtual ruler of Poland, and the favor of the highest officials at St. Petersburg. His associate in the righteous fight, Bima Speir of Mohilev, was also possessed of a thorough command of the language of Russia, and was well posted in its literature, history, and politics. The Pinczovs, descendants of Rabbi Polack, connected with the most eminent rabbinical families, and themselves famous for piety and erudition, produced many works on mathematics and philosophy. Mendelssohn's translation of the Pentateuch was at first hailed with joy, and was recommended by the most zealous rabbis. Doctor Hurwitz of Vilna did not hesitate to dedicate his *Ammude Bet Yehudah* to Wessely, who was more popular in Russo-Poland than in Germany. The whole edition of his *Yen Lebanon,* which fell flat in the latter country, though offered gratis, was sold when introduced into the former." Joseph Pesseles' correspondence concerning Dubno, with David Friedländer, the disciple of Mendelssohn (1773), proves the high esteem in which the liberal-minded savants of Berlin were held in Russia. The rabbis of Brest, Slutsk, and Lublin gave laudatory recommendations to Judah Löb Margolioth's popular works of natural science, which form a little encyclopedia by themselves. Margolioth was the grandson of Mordecai Jaffe, himself rabbi successively at Busnov, Szebrszyn, Polotsk, Lesla, and Frankfort-on-the-Oder (d. 1811). The writings of Baruch Schick of Shklov, referred to above, were accorded the same welcome. His translation of Euclid and his treatises on trigonometry, astronomy (*Ammude ha-Shamayim*), and anatomy (*Tiferet Adam*) won the admiration of rabbis as well as laymen. Epitaphs of the day contain the statement that the deceased was not only " at home in all the chambers of the Torah," but also in " philosophy and the seven sciences." And this, exaggerated though it may be, must be seen to contain a kernel of the truth, when we recall that among Maimon's intimate friends was the rabbi of Kletzk, Lithuania; that in the humble dwelling of his father there were works on historical, astronomical, and philosophical subjects; that the chief rabbi of a neighboring town, Rabbi Samson of Slonim, who, according to Fünn, " had in his youth lived for a while in Germany, learned the German language there, and made himself acquainted in some measure with the sciences," continued his study of the sciences, and soon collected a fair library of German books." Saadia, Bahya, Halevi, Ibn Ezra, Crescas, Bedersi, Levi ben Gerson (whom Goldenthal calls the Hebrew Kant), Albo, Abarbanel, and others whose works deserve a high place in the history of Jewish philosophy, were on the whole fairly represented in the libraries, and diligently studied in the numerous yeshibot and batte midrashim.

Thus the enlightenment which dawned upon

France, Germany, and England cast a glow even on the Slavonic Jews, despite the Chinese wall of disabilities that hemmed them in. Unfortunately, this only helped to render them dissatisfied with their wretched lot, without affording them the means of ameliorating it. While the Jews in Western Europe profited and were encouraged by the example of their Christian neighbors; while, in addition to their innate thirst for learning, they had everywhere else political and civil preferments to look forward to, in Russo-Poland not only were such outside stimuli absent, but the Slavonic Jews had to struggle against obstacles and hindrances at every step. No such heaven on earth could be dreamed of there. The country was still in a most barbarous state. Those who wished to perfect themselves in any of the sciences had to leave home and all and go to a foreign land, and had to study, as they were bidden to study the Talmud, " lishmah," that is, for its own sake. This is the distinguishing feature between the German and Slavonic Maskilim during the eighteenth century. The cry of the former was, " Become learned, lest the nations say we are not civilized and deny us the wealth, respect, and especially the equality we covet ! " The latter were humbly seeking after the truth, either because they could better elucidate the Talmud, or because, as they held, it was *their* truth, of which the nations had deprived them during their long exile.[43] They were unlike their German brethren in another respect. Almost all of them were " self-made men," autodidacts in the truest sense. Lacking the advantages of secular schools, they culled their first information from scanty, antiquated Hebrew translations. Maimon learned the Roman alphabet from the transliteration of the titles on the fly-leaves of some Talmudic tracts; Doctor Behr, from Wolff's *Mathematics*. But no sooner was the impetus given than it was followed by an insatiable craving for more and more of the intellectual manna, for a wider and wider horizon. " Look," says Wessely, " look at our Russian and Polish brethren who immigrate hither, men great in Torah, yet admirers of the sciences, which, without the guiding help of teachers, they all master to such perfection as to surpass even a Gentile sage! " [44] Such self-education was, of course, not without unfavorable results. Never having enjoyed the advantage of a systematic elementary training, the enthusiasts sometimes lacked the very rudiments of knowledge, though engaged in the profoundest speculations of philosophy. " As our mothers in

Egypt gave birth to their children before the mid-
wife came," writes Pinsker somewhat later," " even
so it is with the intellectual products of our brethren: before one becomes acquainted with the grammar of a language, he masters its classic and scientific literature! "

Steadily though slowly, brighter, if not better,
days were coming. " Thought once awakened shall
not again slumber." As Carlyle says of the French
of that period, it became clear for the first time
to the upturned eyes of the Jews, " that Thought
has actually a kind of existence in other kingdoms
[than the Talmud] ; that some glimmerings of civilization had dawned here and there on the human
species." They begin to try all things; they visit
Germany, France, Denmark, Holland, even England; learn their literatures, study in their universities, and contribute their quota to the apologetic,
controversial, scientific, and philosophic investiga-
tions " with a candor and real love of improvement which give the best omens of a still higher
success." Fortune, indeed, has cast them also into
a cavern, and they are groping around darkly. But
this prisoner, too, is a giant, and he will, at length,
burst forth as a giant into the light of day.

[Notes, pp. 310-314.]

## CHAPTER III

# THE DAWN OF HASKALAH

## 1794-1840

A glimmer of light pierced the Russian sky at the accession of Catherine II (1762-1796). This "Semiramis of the North," the admirer of Buffon, Montesquieu, Diderot, and, more especially, Voltaire, whose motto, *N'en croyez rien,* she adopted, endeavored, and for a while not without success, to introduce into her own country the spirit of tolerance which pervaded France. Her ukases were intended for all alike, "without distinction of religion and nationality." Her regard for her Jewish citizens she showed by allowing them to settle in the interior, establish printing-presses (January 27, 1783), and become civil and Government officers (April 2, 1785). In the edict promulgated by Governor-General Chernyshev it is stated that "religious liberty and inviolability of property are hereby granted to all subjects of Russia and certainly to the Jews; for the humanitarian principles of her Majesty do not permit the exclusion of the Jews alone from the favors shown to all, so long as they, as faithful subjects, continue to employ themselves, as hitherto, with commerce and trade, each according to his vocation." That she remained true to her promise, we see from the numerous privileges enjoyed by many Jews, who began to frequent Moscow and St. Petersburg and reside there for business purposes.

Paul (1796-1801), too, was kindly disposed toward the Jews, and permitted them to live in Courland; and when Alexander I (1801-1825) became czar, their hopes turned into certainty. Alexander I did, indeed, appear a most promising ruler at his accession. The theories he had acquired from Laharpe he fully intended to apply to practical life. Like Catherine, he wished to rule in equity and promote the welfare of his subjects irrespective of race or creed. He ordered a commission to investigate the status of the Russian Jews (December 9, 1802). The result was the polozheniye (enactment) of December 9, 1804, according to which Jews were to be eligible to one-third of all municipal offices; they were to be permitted to establish factories, become agriculturists, and either attend the schools and colleges of the empire

on the same footing as subjects of the Christian
faith, or, if they desired, found and maintain
schools of their own. The approach of the great
Usurper and the crushing defeat the Russians sustained at the battle of Friedland (June 4, 1808)
also favored the advance of the Jews. As the short,
but troublous, reign of Paul and his wars with Turkey, Persia, Prussia, Poland, and Sweden had impoverished the country and depleted the treasury,
the shrewd Alexander was not averse from appeal-
ing to Jews for help. Of course, as in many more
enlightened countries and in more modern times,
most of the privileges were merely paper privileges. Few of them ever went into effect. The
noble intentions of the enlightened rulers were
steadily thwarted by bigoted councillors and jealous
merchants. Every favor shown the Jews aroused
a storm of protests, which resulted in numerous in-
fringements. The Jews were compelled to pay
for the good intentions of Catherine with a double
tax (June 25, 1794), and, during Paul's reign, without the emperor's knowledge, a law was enacted
requiring of Jews double payment of the guild
license. In spite of all efforts, the Jews, instead of
being emancipated politically, were burdened with
additional discriminations.[1]

Had not the wheel of progress suddenly stopped revolving, Russian Jews might have constituted one of the most useful as well as most intellectual elements in the vast empire. As it was, the kindly intention of czar or czarina sufficed to arouse them from the asthenia to which they were reduced for want of freedom. The times were rife with excitement, and the Jewish atmosphere with expectancy. The mighty changes which were taking place in Russia and Poland; the dismemberment of the latter; the annexation of Balta (1791), Lithuania (1794), and Courland (1797) to the former; the short-lived yet potent German rule in Byelostok (1793-1807), and the rude but memorable contact with France (1807-1812), these and many other important happenings in a brief span of time had a telling effect upon the diverse races under the dominion of Russia, and among them not the least upon the Jewish race. Everywhere the desire for " liberty, equality, and fraternity " began to manifest itself. In Courland, the most German of Russian provinces, Georg Gottfried Mylich, a Lutheran pastor at Nerft, made a touching appeal (ab. 1787) in German on behalf of the Jews, insisting that the word Jew " should not be taken to indicate a class of people different from us, but only a different religious body; and as regards his nationality, it should not hinder him from obtaining citizen's rights and liberties equal to those of the people of Sleswick, the Saxons, Danes, Swedes, Swiss, French, and Italians, who also live among us." In Poland, Tadeusz Czacki, the historian, wrote his *Discourse on the Jews* (*Rosprava o Zhydakh,* Vilna, 1807), in which he deplores that Jews " experienced indulgence rarely, oppression often, and contempt nearly always " under the most Christian governments, and suggests a plan for reforming their condition. But the main appeal for freedom came, as might have been expected, from the Jews themselves. Contemporaneous with, if not before, Michel Beer's *Appel à la justice des nations et des rois,* a Lithuanian Jew, during his imprisonment in Nieszvicz on a false charge, wrote a work in Polish on the Jewish problem,[2] while in 1803 Löb, or Leon, Nebakhovich, an intimate friend of Count Shakovskoy, published *The Cry of the Daughter of Judah* (*Vopli Docheri Yudeyskoy*), the first defence of the Russian Jew in the Russian language. The followers of the religion of love are implored to love a Jew because he is a Jew, and they are assured that the Jew who preserves his religion undefiled can be neither a bad man nor a bad citizen.

114

But the Jews did not wait for their dreams to be realized. They threw themselves into the swirl of their country's ambition, as if they had never received anything other than the tenderness of a devoted mother at her hands. They were "kindled in a common blaze " of patriotism with the rest of the population. That in spite of all accusations to the contrary they remained loyal to Poland, is amply proved by the history of that unfortunate country. The characteristic kapota of the Polish Jew, his whole garb, including the yarmulka (under cap), is simply the old Polish costume, which the Jews retained after the Poles had adopted the German form of dress.[2] "When, in the year 1794," says Czacki, "despair armed the [Polish] capital, the Jews were not afraid of death, but, mingling with the troops and the populace, they proved that danger did not terrify them, and that the cause of the fatherland was dear to them." With the permission of Kosciusko, Colonel Joselovich Berek, later killed at the battle of Kotzk (1809), formed a regiment of light cavalry consisting entirely of Jews, which distinguished itself especially at the siege of Warsaw. Most of the members perished in defence of the suburb of Praga. In the agony of death, Rabbi Hayyim longed for good tidings, that he might die in peace. And when the fight was over, Zbitkover expended two barrels of money, one filled with gold ducats and one with silver rubles, for the live and dead soldiers who were brought to him.⁴ Indeed, Prince Czartorisky was so convinced of their patriotism, that he always advocated the same rights for the Polish Jews as were claimed for the Polish Gentiles, entrusted his children to the care of Mendel Levin of Satanov, and instructed his son, Prince Ladislaus, always to remain their friend.⁵

But when, in spite of struggle and sacrifice, the doom " finis Poloniae " was sounded, and a large portion of the once powerful empire was incorporated into Russia, we find the Jews bearing their sorrow patiently, and willingly performing their duties as subjects to their new masters. Their attachment to their czar and country was not shaken in the least when, in 1812, Napoleon made them flattering promises to secure their services in his behalf. Rabbi Shneor Zalman, the eminent leader of the Lithuanian Hasidim, hearing of the invasion of the French army, spent many days in prayer and fasting for the success of the Russians, and fled on the Sabbath day, not to be contaminated by contact with the " godless French." When Na-

poleon was finally defeated, the event was celebrated both at home and in the synagogue, and Russian soldiers were everywhere welcomed by Jews
with gifts and good cheer.[6] Lilienthal relates that
the Jews succeeded in intercepting a courier who carried the plan of operations of the French army,
and Alexander declared in a dispatch that Jews had
opened the eyes of the Russians, and the Government, therefore, felt itself bound to them by eternal
gratitude.[7] It is to this proof of patriotism that
some attribute Alexander's interest in the Jews and
his order that three deputies should reside in St.
Petersburg to represent them in Russia, and in
Poland a committee consisting of three Christians
and eight Jews should be appointed to devise ways
and means of ameliorating their condition.[8]

The times were promising in other respects. In
that critical period, the Government, reposing but
little confidence in Russian merchants, whose business motto was " No swindle, no sale," allowed
several Jews to become Government contractors
(podradchiki). These, while rendering valuable
services, amassed considerable fortunes. Notwithstanding the law restricting Jewish residence to
the Pale of Settlement, Catherine II speaks of Jews
who resided in St. Petersburg for many years, and

lodged in the house of a priest, who had been her confessor. Moreover, Jews contributed not a little to the liberal policy of Alexander I. Among them were Eliezer Dillon of Nieszvicz (d. 1838), who was honored by the emperor with a gold medal " for faithful and conscientious services," and was given an audience by his Majesty, at which he pleaded the cause of his coreligionists; [9] Nathan Notkin, who mitigated the possible effect of Senator Dyerzhavin's baneful opinions concerning Jews, as expressed in his report (*Mnyenie*, September, 1800), and who suggested the establishment of schools for children and for adults in Yekaterinoslav and elsewhere; Abraham Peretz, the personal friend of Speransky, Dyerzhavin, and Potemkin, and a brilliant financier, whose high standing enabled him to be a power for good in the councils concerning Jews; [10] and his father-in-law, Joshua Zeitlin (1724-1822). Zeitlin was a rare phenomenon, reminding one of the golden days of Jewish Spain. His knowledge of finance and political economy won him the admiration of Prince Potemkin, the protection of Czarina Catherine, and the esteem of Alexander I, who appointed him court councillor (nadvorny sovyetnik). But his mercantile pursuits did not hinder him from study, and his high living did not interfere with his high thinking. His palatial home at Ustye, in Mohilev, became a refuge for all needy Talmudists and Maskilim, whom he helped with the liberality of a Maecenas; he conducted an extensive correspondence on rabbinic literature, and for many years supported Doctor Schick and Mendel Levin. For Doctor Schick he built a laboratory, and filled his library with rare manuscripts and works on Jewish and secular subjects.[11]

Even among the conservative Talmudists signs of improvement were not wanting. The Gaon became the centre of a group of enlightened friends and disciples, who continued in his footsteps after his death. His son, Rabbi Abraham, who published and edited many of his works, a task requiring no small amount of acumen and Talmudic erudition,[12] was also the author of books on geography, mathematics, and physics. His pupils, such as Doctor Schick and Rabbi Benjamin and Rabbi Zelmele, influenced their contemporaries either directly, by bringing them in touch with the new learning, or indirectly, by reforming the school system and the method of Talmud study.[13] Of Rabbi Zelmele, who like his master became the hero of a wonder-biography written by his disciple Ezekiel Feivel of Plungian, we are told that he regarded grammar as indispensable to a thorough knowledge of the Bible and the Talmud, pleaded for a return to the order of study prescribed in the *Pirke Abot,* and complained that, owing to the neglect of Aramaic, the benefits of comparative philology were lost and unknown. He declared also that while he believed in all the Bible contains, the stories in the Talmud are, for the most part, legends and parables used for the purpose of illustration.[14]

Towering above all the disciples of the Gaon, the most outspoken in behalf of enlightenment is Manasseh of Ilye (1767-1831). At a very early age he attracted the attention of Talmudists by his originality and boldness. In his unflinching determination to get at the truth, he did not shrink from criticising Rashi and the *Shulhan 'Aruk,* and dared to interpret some parts of the Mishnah differently from the explanation given in the Gemara. With all his admiration for the Gaon, but for whom, he claimed, the Torah would have been forgotten, he also had points of sympathy with the Hasidim, for whose leader, Shneor Zalman of Ladi, he had the highest respect. Like many of his contemporaries, he determined to go to Berlin. He started on his way, but was stopped at Königsberg

MAX LILIENTHAL
1815-1882

by some orthodox coreligionists, and compelled to return to Russia. This did not prevent his perfecting himself in German, Polish, natural philosophy, mechanics, and even strategics. On the last subject he wrote a book, which was burnt by his friends, " lest the Government suspect that Jews are making preparations for war! " But it is not so much his Talmudic or secular scholarship that makes him interesting to us to-day. His true greatness is revealed by his attempts, the first made in his generation perhaps, to reconcile the Hasidim with the Mitnaggedim, and these in turn with the Maskilim. He spoke a good word for manual labor, and proved from the Talmud that burdensome laws should be abolished. His *Pesher Dabar* (Vilna, 1807) and *Alfe Menasheh* (ibid., 1827, 1860) are monuments to the advanced views of the author. In the Hebrew literature of his time, they are equalled only by the *'Ammude Bet Yehudah* and the *Hekal 'Oneg* of Doctor Hurwitz.[15]

This short period of enlightenment and tolerance, inaugurated by a semblance of equality, indicates the native optimism of the Slavonic Jew. For a while a cessation of hostilities was evident in the camp of Israel. The reforms introduced by the Gaon, and propagated by his disciples, began to bear fruit. Hasidism itself underwent a radical change under the leadership of Rabbi Shneor Zalman of Ladi (1747-1813) and Jacob Joseph of Polonnoy, who, unlike their colleagues of the Ukraine, were learned in the Talmud and familiar with the sciences. Protests by Hasidim themselves against the irreverent spirit that developed after the death of the Besht, had in fact been heard before. The saintly and retiring Abraham Malak (d. 1780) had denounced, in no uncertain terms, the gross conception held by the Hasidim of the sublime teachings of their own sect. He drew a beautiful picture of the ideal zaddik, who is " so absorbed in meditation on the Divine wisdom that he cannot descend to the lower steps upon which ordinary people stand." [16] But the more active Rabbi Shneor, or Zalman Ladier, as he was usually called, insisted on putting the zaddik on a par with the rabbi, whose duty it is not to work miracles but to teach righteousness. Assuming for his followers the name HaBaD, the three letters of which are the initials of the Hebrew words for Wisdom, Reason, and Knowledge, he furthered the cause of enlightenment in the only way possible among his adherents.[17] How well he succeeded may be inferred from the fact, trivial though it be, that the

biography of the Besht, *The Praises of the Besht*
(*Shibhe ha-Besht*), by Dob Bär, published in
Berdichev (1815), omits many of the legends
about the Master included in the version published
the same year in Kopys. The omission can be ex-
plained only on the ground that the editor, Judah
Löb, who was the son of the author, did not wish
to give offence, or he had outgrown the credulity
of his father.[18]

The feeling of tolerance manifested itself also
in the Jewish attitude towards the Gentiles. " O
that we were identified with the nations of our time,
created by the same God, children of one Father,
and did not hate each other because we are at
variance in some views! " This exclamation of
Doctor Hurwitz [19] found an echo in the works of
the other Maskilim that wrote in Hebrew, but more
especially of those who used a European language.
They were deeply interested in whatever marked a
step forward in their country's civilization. The
opening of a gymnasium in Mitau (1775) was a
joyful occasion, which inspired Hurwitz's Hebrew
muse, and at the centennial celebration of the surrender of Riga to Peter the Great (July 4, 1810),
the craving of the Jewish heart, avowed in a German poem, was expressed " in the name of the local

Hebrew community to their Christian compatriots."
The last stanza runs as follows:

> Grant us, who, like you, worship the God above,
> Also on earth to enjoy equality with you!
> To-day, while your hearts are open to love,
> Let us seal our happiness with your love, too! [20]

This desire for naturalization brought with it
an attempt at " Russification." To show the beauty
of the Russian language, Baruch Czatzskes of Volhynia translated some of the poems of Khersakov
into Hebrew, and others published manuals for the
study of Russian and Polish.[21] Among the first
books issued from the newly-established printing-
press in Shklov, the centre of Jewish wealth, re-
finement, and culture at that time, was the *Zeker
Rab* with a German translation (1804). In an
appendix thereto the Shklov Maskilim announced
their intention to publish a weekly, the first in the
Hebrew tongue. Yiddish was also resorted to as a
medium for educating the masses, and as early
as 1813 some Vilna Jews applied to the Government for permission to publish a paper in that language, though it was not until ten years later (1823-
1824) that a Yiddish periodical, Der Beobachter
an der Weichsel, appeared in Warsaw. Nor do

we hear of any opposition to the Government decrees, issued probably at the request of Dillon, Notkin, Peretz, or Nebakhovich, that the elders of the kahals in and after 1808, and the rabbis of the congregations in and after 1812, be conversant with either Russian, German, or Polish. This sudden Russification of the Jews amounted sometimes to no more than a superficial imitation of Russian civilization, which pious rabbis as well as liberalminded men like Schick, Margolioth, Ilye, and Hurwitz, felt impelled to call a halt to. Jews, especially the rich, aped the Polish pans. Their wives dressed in Parisian gowns of the latest fashion, and their homes were conducted in a manner so luxurious as to arouse the envy of the noblemen. Israel waxed fat and kicked. Their greatest care was to become wealthy; they pampered their bodies at the expense of the impoverishment of their souls, and some feared that " with the passing away of the elder generation there would not remain a man capable of filling the position of rabbi." [22]

The privilege of attending public schools and colleges further stimulated the Russification of the Jews. As soon as these institutions of learning were thrown open to them, numerous Jewish youths made headway in all branches taught, especially in

125

medicine. That Alexander's benign decree of November 10, 1811, issued through the Secretary of State Speransky, was not always executed by his officials goes without saying. Simeon Levy Wolf, one of the first Russo-Jewish graduates, was denied his degree of doctor of jurisprudence in Dorpat unless he embraced Christianity.[23] When, in 1819, some of the Vilna graduates applied for the privilege of not paying the double tax, they were told that they must first renounce their faith, an exception being made only in favor of Arthur Parlovich. Still the number of Jewish graduate physicians was on the increase. Osip Yakovlevich Liboschüts, who was the son of the famous physician of Vilna, took his doctor degree at Dorpat (1806), became court physician in St. Petersburg, where he founded a hospital for children, and wrote extensively in French on the flora of his country.[24] The medical institute of Vilna (1803-1833), afterwards transferred to Kiev, became the centre of attraction for the Russian Jewry. Padua, Berlin, Königsberg, Göttingen, Copenhagen, Halle, Amsterdam, Cambridge, and London were for a third of a century replaced by the home of the Gaon and of Doctor Liboschüts. The first students were recruited from the bet ha-midrash, and they frequently joined, as in former days, knowledge of the Law with the practice of their chosen profession. Such were Isaac Markusevich, whose annotations to the *Shulhan 'Aruk* (ab. 1830) were published fifty years later;[25] Joseph Rosensohn, the promising Talmudist who became rabbi of Pyosk at the age of nineteen;[26] and Kusselyevsky of Nieszvicz, a stipendiary of a Polish nobleman and a great favorite with Professor Frank. Because of his proficiency, he was exempted from serving as a vratch (interne), and for his piety and learning he was addressed by Jews and Gentiles as " rabbi."[27]

With what dreams such happenings filled the Jewish heart! " Thank God," writes a merchant of the first guild in reply to an inquiry from distant Bokhara, " thank God, we dwell in peace under the sovereignty of our czar Alexander, who has shown us his mercy, and has put us in every respect on an equality with all the inhabitants of the land."[28] But a rude awakening was soon to make the Jews aware that their visions of better days were still far from realization. In 1815, Alexander I formed the acquaintance of Baroness Krüdener, and since then, to the satisfaction of Prince Galitzin, " with what giant strides the emperor advanced in the pathway of religion! " His humanitarian deeds gave way to a profound religious mysticism. He experienced a revulsion of feeling toward reforms in his vast empire, and, as always, the Jews were the first victims of an ill-boding change. The kindly monarch who, at Paris, had said to a Russo-Jewish deputation, *J'enleverai le joug de vos épaules*, began to make their yoke heavier than he had found it. The enlightened czar, who, in striking a medal commemorating the emancipation of the Jews of his empire, had anticipated Napoleon by a year, suddenly became a bigoted tyrant, whose efforts were devoted to converting the same Jews to Christianity. He who had claimed that his greatest reward would be to produce a Mendelssohn, now resorted to various expedients, to render education unpalatable to the Jews. The Jewish assemblymen, who, in 1816, soon after the Franco-Russian war, had been convoked to St. Petersburg, were not allowed to meet; and when, two years later, they did meet, their every attempt was baffled by the Government. Jews were expelled systematically from St. Petersburg (1818). They were forbidden to employ Christians as servants (May 4, 1820), to immigrate into Russia from abroad (August 10, 1824), and reside in the towns and villages of Mohilev and Vitebsk (January 13,

1825). Several years after the double poll and guild tax had been abolished in Courland (November 8, 1807), it was restored with an additional impost on meat from cattle slaughtered according to the Jewish rite (korobka). All this impoverished the Jews to such an extent that they were forced to sell the cravats of their praying shawls (taletim), in order to defray the expense of a second deputation to St. Petersburg.[29]

Had Alexander I been satisfied with merely restricting the Jews' rights, the favorable attitude towards enlightenment we have noticed above would probably have remained unaltered. Unfortunately, Alexander became a fanatic conversionist. It was a time when missionary zeal became endemic, and Baroness Krüdener's influence was strengthened. The Reverend Lewis Way, having founded (1808) the London Society for Promoting Christianity among the Jews, made a tour through Europe, everywhere urging the Gentiles to enfranchise the Jews as an inducement to them to embrace Christianity, the only means of hastening the advent of the Apostolic millennium. His *Mémoires sur l'état des israélites* presented to the Congress of Aix-la-Chapelle (October 11, 1818) and his visit to Russia resulted in an imperial ukase (March 25, 1817) organizing a Committee of Guardians for Israelitish Christians (Izrailskiye Christyanye). The members of this association were to be granted land in the northern or southern provinces of Russia and to enjoy special privileges. The bait proved tempting, and, as a consequence, some prominent Maskilim, too weak to resist the allurements, precipitated themselves into the Greek Catholic fold. Abraham Peretz, financier and champion of Jews' rights, consented to be converted, as also Löb Nebakhovich, the dramatist, whose plays were produced in the Imperial theatre of St. Petersburg and performed in the presence of the emperor.[30] Equally bad, if not worse, for the cause of Haskalah was the conduct of those who, disdaining, or unable, to profess the new religion, discarded every vestige of traditional Judaism, and deemed it their duty to set an example of infidelity and sometimes immorality to their less enlightened coreligionists. What Leroy-Beaulieu says of Maimon, " that type of the most cultured Jew to be found before the French Revolution," might more justly be applied to many a less prominent Maskil after him: " Despite his learning and philosophy he sank deeper than the most degraded of his fellow-men, because in repudiating his ancestral faith he had lost the staff which, through all their humiliations, served as a prop even to the most debased of ancient Jews." [31] Haskalah thus having become synonymous with apostasy or licentiousness, we can easily understand why the unsophisticated among the Russian Jews were so bitterly opposed to it from the time the sad truth dawned upon them, until, under Alexander II, their suspicions were somewhat dissipated. Previous to the latter part of the reign of Alexander I the "struggle groups" in Russian Jewry were at first Frankists and anti-Frankists, and afterwards Hasidim and Mitnaggedim. It was a conflict, not between religion and science, but between religion and what was regarded as superstition. Secular instruction, far from being opposed, was, as we have seen, sought and disseminated. Long after the pious element in Germany had been aroused to the dangers that lurked in the wake of their "Aufklärung," and had begun to endeavor to check its further progress by excommunication and other methods, the Russian Jews remained "seekers after light." They might have condemned a Maskil, they had not yet condemned Haskalah. Mendelssohn's German translation was welcomed in Russia at its first appearance no less than in

Germany, but when some of the children of Rabbi
Moses ben Menahem embraced the Christian faith,
and their father, as was natural, was suspected of
skepticism, the *Biur* and the Meassefim were pro-
nounced, like libraries by Sir Anthony Absolute,
to be " an evergreen tree of diabolical knowledge." So also with Wessely's Epistles, which
were destroyed in public, together with Polonnoy's
*Toledot Ya'akob Yosef.* Haskalah itself was not
impugned, and as theretofore translations and original works on science were encouraged, and the
wish was entertained that " many shall run to and
fro, and knowledge shall be increased." [32]

But the latest experiences in their own country
put Haskalah in a very different light from that in
which they were wont to regard it. Formerly the
opposition to it had been limited to the very land
that gave it birth. Because of their determination
to study, Solomon Maimon was denied admission
to Berlin, Manasseh of Ilye was stopped in Königsberg, and Abba Glusk Leczeka, better known as
" the Glusker Maggid," the subject of a poem by
Chamisso, was persecuted everywhere. It was Rabbi
Levin, of Berlin, who prohibited the publication of
Wessely's works, and insisted that the author be
expelled from the city.[33] It was Rabbi Ezekiel

Landau of Prague who, though approving of Wessely's *Yen Lebanon,* opposed the translation of the Pentateuch by Mendelssohn, while Rabbi Horowitz of Hamburg denounced it in unmeasured terms, admonishing his hearers to shun the work as unclean, and approving the action of those persons who had publicly burnt it in Vilna (1782). Moses Sofer of Pressburg adopted as his motto, " Touch not the works of the Dessauer " (Mendelssohn)," and seldom allowed an opportunity to pass without denouncing the Maskilim of his country. Now the clarion note of anti-Haskalah, sounded by these luminaries in Israel, found an echo among the Jews in Russia. They had discovered, to their great sorrow, that like Elisha ben Abuya, the apostate in the Talmud, " those who once entered the paradise [of enlightenment] returned no more." The very name of the seat of Haskalah was an abomination to the pious. To be called " Berlinchick " or " Deitschel " was tantamount to being called infidel and epicurean, anarchist and outlaw. The old instinct of self-preservation, which turned Jews from lambs into lions, holding their ground to the last, asserted itself again. As the Talmudic rabbis excluded certain books from the Canon, as the study of even the Jewish philosophers was later proscribed by certain French rabbis, so the Russian rabbis laid the ban upon whatever savored of German " Aufklärerei."

Thus began the bitter fight against Haskalah, in which Hasidim and Mitnaggedim, forgetting their differences, joined hands, and stood shoulder to shoulder. For, after all, was not Judaism in both these phases endangered by the new and aggressive enemy from the West? And did not the two have enough in common to become one in the hour of great need? Hasidism, in fact, was Judaism emotionalized, and since, beginning with Rabbi Shneor Zalman of Ladi, it, too, advocated the study of the Talmud, the distinction between it and Mitnaggedism was hardly perceptible. The study of the Zohar and Cabbala was equally cultivated by both; Isaac Luria and Hayyim Vital were equally venerated by both, and hero worship was common to both. The *Ascension of Elijah* (Gaon) is as full of miracles as *The Praises of the Besht*. It is no wonder, then, that the animosities, which reached their acme during the last few years of the Gaon's life, were weakened after his death, and that the compromise, pleaded for by Doctor Hurwitz and Manasseh Ilye, was somehow effected. But it was otherwise with the Haskalah. " Verily," says the zaddik Menahem Mendel of Vitebsk, "verily, grammar is useful; that our great ones indulged in the study thereof I also know; but what is to be done since the wicked and sinful have taken possession of it?" In the same manner does Rabbi Hayyim of Volozhin inveigh against the followers of Mendelssohn, because of the latitudinarian habits of the Maskilim, who "despise the counsel of their betters, and go after the dictates of their hearts.[85] Both saw in Haskalah a deadly foe to their dearest ideals, a blight upon their most cherished hopes, and, like Elizabeta Petrovna, they would not derive even a benefit from the enemies of their religion.

Still, Alexander I approached his object only tentatively. Haskalah during his reign was like the Leviathan in the Talmud legend which resembled an island, so that wayfarers approached it to moor under its lee and find shelter in its shade, but as soon as they began to walk and cook on it, it would turn and submerge them in the stormy and bottomless sea. The Jews were invited or induced to forsake their religion, and only the less discerning were caught in the snare. It remained for the "terrible incarnation of autocracy," Nicholas I (1825-1855), or, as his Jewish subjects called him, Haman II, to fill their cup of woe to overflowing and employ every available means to convert them to his own religion.

Nicholas's one aim was " to diminish the number of Jews in the empire," but not by expulsion, the means employed by Ferdinand and Isabella. He knew too well their value as citizens to allow them to migrate. He would diminish their numbers by forced baptism. Baptized Jews were exempted from the payment of taxes for three years; Jewish criminals could have their punishment commuted or could obtain a pardon by ceasing to be Jews. But as these inducements could naturally appeal only to comparatively few, more stringent measures were resorted to. Hitherto the Jews had been excused from military service, paying an annual sum of money for the privilege. On September 7, 1827, an ukase was issued requiring them not only to pay the same amount as theretofore, but also to serve in the army; and while Christians had to furnish only seven recruits per thousand, and only at certain intervals, the Jews had to contribute ten recruits for each thousand, and that at every conscription. The only exception was made in the case of the Karaites, who, according to Nicholas's decision, had emigrated from Palestine before the

Christian era, and could not therefore have participated in the crucifixion of Jesus. Jews found outside of their native towns without passports, and those in arrears with their taxes, frequently even those who, having lagged behind in their payment to the Government, eventually discharged their obligations, were to be seized and sentenced to serve in the army, and this meant a lifetime, or at least twenty-five years, of the most abject slavery imaginable. This grievous measure caused the utmost misery. No Jewish youth leaving home could be sure of returning and seeing his dear ones again. The scum of the Jewish population (poimshchiki, or " catchers ") made it their profession to ensnare helpless young men or poor itinerant students suspected of the Haskalah heresy, destroy their passports, and deliver them up as poimaniki (recruits), to spare the rich who paid for the substitutes. To form an idea of the time we need but read some of the numerous folk-songs of that day. Here is one of many:

> Quietly I walk in the street,
> When behind me I hear the rush of feet.
> Woes have come and sought me,
> Alas, had I bethought me.

137

"Your passport," they ask. Alas, it is lost!
" Then serve the White Czar! " that is the cost.
Woe has come and sought me,
Alas, had I bethought me.

There are many rooms, they take me to one,
And strip from my body the poor homespun.
Woe has come and sought me,
Alas, had I bethought me.

They take me to another room,
The uniform—that is my doom.
Woe has come and sought me,
Alas, had I bethought me.

Rather than wear the cap of the czar,
To study the Torah were better by far.
Woe has come and sought me,
Alas, had I bethought me.

Rather than eat of the czar's black bread,
I'd study the Scriptures head by head.
Woes have come and sought me,
Alas, had I bethought me.

Yet this was not all. Knowing that it is easier
to convert the children than their elders, the Government of Nicholas I, out-Heroding Herod, inaugurated a system so cruel as to fill with terror
and pity the heart of the most ferocious barbarian.
Infants were torn from their mothers, boys of the
age of twelve, sometimes of ten and eight, were

herded like cattle, sent to distant parts of Russia, and there distributed as chattels among the officers of the army. Many of these Cantonists, as they were called, either died on the way, or were killed off when they resisted conversion. Those who survived sometimes returned to Judaism, and formed the nucleus of Jewish settlements in the interior of Russia. These " soldiers of Nicholas " (Niko-layevskiye soldati), with their uncouth demeanor and devoted, though ignorant, adherence to the faith of their fathers, furnished much material for the folk-songs of the time and the novelists of the somewhat happier reigns of Nicholas's successors.[38]

One of these Cantonists, the first to give a description of the life of his fellow-sufferers, was Wolf Nachlass, or Alexander Alekseyev. For many years he remained faithful to the religion of his forefathers, though he had been pressed into the service at the age of ten. About 1845 he changed his views, became an ardent Greek Catholic, and converted five hundred Cantonists, to the great delight of Nicholas I, who thanked him in person for his zeal. He lost his leg, and during the long illness that followed Nachlass settled in Novgorod, and wrote several works on Jewish customs and on missionary topics.

Less horrifying, but equally aiming at disintegration, was Nicholas's scheme of colonization. What better means was there for " diminishing the number of Jews " than to scatter them over the wilderness of Russia and leave them to shift for themselves? This, of course, was necessarily a slow process and one involving some expense, but it was fraught with great importance not only for the Russian Church, but for Russian trade and agriculture as well.

" Back to the soil! " Was not this the cry of the romantic Maskilim in Germany, in Galicia, and particularly in Russia? And have not country life and field labor been depicted by them in the most glowing colors? Here was an opportunity to save the honor of the Jewish name and also ameliorate the material condition of the Russian Jews. The permission given to them by Alexander I to establish themselves as farmers in the frigid yet free Siberian steppes was greeted with enthusiasm by all. Nicholas's ukase was hailed with joy. Elias Mitauer and Meyer Mendelssohn, at the head of seventy families from Courland, were the first to migrate to the new region (1836), and they were followed by hundreds more. Indeed, the exodus assumed such proportions that the Christians in the parts of the country abandoned by the colonists complained of the decline in business and the depreciation of property. The movement was heartily approved by the rabbis; the populace, its imagination stimulated, began to dream dreams and see visions of brighter days, and all gave vent to their hopefulness in songs of gladness and gratitude, in strains like these: [37]

> Who lives so free
> As the farmer on his land?
> His farm his companion is,
> His never-failing friend.
>
> His sleep to him is sweet
> After a hearty meal;
> Neither grief nor worry
> The farmer-man doth feel.
>
> He rises very early
> To start betimes his toil,
> Healthy and very happy
> On his ever-smiling soil.
>
> O blessings on our czar,
> Czar Nikolai, then be,
> Who granted us this gladness,
> And bade the Jews be free.

Alas, this joy was of short duration! Very soon Nicholas became suspicious of his Siberian colonization scheme, that it was in reality a philanthropic measure, and in place of saving the Jew's soul it only promoted his physical well-being. This suspicion grew into a conviction when he learned that the Jewish community at Tomsk, still faithful to the heritage of Israel, applied for permission to appoint a spiritual leader. The autocrat, therefore, signed an ukase checking settlement in the hitherto free land, depriving honest men of the privilege enjoyed by the worst of criminals, and enrolling the children of those already there among the military Cantonists (January 5, 1837).

Then began real misery. Believing at first that the czar's intentions were sincere, many Jews had sold their hut and land and left for Siberia. No sooner were they there than they were sent, on foot, to Kherson. The decree of the " little father " was executed in—no other phrase can describe it so well—Russian fashion. The innocent Jews who had come to Siberia by invitation were seized, treated as vagabonds, and deported to their destination. Want and suffering produced contagious diseases, and many became a burden to the Jews of Kremenchug and such Christians as could not witness unmoved the infernal comedy played by the defender of the Greek Catholic Church.

Help could be rendered only secretly, and those who dared complain were severely punished.

At the same time that this was taking place in the wilderness of Siberia, a phenomenon of rare occurrence was to be witnessed in the very heart of the Jewish Pale, in Lithuania. Aroused by the wretched condition of his coreligionists, Solomon Posner (1780-1848) determined to erect cloth factories exclusively for Jews. He sent to Germany for experts to teach them the trade. These Jewish workingmen proved so industrious and intelligent that before the end of three years they surpassed their teachers in mechanical skill. But this attempt of Posner was only prefatory to the greater and more arduous task he set himself. It was nothing less than the establishment of a colony in which some of the most Utopian theories would be applied to actual life. Ten years after Robert Owen founded his communistic settlement at New Harmony, Indiana, several hundred robust Russian Jews settled on some of the thousands of acres in Lithuania that were lying fallow for want of tillers. With these farmers Posner hoped to realize his Utopia. He provided every family with sufficient land, the necessary agricultural implements, as well as with horses, cows, etc., free of charge, for a term of twenty-five years. In return, the members of the community pledged themselves to use simple homespun for their apparel, black on holidays, gray on week-days, not to indulge in the luxuries of city life, and to avoid trading of any sort. As time passed, Posner opened coeducational technical schools for the children and batte midrashim for adults, and soon the homesteads presented the appearance of progressive and flourishing farms. Posner's successful effort attracted the admiration of Prince Pashkevich, and was both a living protest against the accusation of Nicholas that Jews were unfit to be farmers and an eloquent plea for the unfortunate victims of a capricious tyrant in Siberia and Kherson.[38]

In his efforts to curb the stiff-necked Jews by all manner of fiendish persecution, Nicholas did not neglect to try the efficacy of some of the plans advocated by Lewis Way. Undismayed by the failure of the Committee of Guardians for Israelitish Christians, in which Alexander I had put so much confidence, a " Jewish Committee," all the members of which were Christians, was organized by imperial decree (May 22, 1825). This committee established, in 1829, a school at Warsaw where Christian divinity students were to be instructed in rabbinical literature and in Judeo-German, in order to be fully equipped for missionary work among the Jews. It appointed Abbé Luigi Chiarini to translate, or rather expose, the Babylonian Talmud, to which undertaking the Government contributed twelve thousand thalers. To do his work thoroughly, the abbé deemed it advisable to write a preliminary dissertation, presenting his aim and views. This he did in his *Theory of Judaism* (*Théorie du judaisme*, Paris, 1830). He endeavored to show how worthless, injurious, and immoral were the teachings of the Talmud. Only by discarding them would the Jews qualify themselves to enjoy the right of citizenship. He proved, to his own satisfaction, that ritual murder was enjoined in the Talmud, and this he did at a time when many a community was harassed by this fiendish accusation. When early death cut short the abbé's effort (1832), the Government, still persisting in its plans, engaged the services of Ephraim Moses Pinner of Posen, who published specimens of his intended translation in his *Compendium* (Berlin, 1831). But the fickle or restless emperor seems to have tired of the plan, or perhaps he found Pinner too Jewish for his purposes. Of the twenty-eight volumes planned, only one, which was dedicated to Nicholas, appeared during the decade following Chiarini's death, and the work was abandoned entirely.[39]

The crusade against the Talmud, thus headed and backed by the Government, now broke out in all its fury. Anti-Talmudic works in English, French, and German were imported into Russia, translated into Hebrew, and scattered among the people. *The Old Paths,* by Alexander McCaul, a countryman and colleague of Lewis Way, but surpassing him in zeal for the conversion of Jews, was translated into Hebrew and German (Frankfort-on-the-Main, 1839) for the edification of those who knew no English. Jews themselves, either out of revenge or because they sought to ingratiate themselves with the high authorities, joined the movement, and openly came out against the Talmud in works modelled after Eisenmenger's *Entdecktes Judenthum.* Such were Buchner, author of *Worthlessness of the Talmud (Der Talmud in seiner Nichtigkeit,* 2 vols., Warsaw, 1848), and Temkin, who wrote *The Straight Road (Derek Selulah,* St. Petersburg, 1835). The former was instructor in Hebrew and Holy Writ in the rabbinical seminary in Warsaw; the latter was a zealous convert to the Greek Catholic faith, who spared

146

no effort to make Judaism disliked among his former coreligionists.

All these desperate attempts proved of no avail.
Judaism was practiced, and the Talmud was studied
during the reign of Nicholas I more ardently than
ever before. Their sacred treasures attacked by
the Government without and by renegades and
detractors within, the Russian Jews nevertheless
clung to them with a tenacity unparalleled even in
their own history. Danzig's *Life of Man* (*Hayye
Adam,* Vilna, 1810), containing all Jewish ritual
ceremonies, was followed out to the least minutiae.
Despite the poverty of the Jews and the comparatively exorbitant price the publisher had to charge
for the Talmud, and, aside from the many sets of
former editions in the country and those continually
imported, and in addition to the Responsa, commentaries, Midrashim, and other works directly
and indirectly bearing on it, more than a dozen
editions of the Talmud had appeared in Russia
alone since the ukase of Catherine II (October 30,
1795) permitting Russian Jews to publish Hebrew
works in their own country. This ukase had been
intended originally to exclude seditious literature
from Russia, but what was unfavorable for the
rebellious Poles proved, in a measure, very bene-

147

ficial to the law-abiding Jews. Under the supervision of a censor, and with but slight interruptions, the Jews published their own books, and in 1806 Slavuta, in Volhynia, saw the first complete edition of the Talmud on Russian soil. Then followed another edition in the same place (1808-1813), a third in Kopys (1816-1828), and a fourth in Slavuta (1817-1822), and several others elsewhere.

The story of the Vilna-Grodno edition of the Talmud is interesting as well as illuminating. It depicts the relation of the Jews among themselves and to the Government. Begun in 1835, at Ozar, near Grodno, an imperial ukase directed the removal of the work to Vilna, the metropolis of Russo-Poland. When the publishers, Simhah Ziml and Menahem Mann Romm, had completed their work in the new quarters, the copies of the book were destroyed by incendiaries (1840). After some time, an effort was made by Joseph Eliasberg and Mattathias Strashun to continue the publication, but the Warsaw censor prohibited its importation into Poland, where the bulk of the subscribers lived. To add to the calamity, a feud broke out between the head of the Slavuta publishing company, Moses Schapira (1758-1838), and the Vilna publishers. The publication of the Talmud had

always been supervised by the prominent rabbis of
the land, and their authorization was necessary to
make an edition legal. This the rabbi never granted
unless the previous edition was entirely disposed·
of. The Slavuta publishers claimed that their edition had not been sold out when the Vilna publishers started theirs. The litigation continued for
some time, and was finally decided in favor of the
Vilna firm. The publishers of Slavuta, however,
having the Polish rabbis and zaddikim on their
side, continued to publish the Talmud, regardless
of the protests of Rabbi Akiba Eger and the " great
ones " of Lithuania. But a terrible misfortune
befell the Slavuta publishers. On account of some
accusation, the two brothers engaged in the business were deported to Siberia, and their father, the
head of the establishment, died of a broken heart.
This cleared the field for the Romms of Vilna, who
continue to prosper to this day, and have now the
greatest Hebrew publishing house in the world.
" It is the finger of God," the pious ones said, and
studied the Talmud with increased devotion."

The numerous Talmud editions indicate the
demand for the work, and the multiplicity of yeshibot explains the cause of the demand. We have
seen how the yeshibot destroyed by Chmielnicki

were re-established soon after the massacres ceased. Their number increased when the Hasidic movement threatened to render the knowledge of the Talmud unpopular; and when the Maskilim, too, made them a target for their attacks, there was hardly a town in which such institutions were not to be found. But surpassing all the yeshibot of the nineteenth century, if not of all centuries, was the Yeshibah Tree of Life (Yeshibat 'Ez Hayyim) in the townlet of Volozhin. There the cherished hopes of the Gaon were finally realized. Within its walls gathered the elect of the Russo-Jewish youth for almost a century.

The founder of this famous yeshibah was Rabbi Hayyim Volozhin, the greatest of the Gaon's disciples (1749-1821). A prominent Talmudist at twenty-five, he, nevertheless, left his business and household at that age, and went to Vilna to become the humble pupil of the Gaon, whose method he had followed from the beginning. When he felt himself proficient enough in his studies, he returned to his native place, and founded (1803) the Tree of Life College, with an enrollment of ten students, whom he maintained at his own expense. But soon the fame of the yeshibah and its founder spread far and wide, and students flocked to it from all corners of Russia and outside of it. In response to Rabbi Hayyim's appeal contributions came pouring in, a new and spacious school-house was erected, and Volozhin became a Talmudic Oxford. To be a student there was both an indication of superiority and a means to proficiency. Rabbi Hayyim did away with the " Tag-essen," or " Freitisch " custom, and introduced a stipendiary system in its stead, thus fostering the self-respect of the students. But they did not as a rule require much to satisfy them with their lot. They came to Volozhin " to learn," and they well knew the Talmudic statement, that " no one can attain eminence in the Torah unless he is willing to die for its sake."

Rabbi Hayyim was succeeded by his son Rabbi Isaac, who united knowledge of secular subjects with profound Talmudic erudition, was active in worldly affairs, and played a prominent part in the Jewish history of his day. He was of the leading spirits who, in 1842, attended the rabbinical conference at St. Petersburg convoked by Nicholas I. The number of students increased under his leadership, according to Lilienthal, to three hundred. But Rabbi Isaac became so engrossed in public affairs that he found he could no longer do justice to his position. His two sons-in-law, therefore, took his place, and when the older died, in 1854, Rabbi Naphtali Zebi Judah Berlin (1817-1893) entered on his useful career, unbroken for forty years, as the dean of the greatest seat of learning in the Diaspora. Under his administration the Tree of Life College reached both the height of its prosperity and the end of its existence (1892)."

Thus all the schemes and machinations of the Russian Government respecting the Jews proved ineffectual. Nicholas I, with the possible exception of Ivan the Terrible, the greatest autocrat in Russian history, at whose wish seemingly insuperable obstacles were instantly removed, the wink of whose eye was sufficient to kill or revive the millions of his crouching slaves—Nicholas I, with all his herculean strength, yet found himself helpless in the presence of a handful of wretched Jews. Furious at his defeat, he expressed the intention to reduce all Jews to Governmental servitude or to make them, like the Cossacks, lifelong soldiers. Being advised to postpone the execution of this plan and to employ less severe measures meanwhile, he issued the Exportation Law of 1843, ordering the expulsion of Jews from the fifty-vyerst boundary zone and from the villages within the Pale, thereby depriv-

ing fifty thousand families at once of their homes
and their support.

Those from the country—writes a Russo-Jewish eye-witness of
the scenes following the enforcement of this inhuman law—move
first to the neighboring cities, and increase the existing poverty,
rendering the difficulty of finding profitable employment still
greater. God only knows how it will end when the congestion
increases still further. . . . I must also inform you—he proceeds—
that these past four months several imperial commissioners have
visited the frontier towns on the Lithuanian border, from which
the Jews are to be banished, in order that the value of the real
estate may be estimated. But how is the valuation calculated?
Even one who is acquainted with the venality and unscrupulous-
ness of Russian officers cannot form a correct idea of how this
business is conducted. If a man has no connection with those in
authority, or cannot obtain powerful intercession, or is unable to
give heavy bribes, his property is valued at perhaps five per cent,
or is set at so low a figure as to make the appraisal differ little
from downright robbery. We, however, are used to such measures, for when they banished us some time past from certain
districts of the city of Brest-Litovsk, where for centuries celebrated scholars of our people dwelt, nothing better was done by
the crown to compensate us for our houses.[42] The same occurred
at the expulsion from St. Petersburg, Moscow, Kiev, Nikolayev,
Alexandrov, Sebastopol, etc., but as it did not affect so large a
mass, nor injure us to so great an extent, we bore the injury
silently. Alas, this is not the case at present. We should gladly
quit the country, gladly should we emigrate to America, Texas,
and especially to Palestine under English protection, if, on the one

hand, we had the means and, on the other, the Government would permit us.[43]

This Exportation Law of Nicholas I, the result of a lawsuit between a Jew and a nobleman living on the eastern frontier, which had been decided by the supreme court in favor of the former, aroused much excitement in every civilized country of Europe. It was before anti-Semitism was in flower, and the people of the time were more responsive even than during the later Kishinev massacres. Indignation meetings were held. Both Jews and Gentiles, not only abroad, but even in Russia, protested. Prayers were offered for the unfortunate. Crémieux in France and Rabbi Philippson in Germany appealed to the public. All to no effect. Grief was especially manifest among English Jews, always the first to feel when their fellow-Jews in other countries suffer, and Grace Aguilar, like Rachel weeping over her children, lamented over her Russian brethren:

> Ay, death! for such is exile—fearful doom,
> From homes expelled yet still to Poland chain'd;
> Till want and famine mind and life consume,
> And sorrow's poison'd chalice all is drained.
> O God, that this should be! that one frail man
> Hath power to crush a nation 'neath his ban.

At this critical period, Moses Montefiore, encouraged by his success in refuting the blood accusation at Damascus, and stimulated by the many petitions he had received from Russia, Germany, France, Italy, England, and America, undertook the philanthropic mission of interceding with the czar on behalf of his coreligionists. It is natural to suspect that no trouble is entirely undeserved; it is but human to sympathize with our friends, and yet regard their suffering as a judgment rather than a misfortune. But Montefiore's trip to Russia dispelled the last trace of suspicion against the Russian Jews. In spite of their poverty, he saw numerous charitable and educational institutions in every city he visited. He found the Jewish men to be the cream of Russia. "He had the satisfaction," Doctor Loewe, his secretary, tells us, "of seeing among them many well-educated wives, sons, and daughters; their dwellings were scrupulously clean, the furniture plain but suitable for the purpose, and the appearance of the family healthy." To all his pleadings Count Uvarov returned but a single answer: "The Russian Jews are different from other Jews; they are orthodox, and believe in the Talmud" "—a reason for persecution in Holy Russia!

Montefiore's visit to Russia, from which so

much had been hoped, did not improve the situation in the least. For all his strenuous efforts, he was compelled to leave the Jews as destitute as he had found them. Nay, they might truthfully have said to the Moses of England what their ancestors had said to the Moses of Egypt, " Since thou didst come to Pharaoh, the hardness of our lot has increased." From the first of May (1844) they were not allowed to continue to earn the pittance necessary to maintain life, as, for instance, by the slavish labor of breaking stones on the highways, with which three hundred families had barely earned dry bread.[45] The great love and respect shown to the uncrowned king of Israel proved to the czar's officials the existence of some artful design on the part of the Jews, and convinced them especially of the disloyalty of Montefiore. The latter, they maintained, was scheming to set himself up as the Jewish czar. Hence every movement of his was closely watched, every word he uttered carefully noted, and not a few Jews were left with memorable tokens for doing homage to the English baronet. Their disabilities were not removed, their condition was not improved, the hopes they entertained resolved themselves into pleasant dreams followed by a sad awakening.[46]

Yet, though his visit did not, as Sir Moses had anticipated, " raise the Jews in the estimation of the people," it was not without beneficent effect on the Jews themselves. It cemented the " traditional friendship " which has always existed between Anglo-Jews and Russo-Jews more than between any sets of Jews of the dispersion. It disclosed to the latter that there were happier Jews and better countries than their own; that there were men who sympathized with them as effectively as could be. Above all, it convinced them that a Jew may be highly educated and wealthy, and take his place among the noble ones of the earth, and still remain a faithful Jew and a loyal son of his persecuted people. " I leave you," Sir Moses called to them at parting, " but my heart will ever remain with you. When my brethren suffer, I feel it painfully; when they have reason to weep, my eyes shed tears." Had Montefiore's visit resulted merely in arousing his brethren's self-consciousness, he had earned a place in the history of Haskalah, for self-consciousness is the most potent factor in the culture of mankind.

Jews from other lands also came to the rescue of their Russian coreligionists. Jacques Isaac Altaras, the ship-builder of Marseilles, petitioned the

157

czar to allow forty thousand Jewish families to
emigrate to Algeria. Rabbi Ludwig Philippson,
editor of the Allgemeine Zeitung des Judenthums,
appealed to his countrymen to help the Russian
Jews to settle in America, Australia, Africa, any-
where away from Russia. But all attempts were ineffectual. Though Count Kissilyef assured Montefiore that the czar " did not wish to keep them [the
Jews], five or six hundred thousand might leave
altogether," emigration was next to impossible.
Russia was constantly playing the game of the cat
with the mouse. Her nails were set and her eyes
fixed upon her prey, and yet she made it appear to
the outside world that she was anxious about the
welfare of the Jews. For Russian tactics have
always been, and still are, the despair of the diplomat, a labyrinth through which only they who hold
the clue can ever hope to find their way.

The condition of the Jews in Russo-Poland was,
if possible, even worse than in Lithuania and Russia proper. Nothing, in fact, but the auto-da-fé
was needed to give it the stamp of medieval Spain.
As before the division of Poland, the Poles suspected the Jews of disloyalty to Poland, while the
Russians suspected them of disloyalty to Russia.
Hitherto too proud to soil his hand with a manual

or mercantile pursuit, the Polish pan, now that the glory of his country had departed, and he was deprived of his lordly estates, began to engage in business of all kinds, and, finding in the Jewish trader a rival with whose skill and diligence he could seldom compete, he became embittered against the entire race. This was the cause of the innumerable restrictions, the extortion, and exploitation in Russo-Poland, which surpassed those of Russia proper.

The Jewish archives—said Doctor Marcus Jastrow, then Rabbi in Warsaw—were humorously known as " California " or the " Mexican Gold Mines." Jews had to pay at every step. They had to pay a Tagzettel [daily tax] for permission to stay in Warsaw, which permission, however, did not include the luxury of breathing. The latter had to be purchased with an additional ten kopecks per capita. The income from these taxations amounted to over a million and a half, but in spite of all this the Jews were regarded as parasites, as leeches feasting upon the life-blood of their Christian compatriots.[47]

Such is the background upon which the picture of Haskalah is to be drawn—black enough to throw into relief the faintest ray of light. The Russian Jews, during the reign of Nicholas I, found themselves in a position possible only in Russia. They were not allowed to emigrate, nor suffered to stay.

In 1823 they were expelled from the farms, and had to crowd into the cities; in 1838 they were expelled from the cities, and forced to go back to the country. Then Siberia was opened to them, but when it was found that even the land of the outcasts was hailed as a place of refuge by the Jews, they were told to go to Kherson. At last arrangements were perfected to allow them to colonize Lithuania—all at once even this was interdicted. They had been conquered with the Poles, yet were left unprotected against the Poles. Could they help suspecting the tyrant of what he really intended to do—of seeking to diminish their numbers by conversion? Is it surprising that when he determined to open public schools and establish rabbinical seminaries, Jews looked upon these, too, as the sugared poison with which he intended to extirpate Judaism? Or can we blame them for being determined to the last to baffle him? Nicholas did not understand the great lesson taught by the history of the Jews and inculcated in the old song,

> To destroy all these people
> You should let them alone.

All that tyranny could inflict, the Russian Jews endured. Yet their number was not diminished.

No coercion could make them leave, in a body, the old paths they were wont to tread. Nicholas's so-called reforms only encouraged a reaction, and the more he afflicted the Jews, the more they multiplied and grew. The behalot of 1754, 1764, and 1793 were repeated in 1833 and 1843; the missionary propaganda only strengthened the devotion of the faithful; and the denial of the means of support only increased the stolidity of the sufferers. And if, like some stepchildren, they were first beaten till they cried, and then beaten because they cried, like some stepchildren they rapidly forgot their lot in the happiness of home and the studies of the bet ha-midrash, and could sing⁴⁵ without bitterness even of the behalah-days, when

> Little boys and little girls
> Together had been mated,
> Tishah be-Ab, the wedding day,—
> Not a soul invited.
> Only the father and the mother,
> And also uncle Elye—
> In his lengthy delye (caftan),
> With his scanty beard—
> Jump and jig with each other
> Like a colt afeared.

[Notes, pp. 314-317.]

## CHAPTER IV

## CONFLICTS AND CONQUESTS

### 1840-1855

The charges brought against the Jews of Russia by henchmen of the czar were grave, indeed, only they did not contain a particle of truth. In Russia itself, not only Jews and non-Russians but even many Christians testified to the innocence of the Jews, and protested against their oppressors. Bibikov, the Governor-General of Podolia and Volhynia; Diakov, the Governor-General of Smolensk; and Surovyetsky, the noted statesman, all write in terms of such praise of their unfortunate countrymen of the Jewish faith that their statements would sound exaggerated, were it not that many other unprejudiced Russians confirm their views.[1] The fact that Nicholas thought the Jews reliable as soldiers speaks against the imputation that they were mercenary and unpatriotic. Neither was the conventional accusation, that they were a people of petty traders, applicable to the Jews in Russia.

Laborers of all kinds were very common among them. It was they, in fact, who rendered all manner of service to their Gentile neighbors, from a cobbler's and blacksmith's to producing the most exquisite *objets d'art* and gold and silver engraving. They were equally well represented among the clerks and bookkeepers, and the bricklayers and stone-cutters. They took up with the most laborious employments, if only they furnished them with an honest even though scanty livelihood.²

But most unfounded of all was the allegation that Jews were opposed to education. The *Memoirs* of Madame Pauline Wengeroff indicate that even among the very strict Jews of her time children were not denied instruction in the German, Polish, and Russian literatures. We have seen how they availed themselves of the permission, granted to them by Alexander I, to attend the schools and universities of the empire. Nor did they fail to open schools of their own. No sooner was the Franco-Russian war over than Joseph Perl of Galicia founded a school in Tarnopol (1813), then under the Russian Government, and two years later he drew upon his own resources to build a schoolhouse large enough to accommodate the great, steadily growing number of students. In 1822

163

we hear of a school that had been in existence for some time in Uman (the Ukraine). It had been established by Meïr Horn, Moses Landau, and Hirsh Hurwitz, all of whom were indefatigable laborers in the cause of Haskalah in the Ukraine. Perl's school was the pattern and model for a multitude of other schools, among them the one founded by Zittenfeld (1826) in Odessa, in the faculty of which were Simhah Pinsker, Elijah Finkel, the grandson of Elijah Gaon, and Abraham Abele, the eminent Talmudist. In 1836 a girls' department was added to it, and when Lilienthal visited Odessa (ab. 1843) it had an attendance of from four to five hundred pupils of both sexes, the annual expense being twenty-eight thousand rubles. A similar school was opened in Kishinev by Stern, and in the early " forties " there was hardly a Jewish community of note without one or more of such Jewish public institutions. Several well-to-do Maskilim not only founded but, like Perl, also maintained such schools, and gave instruction in some or all of the subjects taught in them.[3]

The " forties " began auspiciously for Haskalah in Russia. On January 15, 1840, the Riga community, amid pomp and rejoicing, opened the first

Jewish school affiliated with a university. The teaching staff consisted of three Jews and one Christian, with Doctor Max Lilienthal (1815-1882), the young, highly recommended, and recently chosen local rabbi, as its principal. In the same year, the indefatigable Basilius Stern succeeded in forming a committee, of which Hayyim Efrusi and Moses Lichtenstadt were members, to deliberate on founding rabbinical seminaries in Russia. In 1841, forty-five delegates, representing the six chief committees of the Lovers of Enlightenment, assembled in Vilna, and thence issued an appeal in which they adopted as their platform the elevation of the moral standards of adults by urging them to follow useful trades and discouraging the Jewish proclivity to business as much as possible; a reform of the prevailing system of the education of the young; the combating, if possible the eradication, of Hasidism, the fountainhead, as they thought, of ignorance and superstition; the establishment of rabbinical seminaries, after the model of those in Padua and Amsterdam, to supply congregations with educated rabbis. It was further agreed that a Consistory be created, to supervise Jewish affairs and establish schools and technical institutes wherever necessary. To these main points were added several others of minor importance. The Maskilim of Besascz insisted that steps be taken to stop the prevailing custom of premature marriages. Those of Brest proposed that Government aid be invoked to compel Jews to dress in the German style, to use authorized text-books in the hadarim, and interdict the study of the Talmud except by those preparing themselves for the rabbinate.[4]

Even in Vilna and Minsk, towns which later put themselves on record as opposed to Government schools, the Jews yielded gladly to the innovations of such Maskilim as S. Perl, G. Klaczke, I. Bompi, and the distinguished philanthropist David Luria, who took the initiative in transforming the educational system of these cities. Under the superintendence of Luria, the Minsk Talmud Torah became a model institution; the training conferred there on the poor and orphaned surpassed that given to the children of the rich in their private schools. This aroused jealousy in the parents of the latter, and at their request Luria organized a merchants' school, for the wealthier class. He then established what he called Midrash Ezrahim, or Citizens' Institute, in which he met with such success that he attracted the attention of the authorities, and received a special acknowledgment from the czar.[5]

Russian Jewry was astir with new life. In many places secular education was divorced for the first time from rabbinical speculation. Knowledge became an end in itself, and learning increased greatly. An investigation by Nicholas I convinced all who were interested that though the Talmud remained the chief subject of study, the number of educated Jews was far greater than commonly supposed. The upliftment of the masses was the beau-ideal of every Maskil, and Hebrew and even the much-despised Yiddish were employed to effect it. Ignorance was regarded as the bane of life, and enlightenment as the panacea for all the ills to which their downtrodden brethren were heirs. As their pious coreligionists deemed it the universal duty to be well-versed in the Talmud, so the Maskilim thought it incumbent upon everybody to be highly cultured. No obstacle was great enough to discourage them. They were willing martyrs to the goddess of Wisdom, at whose shrine they worshipped, and whose cult they spread in the most adverse circumstances.

Had the Government not interfered with the efforts of the Maskilim, or had it chosen a commission from among the Russian Jews themselves, among whom, as soon became evident to Nicholas himself, there were more than enough to do justice to an educational inquiry, the Haskalah movement would have continued to spread, notwithstanding the obstacles put in its way. But Nicholas was determined to reduce the number of Jews also by " re-educating " them in accordance with his own ideas. Every attempt made by the Jews to educate themselves was, therefore, checked. Even the noble efforts of Luria were stopped, his schools were closed, and his only rewards were " a gold medal from the czar and a short poem by Gottlober."

In Germany, since the time of Mendelssohn, the study of the Talmud had been on the wane. The great yeshibot formerly existing in Metz, Frankfort, Hamburg, Prague, Fürth, Halberstadt, etc., disappeared, and the reforms introduced in the synagogue and the numerous converts to Christianity impressed the outside world with the idea that Judaism among German Jews was writhing in the agony of death. If the same disintegrating elements were introduced among the Russian Jews, the Government believed that they would ultimately come over to the Greek Catholic Church of their own accord. Hence it was anxious to learn the secret of this power and beamed graciously on several learned Jews of Germany.

David Friedländer (1750-1834) was then considered the legitimate successor of Mendelssohn, whose friend he had been for more than twenty years. He resembled his master in many respects, though he lacked both his genius and his sympathy. Mendelssohn translated the Pentateuch and the Psalms into German, Friedländer translated the Haftarot (selections from the Prophets) and the prayer book. Mendelssohn encouraged the publication of the Meassef; he did likewise, and contributed several articles to the journal. But, unlike his master, or, as he claimed, like his master in secret, he held exceedingly latitudinarian views on Judaism. In his later years he advocated abolishing the study of Hebrew in the schools and discarding it from the prayer book. He even rejoiced that by attending the services in Protestant churches many Jewish families were becoming acquainted with the religion he himself would have accepted on certain conditions.[6]

It was to Friedländer that Bishop Malchevsky, actuated, as he maintained, by a desire to render the Jews worthy of the enjoyment of civil rights,

applied for suggestions, in 1816, when the missionary zeal of Alexander I was first aroused. He
responded in a pamphlet, *On the Improvement of
the Israelites in the Kingdom of Poland,*[1] in which
he declared that the quickest way of " civilizing "
the Jews would be to deprive their rabbis of power
and influence, to force them to dress in the German
fashion, and use the Polish language, to admit them
to the public schools and other educational institutions, and, above all, to abrogate the laws discrim-
inating between them and their Gentile countrymen.

Friedländer's advice regarding the removal of
civil disabilities was never executed, but his other
suggestions were followed out with more vigor than
was necessary or good. To do away with the rabbis, and consequently with the Talmud, was just
what was desired. It was partly with this end in
view that Alexander I permitted, that is, commanded, the establishment of the rabbinical seminary in Warsaw. But when it was found that,
although the seminary students were provided with
all necessaries, and notwithstanding the decree that
six years from the date of its opening none but
seminary graduates would be eligible to the rabbinical office, few students availed themselves of
the opportunity afforded, and none obtained posi-

tions, the whole plan fell into disfavor.' The Government, nevertheless, remained as stubbornly determined as ever, and unable to turn all the children into Cantonists, it decided to have those who remained at home gradually converted by means of a method worked out by the Minister of Education, Uvarov. They were forced to attend what became known as Government schools, though maintained exclusively with Jewish funds. In order to win the confidence of the Jews for the project, Doctor Lilienthal, whose speech at the dedication of the Riga School secured him a diamond ring as a token of the czar's approval, was sent from St. Petersburg on a mission of investigation, more especially of persuasion.

For more than three years Lilienthal was one of the most popular personages in Europe. The eyes of all who had the amelioration of the lot of the Russian Jew at heart, it may be said the eyes of the civilized world, were fixed upon him as an epochmaker in the history of the Jews. Nature had formed him, physically and mentally, to be a leader among his people, and his training and temperament made it easy for him to ingratiate himself into the favor of the great. It seemed that he was just the man to be the successful executor of the czar's plan. The Maskilim, above all, hailed him as the champion of the cause of Haskalah. He was their Moses or Ezra, the God-sent redeemer of their benighted brethren out of the quagmire of fanaticism. From various cities numerous urgent appeals came to him to hasten the execution of his great plan. Wherever he went, he was enthusiastically received, a truly royal welcome was extended to him. The Vilna community appropriated five thousand rubles for the school fund, and pledged itself to raise more if it were found necessary; and he was invited also to Minsk by the kahal of the city.

Unfortunately, Lilienthal's tactics exposed him to suspicion, and the seed of discord was soon sown between him and his former admirers. He tried to serve two masters, the czar and the Jews, and he alienated both. The pious regarded him as a mere tool in the hands of the Government, for, they maintained, *education without emancipation leads to conversion.* The enlightened element also lost confidence in one who, instead of boldly attacking superstition, preferred, while in Minsk, to identify himself not only with the Mitnaggedim, but even with the Hasidim. He was also too headstrong and too vain of his achievements. Benjamin Mandelstamm, who, as he tells us in his letters, considered Lilienthal " as wise as Solomon and as enterprising as Moses," complains a little later of his arrogance, and at the last speaks of him with contempt. His assumed superiority grieved the Maskilim, and their former enthusiasm was rapidly replaced by hatred and persecution. He found it necessary to put himself under the protection of the police while in Minsk, and when he returned to Vilna his reception was far less hearty than it had been before.

In order to regain the confidence of the Russian Jews, Lilienthal obtained a permit from the Minister of Education to call an assembly of prominent Jews at St. Petersburg, to decide for themselves how to better the condition of the existing schools and to consider the practicability of establishing rabbinical seminaries. For he, too, like the Maskilim, considered the rabbis the chief menace to Haskalah. Rabbinical authority was supreme, and if the rabbis could be won over, all would be gained. The bell-wethers once secured, the flocks were sure to follow. It took a long time for Lilienthal, and still longer for the Maskilim, to find out that what they regarded as the cause was in reality the consequence. Eight years later Lilienthal himself admitted the sad truth, that the rabbinical seminaries in Russia could not effect the coveted end. " It must not be lost sight of," says he in his *Sketches of Jewish Life in Russia*,⁹ " that the Russian Jews live strictly in accordance with our received laws, and they are sufficiently learned in them to know that the many cases of conscience which are of constant occurrence cannot be decided understandingly by any one who has but a superficial knowledge of the Talmud and of the decisions of the later doctors of the Law, but that it requires the study of an entire lifetime to become thoroughly acquainted with those stupendous monuments of learning and deep research in the great concerns of life."

After several busy months at St. Petersburg and frequent consultations with Count Uvarov, Lilienthal returned to Vilna, and two weeks later he published his circular letter, *Maggid Yeshu'ah* (*The Announcer of Good Tidings*).¹⁰ The " good tidings " were that an imperial ukase (June 22, 1842) would convene a council of distinguished Jews at St. Petersburg, to deliberate how to " re-educate " the Jews. Accordingly, in the early part of April, 1843, the notables, from different places and with diametrically opposed views, assembled in the Rus-

**ALEXANDER ZEDERBAUM**
1816-1893

sian capital. Representing the Jews, there were Rabbi Isaac Volozhin, the dean of the Tree of Life Yeshibah, perhaps the strongest man present; Rabbi Menahem Mendel Shneersohn of Lubavich, leader of the Hasidic reform sect; Joseph Heilprin, the financier and banker of Berdichev, and Bezalel (Basilius) Stern, principal of the Jewish public schools of Odessa. Representing the Government were Count Uvarov, Chevalier Dukstaduchinsky, and others, with de Vrochenko, Minister of State, as chairman and Lilienthal as secretary. Montefiore of England, Crémieux of France, and Rabbi Philippson of Germany had been invited, but they failed to come. The council decided to open Jewish public schools in every city where Jews reside, and also two rabbinical seminaries, the one in Vilna, the other in Zhitomir, the former being considered the Jewish metropolis of the northwestern part, the latter, of the southwestern part, of Russia. They also proposed to do away with the Judeo-Polish garb, and suggested certain alterations in the prayer book.

The delegates met, deliberated, and disbanded, but the tidings announced in Lilienthal's epistle did not prove to be good. In one of the fables of Kryloff, the Russian Æsop, we are told that once a swan, a pike, and a crab, decided to make a trip together. No sooner had they started than, in accordance with their nature, the swan began to fly, the pike to shuffle along, the crab to crawl backward. It was so with the delegation of 1843. Rabbi Isaac, the rabid Mitnagged, could find but little to admire in the proposals of Rabbi Menahem Mendel, the ardent Hasid, and both were bitterly opposed to the view preached by Doctor Lilienthal, that the salvation of the Jews and Judaism would be brought about by a system of education adopted in accordance with an ukase by Nicholas. Stern, too, had little use for Lilienthal, whom he declared to be ignorant of the condition of Russian Jews and incapable of working in their behalf. From such discord nothing good could come. The fact is, that the few resolutions mentioned had been drawn up beforehand by the Government officials, and the time and trouble and expense which the council involved were, à la Russe, for appearance sake. Finding his efforts an utter failure, Lilienthal went to Odessa with letters of recommendation from Uvarov to Vorontzov, the patron of Stern, and was elected rabbi of that enlightened and wealthy community. But, for some inexplicable reason, he suddenly left the city on the plea of visiting friends in

Germany, and went to the United States, where he remained to the end of his life, and became one of the leading rabbis and communal workers among his coreligionists whose lines had fallen in pleasanter places than the fortunes of those he had left behind in Russia."

For Lilienthal's disillusionment came apace, and he finally recognized the error of his ways. In his book, *My Travels in Russia*, published both in English and in German, he admits that the opponents of the schools he advocated were after all in the right. Education without emancipation was indeed the straightest road to conversion. Witness the thirty thousand Jewish apostates in St. Petersburg and Moscow alone, most of whom hailed from the Baltic provinces, where the Jews were more cultured, but not less oppressed, than their brethren.

Those men—says he—who have acquired from study an idea of the rights of man, and that the Jew ought to enjoy the same privileges as every other citizen; those men who tried, by the knowledge they had obtained, to open for themselves better prospects in life, and now saw every hope frustrated by laws inimical to them only as Jews, ran, from mere despair, into the bosom of the Greek Church. The harassing care for a living, the terrible difficulties in surmounting them forced them, in an hour of distress, to deny their faith. I always compared them with the Anusim [forced converts] of Spain. Among them there is no religious indifference, as is the case in Western Europe and Germany; and I have met with many converted Jews there, who, with tears in their eyes, complained of heart-burnings and pangs of conscience; and they look upon themselves as eternally lost. Those tears will show a heavy balance against Czar Nicholas, when, bereft of his earthly power, he stands before the eternal tribunal.

The other charge—he says again after refuting several accusations of the kind stated above—the other charge, that the Jews are averse to secular studies, rests upon an equally erroneous foundation. For even in Germany Jewish parents have at length found out that it is absolute folly to let their sons devote themselves to the study of science, since they never can hope for obtaining the least office; and since many a one, after the best years of his youth are passed, tired of waiting, and fearful of not having in his old age any means of support, finds in the baptismal font the last anchor of his shattered hopes. How much more must this consideration have weight in Russia? Nicholas, instead of encouraging the Jews to study, ordered, on the contrary, that all such of them as held offices and insignia of distinction under Alexander should either resign or become apostates. I know myself several collegiate councillors and men attached to the court, who went to the synagogue on the Day of Atonement with the insignia of the order of St. Anna around their neck, and prayed there with devotion and fervor, who still were forced into apostasy. Such instances are not calculated to encourage Jewish parents to let their children study; and it is but too true that many whose inclination led them to study were carried thereby into the bosom of the Christian Church.[12]

178

After almost half a decade of indefatigable labor, Lilienthal finally came to understand the Russian State policy, " to assign a plausible reason for every act done by the Government, in order to stand justified in the estimation of Europe, whilst they, by throwing dust in the eyes of the public, conceal their true purpose." The laws which seemed favorable to the Jews, and apparently aimed at promoting culture among them, went hand in hand with laws of the most rigorous character. It is true that the Jews were not the only unfortunates whom the fanatic autocrat wished to Russify, that is, compel to see the pure light of Greek Orthodoxy. But they, of course, suffered the most. The slightest laws were enforced by the chinovniks (officials) with the knout and the leaden lash. When the Judeo-Polish gaberdine, the long side-curls (peot), and the wig or turban (knup) fell into disfavor with the Government, the miserable offender caught by an officer seldom saved himself with the mere sacrifice of knup, coat, peot, and beard. And when the time arrived for the execution of the more important laws, such as the Exportation Act of April 20, 1843, no fiendish ingenuity could surpass the cruelty of the Cossacks. This ukase more than any other, it is claimed, em-

bittered Lilienthal against Russia, and caused him
to flee to where he could say as one awakening from
a nightmare: " The horrible hatred against the
Jews in Russia is nothing more to me than a hazy
remembrance. My soul is no longer oppressed by
frightful pictures of tyranny and persecution." [13]
He was in the land of the free!

The Lilienthal tragedy thus came to a premature
close. The hero disappeared at the beginning of
the play. He had the potency, but he lacked the
conditions, for producing great results. His German birth and training, the very qualities which
recommended him to the Government, operated
against him when he came to deal with Russian
Jews. Yet he succeeded in giving a strong impetus
to the Haskalah movement, and builded better than
he knew. The statement in his address at the dedication of the Riga school,[14] " This hour we may
call the hour of the renaissance of the mental education of Israel," which reads like an oratorical
platitude, was not entirely visionary. The real
history of Haskalah in Russia commences with
Lilienthal.

Time helped greatly to restore, even to deepen,
the affection of the Maskilim for Lilienthal. A
modern critic speaking of " life and literature " in

Hebrew, pictures him in glowing colors, and finishes his description thus:

> I have presented to you, reader, a man of deep culture, known and respected in the highest circles, and yet inseparably connected with his race and religion, and ready to offer his life for their welfare; a man who worked with might and main for others at the sacrifice of his own comfort and advancement; an orator whose exalted phrases shattered the pillars and foundations of ignorance and superstition; a hero who in time of peril was proof against the arrows and missiles of the enemy, and who did not relax his hand from the flag. But what was the fruit he reaped? Mostly ingratitude and persecution, a heart lacerated with despair, a soul writhing under the pangs of frustrated hopes. Such a personality with its fine shades, and with the poetry of the artist superimposed, would afford splendid material for the hero of a novel—a hero to captivate the eye and heart of the reader by his nobility and grandeur.[15]

For a long time Russian officialdom discussed the question, whether the establishment of exclusively Jewish schools would prove beneficial, but nobody doubted the efficacy of rabbinical seminaries. Yet it was these latter institutions that evoked the strongest protests from the Jews. The advocates of Haskalah gradually came to recognize the truth, which Lilienthal admitted afterwards, that for a Russian rabbi a thorough knowledge of the Talmud was absolutely indispensable. But it was with the

181

object of discouraging such knowledge that the seminaries had been suggested by Uvarov, and it was this study that was almost entirely ignored in them. What congregation, many of whose members were profound Talmudists, would accept a rabbi to whom unvocalized Hebrew was a snare and a stumbling-block? Moreover, the whole atmosphere of the seminaries was Christian, nay, military. Not a few members of their faculties or boards of governors were discharged police officers or superannuated soldiers, and at the head of the seminary in Vilna, the metropolis of Russian Jewry, stood an apostate Jew! They became, as it were, infirmaries of the bureaucracy, where, at the expense of the Jews, it could stow away anyone who had proved a failure or was no longer useful. The Government also undertook to provide the graduates with positions, patronage which rendered the students insolently independent of their coreligionists, and encouraged some of them to indulge in a *modus vivendi* distasteful to their future flocks. The graduates, therefore, proved failures as rabbis, and the Government was forced to provide for them by appointing them as teachers.[16]

If this was the case with the rabbinical seminaries, we can easily imagine the state of the subordinate schools. The Christian principals were coarse and uneducated as a rule, and did their best to prejudice the children against their religion. Scattered all over the Pale were to be found Jews competent to fill positions not only as teachers in inferior grades but as professors in the universities. Yet Lilienthal was advised ( 1841 ) to advertise for three hundred teachers in Germany. Finally the Government decided to employ Jews as teachers of Hebrew only, the least important subject in the curriculum; for instruction in the secular branches none but Christians were eligible. No Jews were allowed to become rectors in their own schools, and their salaries were so small that they could not support themselves without teaching an additional class, which was prohibited. A Jew might, indeed, become an " honorable overseer " (pochotny blyus-tityel), to mediate between pupils and parents, but the title was the only pay attached to the office. Respectable parents, therefore, kept their children at home, or rather in the heder, and many a child's name was on the roll of attendance who was not even aware of the existence of the school. " Every year in the autumn," relates a writer a quarter of a century later, " there was a kind of compulsory recruiting of Jewish children for the Government school, accompanied sometimes by struggles between the victims and their enemies,—scenes without a parallel, in some respects, in the civilized world. I remember how poor mothers and sisters wept with despair when some boy of the family was carried off or enlisted by the officers to be a pupil of a Government school." Like the poimaniki, the poor and the orphaned were compelled, or induced, to fill the class-rooms shunned by the rich and respectable, and though the Government not only condemned the ancient Hebrew institutions, but declared the twenty thousand teachers who imparted instruction in them to be outlaws and criminals, the melammedim pursued their vocation as ever, and the hadarim, Talmud Torahs, yeshibot, and batte midrashim swarmed with students of the prohibited learning."

Nicholas was paid measure for measure, and the cunning of his ministers was made of no avail by the shrewdness of his Jewish subjects. The report of the Minister of Education, at the end of 1845, shows incredible progress. It states that since the ukase of November 13, 1844, *i. e.* in the course of a single year, more than two thousand schools of different grades were established in various cities of the Pale, with more than one hundred and eighty thousand pupils, not including the technical schools in Odessa, Riga, Kishinev, Vilna, and Uman, with their hundreds of students! The truth was that, instead of the reported Russification, there had set in a vigorous reaction, which rendered the position more critical. Both sides had become desperate.[18] Some Maskilim, emboldened by the interest the Government evinced in their efforts, had resorted to all manner of means to accomplish their object, and frequently allied themselves with the oppressors. The Slavuta publishing house, it is claimed, was closed, and the Schapiras met with their tragic end, because " as printers they scrupulously abstained from publishing Haskalah literature." Maskilim were employed by the authorities as tax collectors, and these, as is ever the case with rapacious farmers of taxes, besides executing the harsh laws of the tyrant, looked also to their own aggrandizement, and harassed their pious coreligionists in all ways conceivable. Many of them even hindered the colonization movement, because, if allowed to mature, it would deprive them of their income.[19] In addition to this, the Jews were now burdened, through the instrumentality of the Maskilim, with a tax on the candles lighted on Sabbath eve, yielding annually over one million rubles, the greater part of which went into the coffers of greedy officials. Another tax, also for the maintenance of the newly-organized Government schools, was levied—one kopeck and a half per page!—on text-books, whether imported from abroad or published in Vilna or Zhitomir, and the text-books were published with unnecessarily large type and wide margins to increase the number of pages. The abridgment and translation of Maimuni's *Mishneh Torah* (St. Petersburg, 1851), superintended by Leon Mandelstamm, cost the Russian Jews tens of thousands of rubles, notwithstanding the expenditure of two or three millions on their own educational institutions, and at a time when every kopeck was needed for the support of the host of victims of fire, famine, and cholera, which ravaged many a city. Hence the reaction became more and more formidable. The cry grew louder and louder, *Znaty nye znayem, shkolles nye zhelayem!* ("We want no schools!"). The opposition, which began in the latter years of Alexander I, reached its culmination in the last decade of the reign of Nicholas I. "Israel," laments Mandelstamm, "seems to be even worse than formerly; he is like a sick person who has convalesced only to relapse, and the physicians are beginning to despair." It was a struggle

186

not unlike that all over Europe at the beginning of the Renaissance, a struggle between liberty and authority, between this world and other-worldliness, between the spirit of the nineteenth century and that of the millenniums which preceded it.

Here is a description, by Morgulis, of the struggles and conquests of the new, small, but zealous, group of Maskilim in Russia at about that time:[20]

Those upon whom the sun of civilization and freedom happened to cast a ray of light, showing them the path leading to a new life, were compelled to study the European literatures and sciences in garrets, in cellars, in any nook where they felt themselves secure from interference. Neither unaffiliated Jews nor the outer world knew anything about them. Like rebels they kept their secrets unto themselves, stealthily assembling from time to time, to consider how they might realize their ideal, and disclose to their brethren the fountainhead of the living waters out of which they drank and drew new youth and life. Whatever was novel was accepted with delight. They looked with envy upon the great intellectual progress of their western brethren. Fain would they have had their Jewish countrymen recognize the times and their requirements, but they could not give free utterance to their thoughts. On the contrary, they found it expedient to assume the mask of religion in order to escape the suspicion of alert zealots, and gain, if possible, new recruits. In many places societies were founded under the name of Lovers of the New Haskalah, the members of which observed such secrecy that even their kinsmen and those among whom they

187

dwelt were unaware of their existence. If through the discovery of some forbidden book any of them happened to be detected, he never betrayed his friends. Such a one was usually compelled to marry, so that, being burdened with family cares, he might desist from his unpopular pursuits.

From which it would appear that though the opposition to Haskalah in Russia was by no means as violent as had been the opposition to enlightenment in France, for instance, or even among the Jews of Germany and Austria,[21] it was a bitter and stubborn conflict between parents and children in the adjustment of old ideals to a new environment.

Aside from the hindrances which Haskalah encountered because of Nicholas's conversionist policy, it was greatly hampered by the geographical distribution of the Jews. Here again the czar defeated his own end by segregating the three or four million of his Jewish subjects in certain districts, technically called the Pale, the greatest ghetto the world has ever known. It was a Judea in itself. The Jews there seldom came in contact with outside civilization. The languages they used were Hebrew as the literary tongue, Yiddish among themselves, and the local Slavonic dialect with their non-Jewish neighbors. Russian was strange, not only to the great majority of Jews, but to the Russians themselves. It was merely the State language, and even the Government officials fell back on their mother tongue whenever they were at liberty to do so. It was this that made it very difficult for the Jews to be Russified.

But even if Russification had been a much easier process, Russian civilization was hardly worth the having.[22] To become Russified would have meant not only religious but also intellectual suicide. Whatever was good in the Russia of that day was an importation. The language was scarcely beyond the barbarous state. Its literature possessed neither original nor adopted writings, no profound philosophical systems, no Rousseau or Goethe, no Franklin or Kant, not even any practical information with which to reward the student. The best writers were Kryloff, Pushkin, Zhukovsky, and Dyerzhavin. The prices of books were so high as to make them unattainable. Karamzin's *History of the Russian Empire* sold at fifty-five rubles per copy. The royal library, which had been founded by the Jewish court physician Sanchez, contained only eight Russian books during the reign of Alexander I, and not many more were added by his successor. The dramatic art developed by the Jewish playwright Nebakhovich remained for a long time in the same state as when he ceased his work.[23] If Russia was the most powerful, it continued to be the most fanatical and uncivilized country in Europe. All who had occasion to visit and study it during the first half of the nineteenth century testify to its deplorable intellectual status. According to a very ingenious and observing writer, quoted by Buckle in his *History of Civilization,* it consisted of but two ranks, the highest and the lowest, or the nobility and the serfs: *Les marchands, qui formaient une classe moyenne, sont en si petit nombre qu'il ne peuvent marquer dans l'état; d'ailleurs presque tous sont étrangers.* The higher classes were distinguished for " a total absence of all rational tastes on literary topics."

Here [in Russia]—the same writer continues—it is absolutely *mauvais genre* to discuss a rational subject—pure *pédanterie* to be caught upon any topics beyond dressing, dancing, and a *jolie tournure.* Military prowess is ranked far above scholarly attainment, and a man in a uniform, no matter how depraved, takes precedence of one in plain clothes, whatever his achievements. All the energies of the nation are turned towards the army. Commerce, the law, and the civil employments are held in no esteem; all young men of any consideration betake themselves to the profession of arms. Nothing astonished them more than to see the estimation in which the civil professions, and especially the bar, are held in Great Britain.[24]

How different was the position of the Jews in other countries, especially in Germany! Culture streamed upon them from all sides. As their numbers were small, and as they lived, in most cases, in the larger cities of the empire, their contact with the Christian world was immediate and continuous. And then the irresistible fascination of German literature, and the easy, almost imperceptible transition from the Judeo-German to the Teutonic-German! All this and many minor allurements were potent enough to draw even the heretofore callous German Jews out of their isolation, and their Germanization by the middle of the nineteenth century was an established fact. No wonder, then, that, unlike Russian Jewry, the German Jews experienced an unprecedented revolution; that the difference between the Mendelssohnian generation and the next following was almost as great as that between the modern American Jew and his brother in the Orient. No wonder, also, that when Haskalah finally took root in Russia, it was purely German for fifty years and more; that Nicholas's vigorous attempts, instead of making the Slavonic Jews better Russians, merely helped to make those he " re-educated " greater admirers of Germany. The most puissant autocrat of Russia unwittingly contributed to the downfall of Russian autocracy, and Gregori Peretz, the Dekabrist, son of the financier who became converted under Alexander I, was the first of those who were to endeavor, with book and bomb, to break the backbone of tyranny under Nicholas II.[25]

Till about the " sixties," then, the Russo-Jewish Maskilim were the recipients, and the German Jews were the donors. The German Jews wrote, the Russian Jews read. Germany was to the Jewish world, during the early Haskalah movement, what France, according to Guizot, was to Europe during the Renaissance: both received an impetus from the outside in the form of raw ideas, and modified them to suit their environment. Berlin was still, as it had been during the days of Mendelssohn and Wessely, the sanctuary of learning, the citadel of culture. In the highly cultivated German literature they found treasures of wisdom and science. The poetical gems of Goethe, Schiller, Lessing, and Herder captivated their fancy; the philosophy of Kant and Fichte, Schelling and Hegel nourished their intellect. Kant continued to be the favorite guide of Maimon's countrymen, and in their love for him they interpreted the initials of his name to mean " For my soul panteth after thee." [26]

But more efficacious than all other agencies was Mendelssohn's German translation of the Bible, and the *Biur* commentary published therewith. Renaissance and Reformation, those mighty, revolutionary forces, have entered every country by side-doors, so to say. The Jewish Pale was no exception to the rule. What Wycliffe's translation did for England, and Luther's for Germany, Mendelssohn's did for Russian Jewry. Like the Septuagint, it marked a new epoch in the history of Jewish advancement. It is said that Mendelssohn's aim was chiefly to show the grandeur of the Hebrew poetry found in the Bible, but by the irony of fate his translation displayed to the Russian Jew the beauty and elegance of the German language. To the member of the Lovers of the New Haskalah, surreptitiously studying the Bible of the " Dessauer," the Hebrew was rather a translation of, or commentary on, the German, and served him as a bridge to cross over into the otherwise hardly accessible field of German literature.

The cities on the borders of Russia were the first strongholds of Haskalah, and among them, as noted before, few struggled so intensely for their intellectual and civil emancipation as those in the provinces of Courland and Livonia. Though their lot was not better than that of their coreligionists, yet, having formerly belonged to Germany, and being surrounded by a people whose culture was superior to that of the rest of Russia, they were the first to adopt western customs, and were surpassed only by the Jews in Germany in their desire for reform. Their strenuous pleadings for equal rights were, indeed, ineffectual, but this did not lessen their admiration for the beauties of civilization, nor blind them to its benefits. " Long ago," remarks Lilienthal, " before the peculiar Jewish dress was prohibited, a great many could be seen here [in Courland] dressed after the German fashion, speaking pure German, and having their whole household arranged after the German custom. The works of Mendelssohn were not *trefah pasul* [unclean and unfit], the children visited the public schools, the academies, and the universities." [27]

The beautiful city of Odessa, on the Black Sea, at that time just out of its infancy and full of the virility and aspiration of youth, was also in the full glare of the German Haskalah movement. With its wide and straight streets, its public and private parks, and its magnificent structures, it presents even to-day a marked contrast to other Russian cities, and the Russians, not without pride,

speak of it as " our little Paris." In the upbuilding
of this southern metropolis Jews played an exceedingly important part. For, as regards the promotion of trade and commerce, Russia had outgrown
the narrow policy of Elizabeta Petrovna, and did
not begrudge her Jews the privilege of taking the
lead. The " enemies of Christ " were permitted,
even invited, to accomplish their " mission " also
in Odessa, and thither they accordingly came, not
only from Volhynia, Podolia, and Lithuania, but
also from Germany, Austria, and especially Galicia.
Erter, Letteris, Krochmal, Perl, Rapoport, Eichenbaum, Pinsker, and Werbel became better known
in Russia than in their own land. As the Russo-
Polish Jews had carried their Talmudic learning
back to the countries whence they originally received it, so the Galician Jews, mostly hailing from
the city of Brody, where Israel Zamoscz, Mendel
Levin, Joseph Hakohen, and others had implanted
the germs of Haskalah, now reimported it into
Russia. The Jews of Odessa were, therefore, more
cultured than other Russian Jews, not excepting
those of Riga. Prosperous in business, they lav-
ished money on their schools, and their educational
system surpassed all others in the empire. In 1826
they had the best public school for boys, in 1835

a similar one for girls, and in 1852 there existed
fifty-nine public schools, eleven boarding schools,
and four day schools. The children attended the
Richelieu Lyceum and the " gymnasia " in larger
proportion than children of other denominations,
and they were among the first, not only in Russia,
but in the whole Diaspora, to establish a " choir-
synagogue " (1840). " In most of the families,"
says Lilienthal, " can be found a degree of refine-
ment which may easily bear comparison with the
best French salon." Even Nicholas I found words
of praise for the Odessa Jews. " Yes," said he,
" in Odessa I have also seen Jews, but they were
men "; while the zaddik " Rabbi Yisrolze " declared that he saw " the flames of Gehennah round
Odessa." [28]

Warsaw, too, was a beneficiary of Germany,
having been occupied by the Prussians before it
fell to the lot of the Russians. It was there that
practically the first Jewish weekly journals were
published in Yiddish and Polish, Der Beobachter
an der Weichsel, and Dostrzegacz Nadvisyansky
(1823). There was opened the first so-called rabbinical seminary, with Anton Eisenbaum as principal, and Cylkov, Buchner, and Kramsztyk as
teachers. The public schools were largely attended,

owing to the efforts of Mattathias Rosen, and a year after a reformed synagogue had been organized in Odessa another was founded in Warsaw, where sermons were preached in German by Abraham Meïr Goldschmidt.

But Riga on the Baltic, Odessa on the Black Sea, and Warsaw on the Vistula were outdone by some cities in the interior. Haskalah lovers multiplied rapidly, and were found in the early " forties " in every city of any size in the Pale. " The further we go from Pinsk to Kletzk and Nieszvicz," writes a correspondent in the Annalen,[29] " the more we lose sight of the fanatics, and the greater grows the number of the enlightened." With the establishment of the rabbinical seminaries in Zhitomir (1848), this former centre of Hasidism became the nursery of Haskalah. The movement was especially strong in Vilna, the " Jerusalem of Lithuania," as Napoleon is said to have called it. From time immemorial, long before the Gaon's day, it had been famous for its Talmudic scholars. " Its yeshibot," says Jacob Emden in the middle of the eighteenth century, " were closed neither by day nor by night; many scholars came home from the bet ha-midrash but once a week. They surpassed their brethren in Poland and in Germany in learning and

197

knowledge, and it was regarded of much consequence to secure a rabbi from Vilna." Now this "city and mother in Israel" became one of the pioneers of Haskalah, all the more because, in addition to the public schools and the rabbinical seminary, the Jews were admitted to its university on equal terms with the Gentiles. "Within six years," exclaims Mandelstamm, "what a change has come over Vilna! Youths and maidens, anxious for the new Haskalah, are now to be met with everywhere, nor are any ashamed to learn a trade." The schools exerted a salutary influence on the younger generation, and the older people, too, began to view life differently, only that they were still reluctant to discard their old-fashioned garb. There also, in 1847, the leading Maskilim started a reform synagogue, which they named Taharat ha-Kodesh, the Essence of Holiness.[30]

It should not be forgotten that, if Lilienthal met with mighty opposition, he also had powerful supporters. There were many who, though remaining in the background, strongly sympathized with his plan. Indeed, the number of educated Jews, as proved by an investigation ordered by Nicholas I, was far greater than had been commonly supposed. Not only in the border towns, but even in the in-

terior of the Pale, the students of German literature and secular science were not few, and Doctor
Loewe discovered in Hebron an exceptional German scholar in the person of an immigrant from
Vilna." The tendency of the time is well illustrated
by an anecdote told by Slonimsky, to the effect that
when he went to ask the approval of Rabbi Abele
of Zaslava on his *Mosde Hokmah,* he found that
those who came to be examined for ordination received their award without delay, while he was put
off from week to week. Ill at ease, Slonimsky approached the venerable rabbi and demanded an
explanation: " You grant a semikah [rabbinical
diploma] so readily, why do you seem so reluctant
when a mere haskamah [recommendation] is the
matter at issue? " To his surprise the reason given
was that the rabbi enjoyed his scientific debates so
much that he would not willingly part with the
young author.

Stories were told how the deans of the yeshibot
were frequently found to have mastered the very
books they confiscated because of the teachings they
inculcated. Before the reign of Nicholas I drew to
its end, Haskalah centres were as numerous as the
cities wherein Jews resided. In Byelostok the
Talmudist Jehiel Michael Zabludovsky was lend-

ing German books to young Slonimsky, the future inventor and publicist; in Vlotslavek Rabbi Joseph Hayyim Caro was writing and preaching in classic German; in Zhagory, Hayyim Sack helped Leon Mandelstamm (1809-1889), the first Jewish " candidate," or bachelor, in philology to graduate from the St. Petersburg University (1844) and the assistant and successor of Lilienthal, in the expurgation and German translation of Maimuni's *Mishneh Torah*. When, in 1857, Mandelstamm resigned, he was followed by Seiberling, for fifteen years the censor of Jewish books in Kiev, upon whom a German university conferred the doctor's degree. The poverty-stricken Wolf Adelsohn, known as the Hebrew Diogenes, formed a group of Seekers after Light in Dubno, while such wealthy merchants as Abraham Rathaus, Lilienthal's secretary during his campaign in Berdichev, Issachar Bompi, the bibliophile in Minsk, Leon Rosenthal, financier and philanthropist in Brest-Litovsk, and Aaron Rabinovich, in Kobelyaki (Poltava), promoted enlightenment by precept and example. In Vilna, Joseph Sackheim's young son acted as English interpreter when Montefiore was entertained by his father, and Jacob Barit, the incomparable " Yankele Kovner " (1793-1833), another of Montefiore's hosts, was master of Russian, German, and French, and aroused the admiration of the Governor-General Nazimov by his learning and his ability.

Yes, the Jews began to pay, if they had ever been in debt, for the good that had for a while been bestowed upon them by Alexander I. Alexander Nebakhovich was a well-known theatrical director, his brother Michael was the editor of the first Russian comic paper Yeralash, and Osip Rabinovich showed marked ability in serious journalism. In 1842 died Abraham Jacob Stern, the greatest inventor Russia had till then produced; and, as if to corroborate the statement of the Talmud, that when one sun sets another rises, the Demidoff prize of two thousand five hundred rubles was the same year awarded to his son-in-law, Hayyim Selig Slonimsky (HaZas, 1810-1904) of Byelostok, for the first of his valuable inventions. Stern's genius was surpassed, though in a different direction, only by that of Elijah Vilna. His first invention was a calculating machine, which led to his election as a member of the Warsaw Society of the Friends of Science (1817) and to his being received twice by Alexander I (1816, 1818), who bestowed upon him an annual pension of three hundred and fifty rubles. This invention was followed by another, " a topographical wagon for the measurement of level surfaces, an invention of great benefit to both civil and military engineers." He also constructed an improved threshing and harvesting machine and a sickle of immense value to agriculture."

But it is scarcely possible, nor would it be profitable, to enumerate either the places or the persons who were, so to speak, inoculated with the Haskalah virus. In Grodno, Kovno, Lodz, Minsk, Mohilev, Pinsk, Zamoscz, Slutsk, Vitebsk, Zhagory, and other places, they were toiling zealously and diligently, these anchorites in the desert of knowledge. Among them were men of all classes and callings, from the cloistered Talmudist to the worldly merchant. The path of Haskalah was slowly yet surely cleared. The efforts of the conservative Maskilim were not devoid of some good results, nor even were those of Nicholas, though aimed at Christianizing rather than civilizing, entirely wasted. With all their shortcomings, and though producing but few rabbis acceptable to Russo-Jewish congregations, the seminaries in Warsaw, Zhitomir, and Vilna were powers for enlightenment. In them the future prominent scientists, scholars, and litterateurs were reared, and there the foundations were laid for the activities of Gold-faden, Gurland, Harkavy, Kantor, Landau, Levanda, Mandelkern, Paperna, Pumpyansky, Rosenberg, Steinberg, and others. Their fate was that of Mendelssohn's Bible translation. The end became a means, the means, an end. But they not only " brought forth " great men, they rendered no less important a service in " bringing out " those already great. Had it not been for their professorships, men like Abramovitsch, Lerner, Plungian, Slonimsky, Suchastover, and Zweifel, who were not blessed with worldly goods like Fünn, Katzenellenbogen, Luria, or Strashun, would probably have sought in private teaching or petty trading a source of subsistence, and Judaism in general and Russian Jewry in particular would have sustained a considerable loss. They helped to prepare the soil, even to implant the germ, and

> Once the germ implanted,
> Its growth, if slow, is sure.

As the history of this period is incomplete without an acquaintance with the lives of some of the Maskilim who sowed the seeds that burst into blossom under the favorable conditions of the " sixties," I shall select, as specimens out of a multitude, the

two who, more than any others, furthered the
cause of Haskalah, Isaac Bär Levinsohn and Mordecai Aaron Günzburg.[33]

Isaac Bär Levinsohn of Kremenetz, Volhynia
(RiBaL, 1788-1860), was for many years a name
to conjure with, not only among the Maskilim of
all shades, but also among their opponents. Long
before he reached man's estate, he had entered
upon the career to which he was to dedicate his life.
Even in those times of numerous child prodigies,
Levinsohn was distinguished for his intellectual
precocity. At the age of three he was ripe for the
heder. At nine he was the author of a work on
Cabbala. At ten he mastered the Talmud, and
knew the entire Hebrew Bible by heart. But what
singled him out among his classmates was his pas-
sionate love of secular knowledge. The son of
Judah Levin, an erudite merchant who knew Hebrew and Polish to perfection, the grandson of
Jekuthiel Solomon, famed for wealth and refine-
ment, he evinced unusual ability in selecting and
retaining what was good and true in everything
he read. At fourteen he was familiar with the
literatures of several nations, so that during the
Franco-Russian war (1812) he easily secured an
appointment as interpreter and secretary in the

local police department. But excessive study caused ill-health, and at the suggestion of his physicians he went to Brody in Galicia, a fortunate incident in the otherwise solitary and gloomy life of the future reformer, for next to Germany Galicia played an important part in the Haskalah movement in Russia. There he met Joseph Perl, the noted educator; Doctor Isaac Erter, the immortal satirist; M. H. Letteris, the distinguished poet; S. L. Rapoport, one of the first and profoundest of Jewish historians, and Nahman Krochmal, the saintly philosopher. Into this circle of "shining ones" Levinsohn was introduced, and each and all left an impression, some greater, some less, upon his plastic soul. It was there and then, in the congenial company of friends of about his own age, that Levinsohn determined to devote himself to improving the educational system of his people and began to plan his work on *Learning in Israel* (*Te'udah be-Yisraël*), which procured for its author the foremost place in the history of the Haskalah movement.

The book was finished in 1823, but, owing to Levinsohn's pecuniary circumstances, it remained unpublished till 1828. Meanwhile it circulated in manuscript among the leading Maskilim of Russia,

Austria, and Germany, and established its author's reputation wherever it was read. Levinsohn was one of those who understand the persuasive power of the still small voice of sweet reasonableness. He knew that a few convincing arguments couched in gentle language will accomplish more for the furtherance of an ideal than the trumpet call of a hundred clamoring militants, and Haskalah will make headway only when it can prove itself to be a help, and not a hindrance, to religion. Accordingly, he aimed to show that the Tanaim, Amoraim, Saboraim, Geonim, and rabbis of later generations were versed in the sciences, were familiar with foreign history, and interested in the affairs of the world. But these he quotes only as exemplars of broadmindedness, they must no longer be regarded as authorities in secular knowledge. "Art and science," he says, "are steadily progressing. . . . To perfect ourselves in them we must resort to non-Jewish sources." This was a bold statement for those times, however mildly expressed. The *Te'udah* became a bone of contention. It was torn and burnt by fanatics, exalted to the skies by friends. The new apostle of enlightenment was forced to leave the city and reside for a while in Berdichev, Nemirov, Ostrog, and Tulchin. But wherever he went, his tribulation was sweetened by the enthusiasm of his admirers and the consciousness that his toil was not entirely wasted. In Warsaw and in Vilna his name was great, and Nicholas presented him with a thousand rubles as a mark of appreciation of the book, the fly-leaf of which bears the inscription " To science."

In the midst of his more serious studies Levinsohn diverted himself occasionally with lighter composition, in which many an antiquated custom served as the butt for his biting satire. In his youth he had a penchant for poetry, and his poem on the flight, or expulsion, of the French from Russia was complimented by the Government. His muse dealt with ephemeral themes, but his *bons mots* are current among his countrymen to this day. A novel sort of plagiarism was the fashion of the time. Authors attributed their work to others, instead of claiming the product of others as their own. Levinsohn's *Hefker Welt,* in Yiddish, and *Sayings of the Saints* and *Valley of the Dead,* in Hebrew, belong to this category. But the deep student did not persist long in this species of diversion. Wittgenstein, the field-marshal, and professors at the Lyceum of his town, supplied him with books, and he, an omnivorous reader, plunged again into his graver work, the result of which was the little book since translated into English, Russian, and German, *Efes Dammim* (*No Blood!*). As the name indicates, it was intended as a defence against the blood, or ritual murder, accusation. It was the right word in the right time and place. In Zaslav, Volhynia, this monstrous libel had been revived, and popular fury rose to a high pitch. Several years later the Damascus Affair stirred the Jewish world to determined action, designed to stamp it out once for all. To wage war against this superstitious belief seems to have fallen to the lot of several of Levinsohn's family. In 1757, when it asserted itself in Yampoly, Volhynia, his great-uncle, by the unanimous consent of the Council of the Four Countries, was sent to Rome to intercede with the Pope. After six years of pleading, he returned to his native land with a signed statement addressed to the Polish king and nobles, which declared the accusation to be utterly false. Another uncle of his had performed a similar task in 1749. True scion of a noble family, Levinsohn followed in their wake, and his effort was declared to be a " sharp sword forged by a master, to fight for our honor."

Everything was against Levinsohn when he

started on his third great work, *The House of
Judah* (*Bet Yehudah*). He found himself poor,
sick, and alone, and deprived of his fine library. In
those days, and for a long time before and afterwards, Hebrew authors were paid in kind. In
return for their copyright they received a number
of copies of their books, which they were at liberty
to dispose of as best they could. Now, while
Levinsohn's copies of his *Bet Yehudah* were still
at the publisher's, a fire broke out, and most of
them were consumed.

The *Te'udah be-Yisraël* had been prompted by
a desire to prove the compatibility of modern civilization with Judaism. Levinsohn's object in writing his *Bet Yehudah* was the reverse. The impetus
came from without the Jewish camp. The book
represents the author's views on certain Jewish
problems propounded by his Christian friend,
Prince Emanuel Lieven, just as Mendelssohn's
*Jerusalem* was written at the instigation of Lavater.
Though there is a similarity in the causes that produced the two books, there is a marked difference
in their methods. Mendelssohn treats his subject
as an impartial non-Jewish philosopher might have
done. He is frequently too reserved, for fear of
offending. Levinsohn, in Greek-Catholic Russia,

is strictly frank. He is conscious of the difficulties under which he is laboring. To discuss religion in Russia is far from agreeable. " It is," he says, " as if a master, pretending to exhibit his skill in racing, were to enter into competition publicly with his slave . . . and at the same time wink at him to slacken his speed." Of one thing he is certain: Judaism is a progressive religion. It had been and might be reformed from time to time, but this can and must be only along the lines of its own genius. To improve the moral and material condition of the Jews by weaning them away from the faith of their fathers (as was tried by Nicholas) will not do. On the contrary, make them better Jews, and they will be better citizens.

The *Bet Yehudah* may justly be called the connecting link between the *Te'udah*, which preceded it, and *Zerubbabel*, which followed it. The latter, though written in Hebrew, was really intended exclusively for the Gentile world, as the former had been mainly for the Jewish world. It is a continuation, but not yet a conclusion, of the self-assigned task of Levinsohn. The Talmud, we have seen, was at that time the object of assaults of zealous Christians and disloyal Jews, and hostile works against Judaism were the order of the day. Most of them, however, like the fabulous snake, vented their poison and died. It was different with McCaul's poignant diatribe against the cause of Judaism and the honor of the Talmud, which had been translated into many languages. Montefiore, while in Russia, urged Levinsohn to defend his people against their traducers, and the bed-ridden sage, almost blind and hardly able to hold a pen, finally consented. What *Zerubbabel* accomplished, can be judged from the fact that in the second Hebrew edition of McCaul's *Old Paths* (1876) are omitted many of the calumnies and aspersions of the first edition, published in 1839.

Levinsohn's life was a continuous struggle against an insidious disease, which kept him confined to his bed, and prevented him from accepting any prominent position. But though, as he said, he had " neither brother, wife, child, nor even a sound body," he impressed his personality upon Russian Jewry as no one else, save the Gaon, had before him. His breadth of view and his sympathetic disposition gradually won him the respect and love of all who knew him. The zaddikim Abraham of Turisk and Israel Rasiner were his lifelong friends; the Talmudist Strashun acknowledged his indebtedness to him, and Rabbi Abele of Vilna remarked jestingly that the only fault to be found with the *Te'udah* was that its author was not the Gaon Elijah. He enjoyed prominence in Government circles, and Prince Wittgenstein was passionately fond of his company. Above all he endeared himself to the Maskilim. To him they looked as to their teacher and guide; him they consulted in every emergency. Lebensohn and Gottlober, Mandelstamm and Gordon, equally sought his criticism and advice. For all he had words of comfort and encouragement. The younger Maskilim he warned not to waste their time in idle versification, not to become intoxicated with their little learning; and the older ones he implored to respect the sentiments of their conservative coreligionists. " Take it not amiss," he would say to the latter, " that the great bulk of our people hearken not as yet to our new teachings. All beginnings are difficult. The drop cannot become a deluge instantaneously. Persevere in your laudable ambition, publish your good and readable books, and the result, though slow, is sure."

Thus lived and labored the first of the Maskilim, an idealist from beginning to end. Persecution did not embitter, nor poverty depress him. And when he passed away quietly (February 12, 1860) in the

obscure little town in which he had been born, and
which has become famous through him, it was felt
that Russia had had her Mendelssohn, too. Strange
to say, he little suspected the tremendous influence
he exerted upon the Haskalah movement, but was
quite sanguine of the success of his fight for " truth
and justice among the nations." His work he mod-
estly summed up in the epitaph which was inscribed
on his tombstone at his request:

> Out of nothing God called me to life.
> Alas, earthly life has passed, and I must
> Sleep again on the bosom of Mother Nature.
> Witness this stone. I fought with God's
> Foes, not with a Sword, but with the Word;
> I fought for Truth and Justice among the Nations
> And *Zerubbabel* and *Efes Dammim* testify thereto.

Contemporaneous with Isaac Bär Levinsohn,
and hardly less distinguished and influential, was
Mordecai Aaron Günzburg (ReMAG, Salanti,
Kovno, December 3, 1795–Vilna, November 5,
1846). His family had been prominent in many
walks of life since the fourteenth century, and,
whether in the land of the Saxons or of the Slavs,
represented the cream of the Jewries in which they
lived. His father was a Maskil of great repute,
who had written several treatises, in Hebrew, on

algebra, geometry, optics, and kindred subjects. He
sought to supplement his son Mordecai Aaron's
heder education with a knowedge of secular sciences.
But at that time and in that place not many were
the books, outside the Talmud, accessible to a lad
eager for learning, the only ones available being
such as the *Josippon, Zemah David,* and *Sheërit
Yisraël* on Jewish History, the *Sefer ha-Berit,* and
a Hebrew translation of Mendelssohn's *Phaedon*
on general philosophy. But the precocious and
clear-minded youth did not need much to stimulate
his love for history and his inclination to philosophy, and his intellectual development continued
in spite of the untoward circumstances in which he
happened to be placed.

Though he was " given " in marriage at a very
early age, the proverbial " millstone " weighed but
lightly upon the neck of young Günzburg. He
never discontinued the habit of secluding himself
in his study for hours, sometimes for days, at a time,
and there writing down his thoughts in painstaking
penmanship. These productions, with all their
crudity, promised, according to a keen critic, the
flowers which would one day " ripen into delicious
fruit, not only pleasant to the sight but also delicious to the taste." In fact, even his religious views

underwent but slight modification in later and maturer years. Ceremonial laws, or minhagim, were to him a social compact among the members of a sect. He who transgresses them is, *eo ipso*, excluded from the sect, as he who disregards the social code, though not immoral, is ostracized from society. This led him to the logical conclusion that every Jew must comply with the customs of his people, though his opinion as to their moral value may differ from that of the rest. He believed in freedom of thought, but would not concede freedom of action or even of expression, and would say with Bolingbroke, " Freedom belongs to a man as a rational creature, he lies under the restraint as a member of society."

At these conclusions, Günzburg arrived only after a long, severe, though silent, struggle in the seclusion of his closet. His active mind would not at first surrender unconditionally to the coercion of custom. But his conception of ceremonialism served him in good stead on many an occasion in his eventful life. Being an expedient to preserve harmony, it may and must vary with change of conditions. Accordingly, Günzburg always accommodated himself to his environment. In Vilna he subscribed to the regulations of the *Shulhan 'Aruk*, in Mitau he quickly and completely became Germanized. Such adaptability rendered him conspicuous wherever he went, and as early as 1829 his name was included among the learned of Livonia, Esthland, and Courland in the Biographical Dictionary then published by Recke and Napyersky.

His claim to fame, however, consists in the influence he exerted upon Russian Jews. Like Levinsohn, he was a constructive force. In his younger days, he had inveighed against the benighted rabbis and the antiquated garb, but moderation came with discretion. He would not sweep away by force the accumulation of hundreds of years. Judaism needed reforms of some sort, but these could not be brought about by the Russo-German-doctor-rabbis, men who could rede the seven riddles of the world, but whose knowledge of their own people and its spiritual treasures was close to the zero point. " For a rabbi," writes he, " Torah must be the integer, science the cipher. Had Aristotle embraced Judaism, notwithstanding his unparalleled erudition, he would still remain a sage, never become a rabbi." But he was as little satisfied with the exclusively Talmudistic rabbis. " O ye modern rabbis," he calls out in one of his essays, in which he stigmatizes Lilienthal's plans as the " gourd of Jonah,"

" you who stand in the place of seer and prophet of yore, is it not your duty to rise above the people, to intervene between them and the Government? And how can you expect to accomplish it, if the language and regulations of our country are entirely unknown to you? "

The impress Günzburg left upon Hebrew literature is of special importance. Until his time, despite the examples set by Satanov and Levin, Hebrew was stamped with the hallmark of medievalism. Like the Spanish entertainment in Dryden's *Mock Astrologer,* at which everything at the table tasted of nothing but red pepper, so the literature of that day was dominated by the style and spirit of the Talmud and saturated with its subtleties. Astronomy, philosophy, mathematics, and poetry swarmed with puns, alliterations, pedantic allusions; they were overladen with irrelevant notes and interwoven with quaint and strained interpretations. Günzburg was the first, with the exception of Erter perhaps, to try to remedy the evil. " Every writer," he maintained, " should guard himself against the fastidiousness or stiffness which results from pedantry, and take great pains not only with the content of his thoughts, but with the language in which these thoughts are couched." Simplicity, perspi-

217

cuity, and conciseness, these he taught by precept and example, and though he was accused of " Germanizing " the Hebrew language, he persisted in his labor until he attained the foremost rank among the neo-Hebraic litterateurs.

In Günzburg we find the artistic temperament developed to a degree rare among Hebraists of even more recent years. He wrote only in moments of inspiration. At times he passed weeks and months without penning a line, but when once aroused he wrote unceasingly until he finished what he had begun. He was careful in the choice of his words, careful in the choice of his books, and would recommend nothing but the best. " I may not have genius enough," he would say, " to distinguish between better and best, but I do not lack common sense, to differentiate tares from weeds." Above all, he possessed a sense of honor, the greatest stimulus, as he maintained, to noble endeavors. " For as marriage is necessary to perpetuate the race, and food to sustain the individual, so is honor to the existence of the superior man."

Of the fifty years of his active life more than one-half was spent in literary labor. His books obtained a wide circulation, and, though they were rather expensive, became rare soon after their publication. Yet, strange to say, this eminent Hebraist seldom, if ever, lauds the beauties of the " daughter of Eber " (Hebrew) like his fellow-Maskilim since the days of the Meassefim, nor does he even think it incumbent on a Jew to be conversant with it.

Three periods have passed over me—he writes to a friend— since I dedicated myself to Hebrew. As a youth I loved it as a Jewish lad loves his betrothed, not because he is enamored of her charms, but because his parents have chosen her for him; as I grew older, I continued to love it as a Jewish man loves his wife, not because of real affection, but because she is the only one he knows; now that I am old, I still love her, as an elderly Jew loves his helpmate: he is aware that she lacks many of the accomplishments of which more educated women can boast, but, for all that, remembering her faithfulness in the past, he loves her also in the present, and loves her till he dies.

Günzburg was different from most of his contemporaries in another respect. He was a voluminous writer, but only a few of his books and essays bear on what we now call Jewish science. Zunz, Geiger, and Jost, seeing that Judaism was gradually losing its hold upon their Jewish countrymen, resorted to exploring and narrating, in German, the wonderful story of their race, in the hope of renewing its ebbing strength. Levinsohn, living amid a different environment, deemed it best to convince his fellow-Jews that secular knowledge was necessary, and religion sanctioned their pursuit thereof. Günzburg, the man of letters, determined to teach through the vehicle of Hebrew the true and the beautiful wherever he found it. He felt called upon to reveal to his brethren the grandeur of the world beyond the dingy ghetto, to tell them the stories not contained in the Midrash, *Josippon,* or the biographies of rabbis and zaddikim. He translated Campe's *Discovery of the New World,* compiled a history of ancient civilization, and narrated the epochal event of the nineteenth century, the conflict between Russia and France. He taught his fellow-Jews to think correctly and logically, to clothe their thoughts in beautiful expressions, and revealed his innermost being to them in his autobiography, *Abi'ezer.* As a writer he appears neither erudite nor profound. We cannot apply to his works what we may safely say of Elijah Vilna's and Levinsohn's, that " there is solid metal enough in them to fit out whole circulating libraries, were it beaten into the usual filigree." But he was elegant, cultured, intelligent, honorable; one who joined a feeling heart to a love for art; a Moses who struck from the rock of the Hebrew tongue

**PEREZ BEN MOSHEH SMOLENSKIN**
1842-1885

refreshing streams for those thirsting for knowledge; a most amiable personality, and an altogether unusual character during the century-long struggle between light and darkness in the Jewry of Russia.

[Notes, pp. 318-322.]

## CHAPTER V

# RUSSIFICATION, REFORMATION, AND ASSIMILATION

## 1856-1881

The year 1856 will always be remembered as the *annus mirabilis* in the history of Russia. It marked at once the cessation of the Crimean war and the accession of the most liberal and benevolent monarch Russia ever had. On January 16, the heir apparent signified his consent to accept Austrian intervention, which resulted in the Treaty of Paris (March 30), granting the Powers involved " peace with honor "; and in August, in the Cathedral of the Assumption at Moscow, amidst unprecedented rejoicing, the czarevich placed the imperial crown upon his head. From that time reform followed reform. The condition of the soldiers, who had virtually been slaves under Nicholas I, was greatly improved, and a proclamation was issued for the emancipation of the peasants, slaves not for a limited time only, but for life and from generation to generation. It cost the United States five years of fratricidal agony, a billion of dollars, and about half a million of lives, to liberate five or six millions of negroes; Russia, in one memorable day (February 19, 1861), liberated nearly twenty-two millions of muzhiks (peasants), and gave them full freedom, by a mere stroke of the pen of the " tsar osvobodityel," the Liberator Czar, Alexander II (1856-1881).

Other innovations, of less magnitude but nevertheless of far-reaching importance, were introduced later. Capital punishment, which still disgraces human justice in more enlightened states, was unconditionally abolished; the number of offences amenable to corporal punishment was gradually reduced, until, on April 29, 1863, all the horrors of the gauntlet, the spur, the lash, the cat, and the brand, were consigned to eternal oblivion. The barbarous system of the judiciary was replaced by one that could render justice " speedy, righteous, merciful, and equitable." Railway communication, postal and telegraph service, police protection, the improvement of the existing universities, the opening of many new primary schools, and the introduction of compulsory school attendance, told speedily on the intellectual development of the people. In the words of Shumakr, Russia experienced " a complete inward revival." Old customs seemed to disappear, all things were become new. New life, new hope, new aspirations throbbed in the hearts of the subjects of the gigantic empire, and better times were knocking at their doors. *Joli tout le monde, le diable est mort!*

This era of great reforms and the resuscitation of all that is good and noble in the Slavonic soul brought about also a moral regeneration. The colossus who, according to Turgenief, preferred to sleep an endless sleep, with a jug of vodka in his clutched fingers, proved that he, too, was human, with a feeling, human heart beating in his bosom. With the restoration of peace and the abolition of serfhood, there began a removal of prejudice even against Jews. Hitherto the foremost litterateurs in Russia, imitating the writers of other lands, had painted the Jew as a monstrosity. Pushkin's prisoner, Gogol's traitor, Lermontoff's spy, and Turgenief's Zhid (Jew) were caricatures and libels, equal in acrimony, and not inferior in art, to Shakespeare's Shylock and Dickens's Fagin. But now the best and ablest men of letters signed a protest against such unjust and impossible characters.

Two thousand years of cruel suffering and affliction—said the historian and humanitarian Professor Granovsky, of the University of Moscow—have at last erased the bloody boundary line separating the Jews from humanity. The honor of this reconciliation, which is becoming firmer from day to day, belongs to our age. The civic status of the Jews is now established in most European countries, and even in the places that are still backward their condition is improved, if not by law, then by enlightenment.

And law and enlightenment radiated their sunshine also upon the Jews of rejuvenated Russia. The Cantonist system was abolished for good; the high schools and universities were opened to Jews without discrimination; and the Governments lying outside the Pale were made accessible to Jewish scholars, professional men, manufacturers, wholesale merchants, and skilled laborers (March 16, 1859; November 27, 1861).[1] Through the efforts of Wolf Kaplan, one of Günzburg's noted pupils, the persecution of Jews by Germans in Riga was stopped, and the eminent publicist Katkoff undertook to defend them in the newspaper Russkiya Vyedomosti. Nazimov, the Governor-General of Vilna, Mukhlinsky, who inspected the Jewish schools in western Russia, Artzimovich, of southern Russia, and many other prominent personages arose as champions of the Jews.[2]

The physician and pedagogue Nikolai Ivanovich Pirogov (1810-1881), the superintendent
of the Odessa and Kiev school districts, is especially deserving of honorable mention in the history
of Haskalah. Of all the Russians of the period
who gloried in their liberal convictions, he was the
most liberal. In him the last vestige of prejudice
and race distinction disappeared, and he conscien-
tiously devoted himself to the study, not only of the
present, but also of the past of the Jews, to be in
a better position to lend them his assistance. To the
Jews he appealed to unite and spread enlightenment
among the masses by peaceful means. To the Gentiles, again, he did not hesitate to point out the good
qualities of the Jews, and in an article on the Odessa
Talmud Torah he held up the institution as a model
for the public elementary schools. He admired
especially the enthusiasm with which Jewish youths
devoted themselves to the acquisition of knowledge.
" Where are religion, morality, enlightenment, and
the modern spirit,'' asked he, " when these Jews,
who, with courage and self-sacrifice, engage in the
struggle against prejudices centuries old, meet no
one here to sympathize with them and extend a
helping hand to them? " His liberality carried
him so far that he established a fund for the support

of indigent Jewish students at the University of Kiev, and he advocated strenuously the award of prizes and scholarships to deserving Jewish students. Such as he were rare in any land, but nowhere so rare as in Russia.'

Pirogov took the initiative in reorganizing the Jewish schools. It required little observation to understand that they had proved a failure. Instead of attracting the Jewish masses to secular education, they only repelled them. The remedy was not far to seek. " The abolition of these schools," said Count Kotzebu, " would drive the Jews back to their fanaticism and isolation. It is necessary to make the Jews useful citizens, and I see no other means of achieving this than by their education." Pirogov's first move was to order that Jewish instead of Christian principals be put at their head, and he set an example by appointing Rosenzweig to that office. The curriculum was changed, making the lower schools correspond with our grammar schools, and adapting their studies to the needs of those who must discontinue schooling at a comparatively early age. The higher schools were arranged so as to prepare the pupils for the gymnasium. The salaries of the teachers were raised, and books and necessaries were provided for pupils too poor to afford them.

The Government's attention having been directed by General Zelenoy to the Jewish agricultural colonies in southern Russia, Marcus Gurovich was appointed to work out a plan to provide them with graded schools. He proposed that secular and sacred subjects alike be taught by Jewish teachers, and these were to be cautioned to be careful not to offend the religious sensibilities of the parents. The plan appealed to the colonists, and they looked forward anxiously to its fulfilment. Having waited in vain till 1868, they offered to defray the expenses of the schools involved, if the Government would advance the money at the first. Accordingly, ten schools for boys and two for girls were opened in that year.

Such disinterested efforts on their behalf would have evoked the gratitude of Jews at any time and in every country, how much more in Russia, and following close upon the darkest period in their history! The struggle for liberty all over Europe in 1848—the spring of nations—had confirmed Nicholas in his policy of exclusion. The last five years of his reign had surpassed the preceding in cruelty and tyranny. The " Don Quixote of Politics," finding that his attempts to quarantine Russia against European influences had proved futile, that the nationalities constituting the empire remained as distinct as ever, and the desired homogeneity was still far from becoming a reality, finally had lost patience and had determined to execute his conversionist policy at all hazards. He had increased the conscription duties, already unbearable (January 8, 1852; August 16, 1852), restricted the study of Hebrew and Hebrew subjects still further in the Government schools, and, as if to embitter the lives of the Jew by all means available, insisted on the use of the Mitnaggedic ritual even in communities exclusively or largely Hasidic.' Even the blood accusation had been revived, and the statements in the pamphlet entitled *Information about the Killing of Christians by Jews for the Purpose of Obtaining Their Blood,* which Skripitzyn, " the manager of Jewish affairs in Russia," published in 1844, found many believers in Government circles, and caused the Saratoff affair which, though suppressed, ruined numerous Jewish families, and made the breach between Jew and Gentile wider than ever.'

Now all this was changed. Christians championed the cause of Jews. The Government, too, appeared to be sincerely anxious for the welfare of its Jewish subjects. It not only promised, but frequently also performed. The Jews were allowed to follow their religious predilections unhindered. The schools were reorganized with rabbinical graduates as their teachers and principals. The Rabbinical Assembly, which, though established by Nicholas (May 26, 1848), had rarely been called together, was summoned to St. Petersburg, and there spent six months in 1857 and five in 1861 in deliberating on means of improving the intellectual and material standing of the Jews. The "learned Jew" (uchony Yevrey) Moses Berlin was invited to become an adviser in the Department of Public Worship (1856), to be consulted concerning the Jewish religion whenever occasion required. Permission was granted to publish Jewish periodicals in Russian, Polish, Hebrew, and Yiddish (1860), and on April 26, 1862, the restriction was removed that limited Jewish publishing houses and printing-presses to Vilna and Zhitomir. The Russia Montefiore saw on his visit in 1872, how different from the Russia he had left in 1846!

These auspicious signs renewed the hope of the Maskilim and intensified their zeal. They were convinced of the noble intentions of the Liberator Czar; they were confident that the emperor who emancipated the muzhiks, and expunged many a *kromye Yevreyev* (" except the Jews ") which his father was wont to add to the few privileges he granted his Christian subjects, would ultimately remove the civil disabilities of the Jews altogether. In a very popular song, written by Eliakum Zunser (Vilna, 1836–New York, 1913), then a rising and beloved Badhan (bard) writing in Yiddish and Hebrew, Alexander II was likened to an angel of God who finds the flower of Judah soiled by dirt and trampled in the dust. He rescues it, and revives it with living water, and plants it in his garden, where it flourishes once more.[6] The poets hailed him as the savior and redeemer of Israel. All that the Jews needed was to make themselves deserving of his kindness, and worthy of the citizenship they saw in store for them. In Russian, in Hebrew, and in Yiddish, in prose and in poetry, the one theme uppermost in the mind of all was enlightenment, or rather Russification. From all quarters the reveille was sounded. Abraham Bär Gottlober (1811-1899) exclaimed:

> Awake, Israel, and, Judah, arise!
> Shake off the dust, open wide thine eyes!
> Justice sprouteth, righteousness is here,
> Thy sin is forgot, thou hast naught to fear.[7]

More impressively still Judah Löb Gordon
(1831-1892) called:

> Arise, my people, 'tis time for waking!
> Lo, the night is o'er, the day is breaking!
> Arise and see where'er thou turn'st thy face,
> How changed are both our time and place.[8]

And in Yiddish, too, an anonymous poet echoed
the strain:

> Arise, my people, awake from thy dreaming,
> In foolishness be not immersed!
> Clear is the sky, brightly the sun is beaming;
> The clouds are now utterly dispersed!

Rapid growth is sometimes the cause of disease,
and sudden changes the cause of disappointment.
This was true of the swift progress of Haskalah
during the reign of Alexander II. To comprehend
fully the tragedies that took place frequently at that
time, the disillusionments that embittered the lives
of many of the Maskilim, the breaking up of homes
and bruising of hearts, one should read *Youthful
Sins* (*Hattot Ne'urim*, 1876) by Moses Löb Lilienblum. The author lays bare a heart ulcerated and
mangled by an obsolete education, a meaningless
existence, and a forlorn hope. The hero of this
little work, masterly less by reason of its artistic

finish than the earnestness that pervades it from beginning to end, is " one of the slain of the Babylonian Talmud, whose spiritual life is artificially maintained by a literature itself dead." His diary and letters grant a glimpse into his innermost being; his childhood wasted in a methodless acquisition of futile learning; his boyhood blighted by a union with a wife chosen for him by his parents; his manhood mortified by the realization that in a world thrilling with life and activity he led the existence of an Egyptian mummy. Impatient to save the few years allotted to him on earth, and undeterred by the entreaties and the threats of his wife, he leaves for Odessa, the Mecca of the Maskilim, and begins to prepare himself for admission into the gymnasium. " While there is a drop of blood in my veins," he writes to his forsaken wife, " I shall try to finish my course of studies. Though the physicians declare that consumption and death must be the inevitable consequence of such application, I will not desist. I will rather die like a man than live like a dog." And on and on he plods over his Latin, his French, his history, geography, and grammar. Two more years and the university will be opened to him, and he will read law, and defend the honor of his people. But in the midst of his ceaseless toil the spectre of his simple wife and his former innocent life appears before him and " will not down." Is Haskalah worth the sacrifices he and his like are daily bringing on its altar? Is not the material-ism of the emancipated Maskilim often greater than the medievalism of the fanatical Hasidim? In his native town, gloomy as it was, there was at least the glow of sincerity. Haskalah had to be snatched by stealth, but it was sweeter because thus snatched. In Odessa, where the fruit of the tree of knowledge could be obtained for the asking, it turned into the apples of Sodom. The " lishmah " ideal, the love of culture for its own sake, yielded to the greed which changes everything into a commodity to profit by. Yet, since life demands it, what a pity that his early training had incapacitated him from following the beaten path! He concludes his self-indictment thus, " I have taken an inventory of the business of my life, and I am heartbroken, because I find that in striking the balance there remains on the credit side only a cipher! "

But the tide of Haskalah was not to be stemmed. The " blessed heritage of noble passion," the burn-ing desire for enlightenment and improvement as-serted itself at all hazards. The note of despair was lost in the call for action. Odessa continued to be in the forefront. There technical institutes for boys and girls were established in addition to the previously existing public schools. A society by the name of Trud (Labor) was organized (October 11, 1864), for the purpose of teaching useful trades. Its school has ever since been the crown of the institutions of the sort. It was provided with the most modern improvements, a workshop for mechanics and an iron foundry, and it offered a post-graduate course. A similar trade school (remeslenoye uchilishche) had been in existence since May 1, 1862, in Zhitomir, where, besides geometry, mechanics, chemistry, physics, etc., instruction was given in carpentry, turning, tin, copper, and blacksmith work.' Through the efforts of Rabbi Solomon Zalkind Minor a Sabbath School and a Night School for artisans were opened in Minsk (1861), and a reference and circulating library for the general public (1863), and similar educational institutions were soon called into existence in many other cities.

Those were the days of organizing and consolidating among Jews and Gentiles alike. At the time when Abraham Lincoln was proclaiming his famous " United we stand, divided we fall," Julius Slo-

vacki in Poland pleaded the cause of the peasantry
of his country, and the Alliance Israélite Universelle issued a call to the entire house of Israel " to
defend the honor of the Jewish name wherever it
is attacked; to encourage, by all means at our disposal, the pursuit of useful handicrafts; to combat, where necessary, the ignorance and vice engen-
dered by oppression; to work, by the power of
persuasion and by all the moral influences at our
command, for the emancipation of our brethren
who still suffer under the burden of exceptional
legislation; to hasten and solidify complete en-
franchisement by the intellectual and moral regeneration of our brethren." A powerful movement
for the upliftment of the masses was also taking
hold of the educated classes among the Russians.
Professor Kostomarov started a systematic campaign for the education of the common people. A
species of philanthropic intoxication seized upon
the more enlightened Russian youth. A society of
Narodniki, or Common People, so-called, was organized. Young men and women renounced high
rank, and students came out of their seclusion and
joined the people, dressed in their garb, spoke their
dialect, led their life, and, having won their confidence, gradually opened their minds to value the

blessings of education, and their hearts to desire them. These examples from within and without resulted in a similar attempt among the Russian Jews. An organization was perfected (December, 1863) which exercised a great civilizing influence for almost half a century, the Society for the Promotion of Haskalah among the Jews of Russia.

To the credit of the Jewish financiers be it said that they were always the banner bearers of enlightenment. It had been so with German Aufklärung, when Ben-David, Itzig, Friedländer, and Jacobson, laid the corner-stone of the intellectual rebirth of their people. It was more especially so in Russia during the " sixties." Odessa was the most enlightened, because it was the wealthiest, of Jewish communities, as the benumbing poverty of the Pale was largely to blame for the unfriendly attitude towards whatever did not bear the stamp of Jewishness on its surface. The Society for the Promotion of Haskalah, too, owes its existence to some of the most prominent Russo-Jewish merchants. Its original officers were Joseph Yosel Günzburg, President; his son Horace Günzburg, First Vice-president; Rabbi A. Neuman, Second Vice-president; the Brodskys, and, the most active of them all, its Secretary, Leon Rosenthal (1817-1887). Busy

237

as he was with his financial affairs, Rosenthal devoted considerable time to the propagation of enlightenment among his coreligionists. Many a youthful Maskil was indebted to him for material as well as moral support, and it was due to him that Osip Rabinovich finally succeeded in publishing the Razsvyet (Dawn, 1860), the first journal in Russian devoted to Jewish interests.

The Society for the Promotion of Enlightenment was not unlike the Alliance Israélite Universelle, only on a smaller scale. Its object was " to spread the knowledge of the Russian language among the Jews, to publish and assist others in publishing, in Russian as well as in Hebrew, useful works and journals, to aid in carrying out the purposes of the Society, and, further, to assist the young in devoting themselves to the pursuit of science and knowledge." For several years, owing to the indifference of the public, it had a hard struggle to live up to its ideal. But continuously, if slowly, it gained in membership, so that in 1884 it had an affiliation of 545. During the first twenty years of its existence its income amounted to 338,685 rubles, its expenditures to 309,998 rubles. In 1880 it endowed an agricultural college for Jewish boys. When, in the same year, medical schools for women were opened, and Jewish girls in large numbers took up the study of medicine, the Society set aside the sum of 18,900 rubles for the support of the needy among them. Many a young man was aided in the pursuit of his chosen career by the Society. It directed its activities principally to the younger generation, yet it did not neglect the older. With its assistance Sabbath Schools and Evening Schools were opened in Berdichev, Zhitomir, Poltava, and other cities; libraries were founded; interesting Hebrew books on scientific subjects were published. Thus it had a two-fold object: in those who were drifting away it aimed to reawaken knowledge or love of Judaism by translating some of the most important Jewish books into Russian (the Haggadah, in 1871, the prayer book, Pentateuch, and Psalms, in 1872) as well as text-books and catechisms; and it popularized science among those who would not or could not read on such topics in Russian or other living tongues. In both directions it was a power for good among the Jews of Russia.[10]

These united efforts of the Government, the Maskilim, and the Jewish financiers produced an effect the like of which had perhaps been witnessed only during the Hellenistic craze, in the period of the second commonwealth of Judea. Russian Jewry

began to " progress " as never before. In almost
all the large cities, particularly in Odessa, St.
Petersburg, and Moscow, the Jews were fast becoming Russified. Heretofore cooped up, choking
each other in the Pale as in a Black Hole, they were
now wild with an excessive desire for Russification.
What Maimon said of a few, could now be applied
to hundreds and thousands, they were " like starving persons suddenly treated to a delicious meal."
They flocked to the institutions of learning in numbers far exceeding their due proportion. They
were among the reporters, contributors, and edi-
torial writers of some of the most influential Russian journals. They entered the professions, and
distinguished themselves in art."

The ambition of the wealthy was no longer to
have a son-in-law who was well-versed in the Torah,
but a graduate from a university, the possessor of
a diploma, the wearer of a uniform. The bahur
lost his lustre in the presence of the " gymnasiast."
This ambition pervaded more or less all classes of
Russo-Jewish society. A decade or two before, especially in the " forties," orthodoxy had been as
uncompromising as it was unenlightened. " To
carry a handkerchief on the Sabbath," as Zunser
says, " to read a pamphlet of the ' new Haskalah,'

or commit some other transgression of the sort, was sufficient to stamp one an apikoros (heretic)." [12] Reb Israel Salanter, when he learned that his son had gone to Berlin to study medicine, removed his shoes, and sat down on the ground to observe shivah (seven days of mourning). When Mattes der Sheinker (saloon-keeper) discovered that his boy Motke (later famous as Mark Antokolsky) had been playing truant from the heder, and had hidden himself in the garret to carve figures, he beat him unmercifully, because he had broken the second commandment. This was greatly altered in the latter part of the " seventies." Jacob Prelooker has a different story to tell.

A remarkable change—he says [13]—had taken place in the minds of my parents since I had overcome all difficulties and become a student of a royal college. Not only were they reconciled to me, but they were distinctly proud of me. Old Rabbi Abraham now delighted in conversation and discussion with his grandson, who seemed to him almost like an inhabitant of another world, of the *terra incognita* of modern knowledge and science. In the town inhabited chiefly by Jews the very appearance of the rabbi's grandson in the uniform of a royal college created an immense sensation, and I became naturally the hero of the day. The older generation lamented that now an end would be put to the very existence of Israel and the sacred synagogue, while the younger people envied me and were inspired to follow my example.

Such scenes occurred not only in Pinsk, but, not infrequently, in other towns of the Pale as well. The striving for intellectual enlightenment manifested itself in the refining of religious customs. Though Russian Jewry " has never experienced any of the ritualistic struggles that Germany has witnessed," <sup>14</sup> yet reform and Haskalah always went hand in hand. The attacks on tradition by the Maskilim of the " forties " and the early " fifties " were mild and guarded compared with the assaults by the generation that followed. With the appearance of the periodicals the combat was intensified. Ha-Meliz, and, later, Ha-Shahar in Hebrew, and Kol Mebasser in Yiddish were the organs of those who were dissatisfied with the old, and sought to introduce the new. It was in the latter that *Dos Polische Yingel (The Polish Boy)*, by Linetzky, first appeared, and it proved so popular that the editor published it in book form long before it was finished in the periodical. In an article on *The Ways of the Talmud,* by Moses Löb Lilienblum, the prevailing Jewish religious observances were vehemently attacked. This was followed by another article from the pen of Gordon, *Wisdom for Those Who Wander in Spirit*, with suggestions for adapting religion to the needs of the times, and a still more powerful one, *The Chaotic World*, by Smolenskin. The muse ceased to content herself with " flame-songs that burn their pathway " to the heart. She preferred to appeal to the head. She no longer tried

> In strains as sweet
> As angels use . . . to whisper peace.

In cutting criticisms and biting satires she exposed time-honored but time-worn beliefs and practices. Gordon was a militant reformer in his younger days, and so were Menahem Mendel Dolitzky and the lesser poets of the period. Needless to say, the Jewish-Russian press was an enemy of ultra-orthodoxy. Osip Rabinovich, the leading Russo-Jewish journalist, made his debut with an article in which he denounced the superstitious customs of his people in unmeasured terms.[15] The motto chosen for the Razsvyet (1860) was " Let there be light," and the platform it adopted was to elevate the masses by teaching them to lead the life of all nations, participate in their civilization and progress, and preserve, increase, and improve the national heritage of Israel.[16]

Yet journalists and poets were outdone by scholars and novelists in the battle for reform. Lebensohn's didactic drama *Emet we-Emunah* (*Truth and Faith*, Vilna, 1867, 1870), in which he attempts to reconcile true religion with the teachings of science, was mild compared with *Dos Polische Yingel* or Shatzkes' radical interpretations of the stories of the rabbis in his *Ha-Mafteah* (*The Key*, Warsaw, 1866-1869), and both were surpassed by Raphael Kohn's clever little work *Hut ha-Meshullash* (*The Triple Cord*, Odessa, 1874), in which many prohibited things are ingeniously proved permissible according to the Talmud. But the most outspoken advocate of reform was Abraham Mapu (1808-1867), author of the first realistic novel, or novel of any kind, in Hebrew literature, the *'Ayit Zabua* (*The Painted Vulture*). His Rabbi Zadok, the miracle-worker, who exploits superstition for his own aggrandizement; Rabbi Gaddiel, the honest but mistaken henchman of Rabbi Zadok; Ga'al, the parvenu, who seeks to obliterate an unsavory past by fawning upon both; the Shadkan, or marriage-broker, who pretends to be the ambassador of Heaven, to unite men and women on earth,—in these and similar types drawn from life and depicted vividly, Mapu held up to the execration of the world the hypocrites who " do the deeds of Zimri and claim the reward of Phinehas," whose outward piety is often a cloak for inner impurity, and whose ceremonialism is their skin-deep religion. These characters served for many years as weapons in the hands of the combatants enlisted in the army arrayed for " the struggle between light and darkness."

The waves of the Renaissance and the Reformation sweeping over Russian Jewry reached even the sacred precincts of the synagogues, the batte midrashim, and the yeshibot. The Tree of Life College in Volozhin became a foster-home of Haskalah. The rendezvous of the brightest Russo-Jewish youths, it was the centre in which grew science and culture, and whence they were disseminated far and wide over the Pale. Hebrew, German, and Russian were surreptitiously studied and taught. Buckle and Spencer, Turgenief and Tolstoi were secretly passed from hand to hand, and read and studied with avidity. Some students advocated openly the transformation of the yeshibah into a rabbinical seminary on the order of the Berlin Hochschule. The new learning found an ardent supporter in Zebi Hirsh Dainov, " the Slutsker Maggid " (1832-1877), who preached Russification and Reformation from the pulpits of the synagogues, and whom the Society for the Promotion of Haskalah employed as its mouthpiece among the less advanced." In the existing reform synagogues, in Riga, Odessa, Warsaw, and Vilna, and even in more conservative communities, sermons began to be preached in Russian. Solomon Zalkind Minor, who lectured in German, acquired a reputation as a preacher in Russian since his election to the rabbinate of Minsk (1860). He was called " the Jellinek of Russia " by the Maskilim." Aaron Elijah Pumpyansky began to preach in Russian at Ponevezh, in Kovno (1861). Germanization at last gave way to Russification. Even in Odessa, where German culture predominated during the reign of Nicholas I, it was found necessary, for the sake of the younger generation, to elect, as associate to the German Doctor Schwabacher, Doctor Solomon Mandelkern to preach in Russian. Similar changes were made in other communities. In the Polish provinces the Reformation was making even greater strides. There the Jews, whether reform, like Doctor Marcus Jastrow, or orthodox like Rabbi Berish Meisels, identified themselves with the

Poles, and participated in their cultural and political aspirations, which were frequently antagonistic to Russification. A society which called itself Poles of the Mosaic Persuasion was organized in Warsaw, an organ of extreme liberalism was founded in the weekly Israelita, and, with the election of Isaac Kramsztyk to the rabbinate, German was replaced (1852) by the native Polish as the language of the pulpit.

Some champions of reform did not rest satisfied with mere innovations and improvements. They went so far as to discard Judaism altogether and improvise religions of their own. Moses Rosensohn of Vilna was the first, in his works *Advice and Help* (*'Ezrah we-Tushiah*, Vilna, 1870) and *The Peace of Brothers* (*Shelom Ahim*, ibid.), to suggest a way to cosmopolitanism and universalism through Judaism.[19] In 1879, Jacob Gordin founded in Yelisavetgrad a sort of ethical culture society called Bibleitsy (also Dukhovnoye Bibleyskoye Bratstvo, Spiritual Bible Brotherhood), which obtained a considerable following among the workmen of the section. It advocated the abolition of ritual observances, even prayer, and the hastening of the era of the brotherhood of man. It preached, in the words of one of its leaders, that " our moral-

247

ity is our religion. God, the acme of highest reason, of surest truth, and of the most sublime justice, does not demand useless external forms and ceremonies." [20] Following the organization of the Bibleitsy, and based on almost the same principles, branches of a Jewish sect, which called itself New Israel (Novy Izrail), were started almost simultaneously in Odessa and Kishinev. In the former city, the organization was headed by Jacob Prelooker, in the latter, by Joseph Rabinowitz. Prelooker, who after graduating from the seminary at Zhitomir became a school-master at Odessa, sought to bring about a consolidation between his own people and Russian Dissenters (Raskolniki: the Molocans, Stundists, and Dukhobortzi). The theme of his book, *New Israel,* is a " reformed synagogue, a mitigation of the cleavage between Jew and Christian, and recognition of a common brotherhood in religion." Rabinowitz went still further, and preached on actual conversion to one of the more liberal forms of Christianity. [21]

These sects, which sprang up in church and synagogue during the latter part of the " seventies," were the outcome of political and social as well as religious unrest. Alexander II fulfilled the expectation which the first years of his reign aroused in

Jewish hearts no more than Catherine II and Alexander I. Those who had hoped for equal rights were doomed to disappointment. Most of the reforms of the Liberator Czar proved a failure owing to the antipathy and machinations of his untrustworthy officials. Russia was split between two diametrically opposed parties, the extreme radicals and the extreme reactionaries, waging an internecine war with each other. The former originated with the young Russians that had served in the European campaigns during the Napoleonic invasion, and who, in imitation of the secret organizations which had so greatly contributed to the liberation of Germany, united to throw off the yoke of autocracy in Russia. These secret orders, the Southern, the Northern, the United Slavonian, and the Polish, Alexander I had endeavored in vain to suppress, and the drastic measures taken by Nicholas I against the Dekabrists (1825) proved of no avail. Nor did the reforms of Alexander II help to heal the breach. On the contrary, seeing that the constitution they expected from the Liberator Czar was not forthcoming, and the democracy they hoped for was far from being realized, they became desperate, and determined to demand their rights by force. The peasants, too, sobering up from the intoxication, the figurative as well as the literal, caused by the vodka drunk in honor of their newly-acquired volyushka (sweet liberty), discovered that the emancipation ukase of the czar had been craftily intercepted by the bureaucrats, and their dream of owning the land they had hitherto cultivated as serfs would never come true. Russia was rife with discontent, and disaffection assumed a national range. The cry was raised for a " new freedom." A certain Anton Petrov impersonated the czar, and gathered around him ten thousand Russians. Pamphlets entitled *Land and Liberty* (*Zemlya i Volya*) were spread broadcast among the masses, the mind of the populace was inflamed, and attempts on the life of the czar ensued.

The extreme reactionaries, consisting mostly of nobles who had become impoverished by the emancipation of the serfs, grasped the opportunity to point out to the bewildered czar the evil of his liberal policy. Slavophilism was rampant. Men like Turgenief, Dostoyevsky, and Tolstoi, were condemned as " Westernists," or German sympathizers, the enemies of Russia. At the recommendation of Princess Helena Petrovna, the czar engaged as the teacher of his children a comparatively unknown professor of history, Pobyedonostsev, who later became the soul of Russian despotism. This man, meek as a dove and cunning as a serpent, easily ingratiated himself with the czar, and soon there began " a war upon ideas, a crusade of ignorance." " Karakazov's pistol-shot," as Turgenief says, " drove back into the shade the phantom of liberty, the appearance of which all Russia had hailed with acclamations. From that moment to the end of his life, the emperor devoted himself to the undoing of all he had accomplished. If he could have cancelled with one stroke the glorious ukase that had proclaimed the emancipation of the serfs, he would have been only too glad to disgrace himself." [22]

And again, as it had been during the reign of Alexander I after his acquaintance with Baroness Krüdener, so it was with the reign of Alexander II after his acquaintance with Pobyedonostsev. The status of the Jews constituted the first indication of the ill-boding change. How little the officials had been in sympathy with the reformatory efforts of their czar, even when the atmosphere had been filled with peace and good-will to all including the Jews, is shown by the fact that when, in 1863, through the efforts of Doctor Schwabacher, the Jewish community of Odessa applied for a charter to build a Home for Aged Hebrews, the charter, though granted by the higher authorities, was withheld for over twenty years! The reaction flaunted its power once again, and sat enthroned in Tsarskoye Syelo. The few rights the Jews had enjoyed were rescinded one by one. Not satisfied with this, the Slavophils tried, under every pretext, to stop the progress of the Jewish people. Every now and then the Society for the Promotion of Haskalah would send some of the brighter seminary students to complete their education in Breslau or Berlin, but at the command of the Government this was soon discontinued. It was the intention of the same organization, from its very incipiency, to have the Bible translated under its auspices into Russian, but it took ten long years before this praiseworthy undertaking could be begun, because of the obstacles the Government placed in the way of its execution. Fortunately, the indomitable courage of the Maskilim could not be subdued. Young men went, or were sent, to Germany to prepare themselves for the rabbinate as before; the Bible and the Book of Common Prayer, too, were translated secretly by Wohl, Gordon, Steinberg, and Leon Mandelstamm, and published in Germany, whence they were smuggled into Russia.[23]

More direct and equally inexplicable, save on the ground of animosity to whatever was not Slavonic, was the ukase to close the Sabbath Schools and the Evening Schools, the only means of educating the laboring men (1870). In 1871, the first of a series of massacres (pogromy) took place in the centre of Jewish culture, Odessa. In 1872, permission was denied to the ladies of that city to organize a society for the purpose of maintaining trade schools, to teach poor Jewish girls handicrafts. The two rabbinical seminaries, of Vilna and Zhitomir, were closed in 1873, and replaced by institutes for teachers, which were managed in the spirit that had prevailed under Nicholas I. And in 1878 the absurd blood accusation, against which four popes, Innocent IV, Paul III, Gregory X, and Clement XIV, issued their bulls, declaring it a baseless and wicked superstition, and which not only the Polish kings Boreslav V, Casimir III, Casimir IV, and Stephen Bathòry, but also Alexander I (March 18, 1817), branded as a diabolic invention—that dreadful accusation which even the commission of Nicholas, despite Durnovo's efforts, had denounced as a disgrace and an abomination, was revived by the newspaper Grazhdanin. The ghost of medievalism began to stalk abroad once more in

erstwhile enlightened Russia and under the aegis of
the Liberator Czar.

As often before in Jewish history, the Jews
helped not a little to aggravate the untoward conditions. At the instigation of a number of students
of the Yeshibah Tree of Life, the doors of that
noble institution were closed (1879), to open again
after two years of untiring efforts on the part of
its self-sacrificing dean, the renowned Naphtali Zebi
Judah Berlin. But at the worst this was the
result of mistaken zeal for the cause of Haskalah.
What was more detrimental was the disgrace
brought upon the Jewish name by several converts
to Christianity. A certain Jacob Brafmann, having proved a failure in all he undertook, tried at the
last the business of Christianity, and succeeded
therein. He was appointed professor of Hebrew
in the seminary of Minsk, and the Holy Synod
charged him with the duty of devising means to
promulgate Christianity among the Jews. Finding
the times auspicious, he devoted himself to writing
libellous articles about his former coreligionists,
and wound up with a *Book on the Kahal* (*Kniga
Kahala*, Vilna, 1869), in which he quoted forged
" transactions," to the effect that Judaism tolerates
and even recommends illegality and immorality

among its adherents. In a conference of Jews and Gentiles convoked by Governor-General Kaufman (1871), Barit proved the falsity and forgery of Brafmann's documents. But, as usual, the defence was forgotten, the charges remained.[24] A certain Lutostansky poisoned the public mind by caricaturing the Jews, and aroused an anti-Semitic agitation among his countrymen. The consequence was that even the liberals began to be suspicious, and the prospect of better days was blighted by the hatred which broke out in fiendish fury, in lightnings and thunders which astounded the world under Alexander III.

It was but natural that the Jews that had become completely Russified should enlist in the ranks of the extreme liberals. They found themselves in every way as progressive and patriotic as the Christian Russians. The language of Russia became their language, its manners and aspirations their manners and aspirations. They contributed more than any other nationality to Russifying Odessa, which, owing to its great foreign population, was known as the un-Russian city of Russia. Proportionately to their numbers, they promoted the trade and industry, the science and literature of their country more than the Russians themselves. Yet the coveted equality was denied them, and the emancipation granted to the degraded muzhiks was withheld from them, because of a religion they hardly professed. They were like Faust when he found himself tempted but not satisfied by the pleasures of life, when food hovered before his eager lips while he begged for nourishment in vain. The liberals, on the other hand, preached and practiced the doctrine of equal rights to all. Socialism, or nihilism, also appealed to the Jews from its idealistic side, for never did the Jews cease to be democrats and dreamers. In the schools and universities, which they were now permitted to attend, they heard the new teachings and imbibed the novel ideas.

Those, therefore, who disdained conversion allied themselves with the secret organizations. " The torrent which had been dammed up in one channel rushed violently into another." A Hebrew monthly, Ha-Emet (Truth, Vienna, 1877), devoted to the cause of communism, was started by Aaron Liebermann (" Arthur Freeman "), in which, in the language of the oldest and greatest socialists, the doctrines of Karl Marx were inculcated among the Hebrew-reading public. The more completely Russified element took a leading part in the activities of the Narodnaya Volya (Rights of the People), propagating socialism among the Russian masses, either by word of mouth or as editors and coworkers in the " underground " publications. Not a few went to Berlin, where, though opulent, they sought employment in factories, the better to disseminate socialism among the working classes. Others, like Aaronson, Achselrod, Deutsch, Horowitz, Vilenkin, and Zukerman, fled to Switzerland, whence, under the assumed names of Marx, Lassalle, Jacoby, etc., or united in a League for the Emancipation of Labor, they directed the socialistic movement in Russia.[25] Chernichevsky's *What to Do*, Gogol's *Dead Souls*, Turgenief's *Virgin Soil* and *Fathers and Sons*, the doctrines of Pisarev and Bielinsky, and of the other writers who then had their greatest vogue, were eagerly read and frequently copied by Jewish young gymnasiasts and passed on to their Christian schoolmates. The revolutionary spirit seized on men and women alike. Women left their husbands, girls their devoted parents, and threw themselves into the swirl of nihilism with a vigor and self-sacrifice almost incredible. When a squad of police came to disperse the crowd clamoring for " land and liberty " in front of the Kazanskaya

Church in St. Petersburg, a Jewish maiden of six-
teen, taking the place of the leader, inspired her
comrades with such enthusiasm that the efforts of
the police were ineffectual.[26] By 1878, Russia became honeycombed with secret societies. It fell
into spasms of nihilism. One general after another
was assassinated. Attempts were made to wreck the
train on which the czar was travelling (1879) and
blow up the palace in which he resided (1880).
Finally, on March 13, 1881, after many hairbreadth
escapes, the carefully laid plans of the revolutionists
succeeded, and the Liberator Czar was no more.

Thus was the deep-rooted yearning for enlightenment finally let loose, and the gyves of tradition
were at last removed. The Maskilim of the
" forties " and " fifties " were antiquated in the
" sixties " and " seventies." They began to see
that the fears of the orthodox and their denuncia-
tions of Haskalah were not altogether unfounded.
A young generation had grown up who had never
experienced the strife and struggles of the fathers,
and who lacked the submissive temper that had
characterized their ancestors. Faster and farther
they rushed on their headlong way to destruction,
while the parents sat and wept. When, in 1872,
in Vilna, the police arrested forty Jewish young

men suspected of nihilistic tendencies, Governor-General Patapov " invited " the representatives of the community to a conference. As soon as they arrived, Patapov turned on them in this wise, " In addition to all other good qualities which you Jews possess, about the only thing you need is to become nihilists, too! " Amazed and panic-stricken, the trembling Jews denied the allegation and protested their innocence, to which the Governor-General replied, " Your children are, at any rate; they have become so through the bad education you have given them." " Pardon me, General," was the answer of "Yankele Kovner " (Jacob Barit), who was one of the representatives, " This is not quite right. As long as *we* educated our children there were no nihilists among us; but as soon as you took the education of our children into your hands, behold the result." The foundations of religion were undermined. Parental authority was disregarded. Youths and maidens were lured by the enchanting voice of the siren of assimilation. The naïve words which Turgenief put into the mouth of Samuel Abraham, the Lithuanian Jew, might have been, indeed, were, spoken by many others in actual life. " Our children," he complains, " have no longer our beliefs; they do not say our prayers, nor have they your beliefs; no more do they say your prayers; they do not pray at all, and they believe in nothing." [27] The struggle between Hasidim and Mitnaggedim ended with the conversionist policy of Nicholas I, which united them against the Maskilim. The struggle between these anti-Maskilim and the Maskilim had ceased in the golden days of Alexander II. But the clouds were gathering and overspreading the camp of Haskalah. The days in which the seekers after light united in one common aim were gone. Russification, assimilation, universalism, and nihilism rent asunder the ties that held them together. Judah Löb Gordon, the same poet who, fifteen years before, had rejoiced with exceeding joy " when Haskalah broke forth like water," now laments over the effect thereof in the following strain:

> And our children, the coming generation,
> From childhood, alas, are strangers to our nation—
> Ah, how my heart for them doth bleed!
> Farther and faster they are ever drifting,
> Who knows how far they will be shifting?
> Maybe till whence they can ne'er recede!

Amidst the disaffection, discord, and dejection that mark the latter part of the reign of Alexander

II, one Maskil stands out pre-eminently in interest and importance,—one whom assimilation did not attract nor reformation mislead, who under all the mighty changes remained loyal to the ideals ascribed to the Gaon and advocated by Levinsohn,—Perez ben Mosheh Smolenskin (Mohilev, February 25, 1842–Meran, Austria, February 1, 1885).[28]

Smolenskin was endowed with the ability and courage that characterize the born leader. He possessed an iron will and unflinching determination, before which obstacles had to yield, and persecution found itself powerless. His talent to grasp and appreciate the true and the beautiful rendered him the oracle of the thousands who, to this day, are proud to call themselves his disciples. To him Haskalah was not merely acquaintance with general culture, or even its acquisition. It was the realization of one's individuality as a Jew and a man. Gordon's advice, to be a Jew at home and a man abroad, found little favor in his estimation; for Haskalah meant the evolution of a Jewish man *sui generis*. He equally abhorred the fanaticism of the benighted orthodox and the Laodicean lukewarmness of the advanced Maskilim. To fight and, if possible, eradicate both, he undertook the publication of The Dawn (Ha-Shahar, Vienna, 1869), a maga-

zine in which he declared " war against the darkness of the Middle Ages and war against the indifference of to-day! "

Not like the former days are these days, he says in his fore-
word to Ha-Shahar. Thirty or twenty years ago we had to fight
the enemy within. Sanctimonious fanatics with their power of
darkness sought to persecute us, lest their folly or knavery be
exposed to the light of day. . . . Now that they, who hitherto
have walked in darkness, are beginning to discern the error of
their ways, lo and behold, those who have seen the light are
closing their eyes against it. . . . Therefore let them know
beforehand that, as I have stretched out my hand against those
who, under the cloak of holiness, endeavor to exclude enlightenment from the house of Jacob, even so will I lift up my hand
against the other hypocrites who, under the pretext of tolerance,
strive to alienate the children of Israel from the heritage of their
fathers!

That the salvation of the Jews lies in their distinctiveness, and that renationalization will prove
the only solution of the Jewish problem, is the central thought of Smolenskin's journalistic efforts.
Jews are disliked, he maintains, not because of their
religious persuasion, nor for their reputed wealth,
but because they are weak and defenceless. What
they need is strength and courage, but these they
will never regain save in a land of their own.
Twelve years before the tornado of persecution

broke out in Russia he had predicted it, and even welcomed it as a means of arousing the Jews to their duties as a people and their place as a nation, and that his conclusion was correct, the awakening which followed proved unmistakably.

For Smolenskin Jews never ceased to be a nation, and to him the Jew who sought refuge in assimilation was nothing less than a traitor. He was thus the forerunner of Pinsker, and of Herzl a decade later. Indeed, in the resurrection of the national hope he was the first to remove the shroud. According to him, " the eternal people " have every characteristic that goes to make a nation. Their common country is still Palestine, loved by them with all the fervor of patriotism; their common language had never ceased to be Hebrew; their common religion consists in the basic principles of Judaism, in which they all agree.

You wish—thus he addresses himself to the assimilationists— you wish to be like the other people? So do I. Be, I pray you, be like them. Search and find knowledge, avoid and forsake superstition, above all be not ashamed of the rock whence you were hewn. Yes, be like the other peoples, proud of your literature, jealous of your self-respect, hopeful, even as all persecuted peoples are hopeful, of the speedy arrival of the day when we, too, shall reinhabit the land which once was, and still is, our own.

But as the soil of Palestine, however regarded, is at present inaccessible to Jews as a national entity, the language once spoken in Palestine is so much the more to be cherished and cultivated by the exiled people.

You ask me—he calls out again—what good a dead language can do us? I will tell you. It confers honor on us, girds us with strength, unites us into one. All nations seek to perpetuate their names. All conquered peoples dream of a day when they will regain their independence. . . . We have neither monuments nor a country at present. Only one relic still remains from the ruins of our ancient glory—the Hebrew language. Those, therefore, who discard the Hebrew tongue betray the Hebrew nation, and are traitors both to their race and their religion.

No less trenchant and outspoken was he against the serried array of self-styled " reformers " of Judaism. He could not forgive the German rabbis and Russian Maskilim for presuming to " dictate " to their coreligionists what to select and what to reject in matters religious. The whole movement he condemned as a mere imitation of Protestant Christianity. To renovate Judaism! What a stigma on a religion that had endured through the ages, and is rich in all that makes for holiness and right living! The old garment needs no new patches. It still fits and will fit " the eternal people " till time is no more. Since the reform movement in Germany went back to the time of Mendelssohn, Smolenskin hurled the missiles of his criticism against the Berlin sage, forgetting that for more than half a century his example and encouragement had served to awaken a love of knowledge in the hearts of his countrymen. But he saw that in the home of Haskalah, the *Biur,* and the Meassefim, apostasy increased, Hebrew was almost forgotten, and Judaism was declining, and he blamed the pellucid water at the source of the stream for the muddy pool at its mouth. Mendelssohn, however, lacked no defenders among his Russo-Jewish coreligionists, and their sentiments were voiced by Abraham Bär Gottlober in an opposition periodical, The Light of Day (Ha-Boker Or, Lublin, 1876). " Why," exclaimed the editor, " were it not for him and his reforms . . . were it not for that grand and noble personality . . . neither you nor I should have been what we are! " It was only the sad sincerity of Smolenskin that mitigated the errors he had committed in regard to the history of his people and the theology of its religion.

But the militant editor of Ha-Shahar, who wielded his pen like a halberd, to deal out blows to those of whose views he disapproved, became as tender as a father when he set out to write about the people. His love for the masses whom he knew so well was almost boundless. Underlying their superstitions, crudities, and absurdities is the " prophetic consciousness," of which they have never been entirely divested. The heder is indeed far from what a school should be, and the yeshibah is hardly to be tolerated in a civilized community; yet what spiritual feasts, what noble endeavors, and what unselfish devotion are witnessed within their dingy walls! Jewish observances are sometimes cumbersome and sometimes incompatible with modern life, but what beauty of holiness, what irresistible influences emanate and radiate from most of them! Under an uninviting exterior and beneath the accumulated drift of countless generations he discerned the precious jewel of self-sacrifice for an ideal. It was this sympathy and broad-mindedness, expressed in his *Ha-Toëh,* his *Simhat Hanef, Keburat Hamor, Gemul Yesharim,* and *Ha-Yerushah* that will ever endear him to the Hebrew reader.

Such, in brief, was the life of the man who bore the chief part in framing and moulding the Haskalah of the " eighties," which was devoted to the development of Hebrew literature and the rejuvenation of the Hebrew people. Loving the Hebrew tongue with a passion surpassing everything else, he censured the German Jewish savants for writing their learned works in the vernacular, and was on the alert to discover and bring out new talent and win over the indifferent and estranged. Dreaming of the redemption of his people, he paved the way for the Zionistic movement, which spread with tremendous rapidity after his death. And his sincerity and ability were repaid in the only coin the poor possess—in love and admiration. Pilgrimages were made, sometimes on foot, to behold the editor of Ha-Shahar and the author of *Ha-Toëh*. The greatest journalists in St. Petersburg united in honoring him when he visited the Russian capital in 1881. And when he was snatched away in the midst of his usefulness, a victim of unremitting devotion to his people, not only Maskilim, but Mitnaggedim and Hasidim felt that " a prince and a mighty one had fallen in Israel! "

[Notes, pp. 322-327.]

## CHAPTER VI

# THE AWAKENING

## 1881-1905

The reign of Alexander III, like that of Nicholas I, was devoid of even that faint glamor of liberalism which, in the days of Alexander I and Alexander II, had aroused deceptive hopes of better times. During the thirteen years of Alexander III's autocracy (1881-1894) not a ray of light was permitted to penetrate into Holy Russia. On May 14, 1881, the manifesto prohibiting the slightest infringement of the absolute power of the czar was promulgated, to continue unbroken till the Russo-Japanese war. The liberal current which had carried away his predecessors when they first mounted the throne was checked, the sluices of Slavophilism were opened, the history of Russian thinkers became again, as Herzen said, " a long list of martyrs and a register of convicts."

Nicholas Ignatiev, a rabid reactionary, a second Jeffreys, became chief of the Ministry of the Interior; Katkoff, a repentant liberal and exile, was appointed the czar's chief adviser, the Richelieu behind the throne; and Pobyedonostsev, whom Turgenief called the " Russian Torquemada," obtained supremacy over Melikoff, and was appointed procurator of the Holy Synod. With such as these at the head of the Russian bureaucracy, there may have been some foundations for the rumor that an imperial ukase decreed the pillage and slaughter of the Jews, and the muzhiks, obedient to the behests of the " little father," and smarting under the pain of disappointment, vented their venom on their Jewish compatriots. Before the new czar had been on his throne three months, Russia was drenched with Jewish blood. There began saturnalia of rape, plunder, and murder, the like of which had been witnessed nowhere in Europe. For half a year the pogroms which began in Yelisavetgrad (April 27, 28) swept like a tornado over southern Russia, visiting more than one hundred and sixty communities with fire and sword, resulting in outrages on women, in the murder of old and young, in the ruin of millions of dollars of property. The Black Hundreds of the nineteenth century put to shame the Haidamacks of the eighteenth and the Cossacks of the seventeenth. In the words of the Bishop of Canterbury to Sir Moses Montefiore, it looked "as if the enemy of mankind was let loose to destroy the souls of so many Christians and the bodies of so many Jewish people."

But it would be a vain attempt, and out of keeping with the object of this work, to describe in detail the "bloody assizes" and the infernal tragedies that ensued upon the accession of Alexander III; the moral degeneracy and the economic ruin that spread over the mighty empire; the shudder that passed over the civilized world, and was expressed in indignation meetings held everywhere, especially in Great Britain and in the United States (February, 1882), to protest, "in the name of civilization, against the spirit of medieval persecution thus revived in Russia." Suffice it to say that even when the mob, tired of carnage, ceased its work of extermination, the bloodthirstiness of those in authority was not assuaged. Such a policy was inaugurated against the Jews as would, according to Pobyedonostsev, "force one-third of them to emigrate, another third to embrace Christianity, and the remainder to die of starvation." With this in view, his Majesty the Emperor, "prompted by a desire to protect the Jews against the Christians," was graciously pleased to give his assent to the Resolutions

270

of the Committee of Ministers, on the third of May, 1882, *i. e.* to the notorious " temporary measures," or " May laws," framed by Ignatiev, against the will of the Council of the Empire. These " temporary measures " have remained in force to this day. With them was resuscitated all the inimical legislation of the past, beginning with the time of Elizabeta Petrovna. What was favorable was suppressed; the unfavorable was most rigorously enforced. Jews living outside the Pale were driven back into it on the slightest pretext and in the most inhuman manner. To increase the already unendurable congestion, the Pale was made smaller than before. In accordance with the first clause of the " May laws," Jews were expelled from the villages within the Pale itself. In 1888 the districts of Rostov and Taganrog, which till then had belonged to the Pale, and had been developed largely through Jewish enterprise, were torn away and amalgamated with the Don district, in which Jews were not permitted to reside. This was followed by expulsions from St. Petersburg (1890), Moscow, (1891), Novgorod, Riga, and Yalta (1893), and the abrogation of the time-honored privileges of the Jews of Bokhara (1896). Even those who, as skilled artisans or discharged

271

soldiers, had been privileged to reside wherever they chose, were expelled with their wives and the children born in their adopted city. Their only salvation lay in conversion. Converts were especially favored, and were offered liberal inducements. By becoming a convert to the Orthodox Russian Church, a Jew is immediately freed from all the degrading restrictions on his freedom of movement and his choice of a profession. Converts, without distinction of sex, are helped financially by an immediate payment of sums from thirteen to thirty rubles, and until recently were granted freedom from taxation for five years. If a candidate for Greek Christianity is married, his conversion procures him a divorce, and, unless she likewise is converted, his wife may not marry again. By conversion, a Jew may escape the consequence of any misdeed against a fellow-Jew, for, to quote the Russian code, "in actions concerning Jews who have embraced Christianity Jews may not be admitted as witnesses, if any objection is raised against them as such." The penal code provides that Jews shall pay twice and treble the amount of the fine to which non-Jews are liable under similar circumstances. Jews were excluded from the professions to which they had turned in the "sixties" and "seventies,"

272

and in which they had been eminently successful; they were not allowed to hold any civil or municipal office; they were forbidden even to be nurses in the hospitals or to give private instruction to children in the homes.

And still persecution did not cease. Not satisfied with starving the bodies of five millions of Jews, Russian legislators were determined to crush them intellectually. The Slavophils could not brook seeing " non-Russians " surpass their own people in the higher walks of life. The Jews, finally successful in emancipating themselves from the trammels of rabbinism, had transferred their extraordinary devotion from the Talmud to secular studies. They filled the schools and the universities of the empire with zealous and intelligent pupils, who carried off most of the honors. They contributed forty-eight pupils to the gymnasia out of every ten thousand, while the Christians contributed only twenty-two. This was regarded an unpardonable sin. " These Jews have the audacity to excel us pure Russians," Pobyedonostsev is reported to have exclaimed, and measures were taken to suppress their dangerous tendency. As early as 1875 a law was passed withholding from Jewish students the stipends they had hitherto received from a fund set aside for that purpose. In 1882 the number of Jewish students in the Military Academy of Medicine was limited to five per cent, and later it was reduced to zero. Thereafter one professional school after another adopted a percentage provision, and some excluded Jews altogether. Finally, " seeing that many Jewish young men, eager to benefit by a higher classical, technical, or professional education," presented themselves every year for admission to the universities, that they passed their examination and continued their studies at the various schools of the empire, the Government deemed it " desirable to put a stop to a state of affairs which is so unsatisfactory." Consequently the ministry limited the attendance of Jews residing in places within the Pale to ten per cent in all schools and universities (December 5, 1886; June 26, 1887), in places without the Pale to five per cent, and in Moscow and St. Petersburg to three per cent, of the total number of pupils in each school and university. Of the four hundred young Jews who had successfully passed their matriculation examination at the beginning of the scholastic year 1887-1888, and had thus acquired the right of entering the university, three hundred and twenty-six were refused admission, and in many schools and universities they were denied even the small per cent the law permitted.

When, nevertheless, in spite of the many restrictions, the Jew at last obtained the coveted degree, the Government rendered it nugatory by depriving him of the right of enjoying the fruit of his labor and self-sacrifice. He could not practice as an army physician or jurist, nor obtain a position as an engineer or a Government or municipal clerk. In the army, he was not allowed to hold any office, and, though he might be an expert chemist, he could never fill the post of a dispenser (March 1, 1888). He was excluded from the schools for the training of officers, and if he passed the examination on the subjects taught there, his certificate could not contain the usual statement that there " was no objection to admitting him to the military schools." [1]

These restrictive measures were not relaxed when Alexander III was succeeded by his son Nicholas II (1894). If anything, they were more rigorously executed, and the mob was encouraged to multiply its outrages upon the defenceless Jews. The closing years of the nineteenth century wiped out the promises of its opening years. Blood accusations followed by riots became of frequent occurrence. Irkutsk (1896), Shpola, and Kiev

(1897), Kantakuzov (Kherson), Vladimir, and
Nikolayev (1899) gave the Jews a foretaste of
what they had to expect when the Black Hundreds,
encouraged by the Government and incited by
Kruzhevan and Pronin, would be let loose to enact
the scenes that took place in Kishinev and Homel
before the Russo-Japanese war, and in hundreds of
towns after it. The difficulties in the way of secur-
ing an education were increased. Russia did not
believe in an " irreducible minimum " where the
rights of her Jews were concerned. Under Nicholas II the number of Jewish women admitted to
medical schools was put at three per cent of the
total number of students; the newly-established
School for Engineers in Moscow was closed to
Jewish young men altogether; and the students of
both sexes in the schools were constantly harassed
by the police because of the harsh laws concerning
the rights of residence. Some splendidly equipped
institutions of learning were allowed to remain
almost empty rather than admit Jewish students.[2]

This was the worst punishment of all, the most
relentless vengeance wreaked on a helpless victim.
" Of all the laws which swept down upon them
from St. Petersburg and Moscow," says Leroy-
Beaulieu with characteristic insight into the soul of

Israel, " those which they [the Jews] find hardest to bear are the regulations that block their entrance to the Russian universities." The bloodless weighed heavier than the bloody pogroms. Consumed with a desire for education, wealthy Russian Jews made an attempt to establish higher schools of their own, without even drawing upon the surplus money of the kosher-meat fund, which had originally been created for such purposes. Baron de Hirsch, too, offered two million dollars for the higher and technical education of the Jews. But every attempt proved fruitless. Baron de Hirsch's munificence was flatly refused. In the school which Mr. Weinstein opened at Vinitza, Podolia, no more than eight Jews were allowed to attend among eighty Christians, and in the one at Gorlovka, founded by another Jew (Polyakov), only five per cent were admitted.[3]

Writers are wont to speak of this as a reactionary period. The description applies to the Russians; among the Jews it was a period of reawakening.[4] They were disillusioned. They saw that Russification without emancipation, as their unsophisticated fathers had told Lilienthal, meant extermination. The first and worst pogroms were perpetrated in those places where the Jews were like their Russian

neighbors in every respect, except in the eyes of the
law, and with the approval of some who were devotees of the Narodnaya Volya. The Jewish consciousness reasserted itself. If Pobyedonostsev accomplished his fiendish design as regards emigration, more than a million Jews having left Russia
within the last twenty years; if he has almost succeeded in causing them to die of starvation; yet his
hope of forcing a third of them to conversion was
a disappointment and a delusion. The Jews showed
that the traditional description applied to them,
" stiff-necked," was not undeserved. While the
Roman Catholics, Lutherans, and Armenians have
undergone conversion in multitudes, they whose
suffering by far exceeded that of any other " non-
Russian " nationality remained, with insignificant
exceptions, loyal to the religion of their fathers.[5]

The Russian Jews—says Zunser—sobered down from the orgies
of assimilation, and its worshippers abandoned their idol. Those
who had almost forgotten that they were of the camp of Israel
began to return to its tents. The Jewish physicians, jurists,
technologists, and the entire so-called Jewish " intelligentia," who
heretofore had never cared to speak a word of Yiddish to a Jew,
resumed their native tongue; they began to send their children to
the Jewish hadarim, and adopted once more Jewish ways and
customs. Several hundred Jewish university students, pro-
verbially irreligious, sent to Vilna for tefillin [phylacteries]!

In many cities fasts were observed and prayers for forgiveness offered, and the prodigal sons of Israel repaired to the synagogue, participated in the services, and wept with their more steadfast though equally unfortunate coreligionists. Many converts, too, began to feel qualms of conscience, and endeavored to make up for their youthful indiscretions. Some of them fled to places of safety, and returned to Judaism. The gifted young poet Simon Yakovlevich Nadsohn died of a broken heart. Sorkin, the classmate and friend of Levanda, committed suicide, while Levanda, the great novelist of assimilation, was so affected by the massacres and their consequences, that he became melancholy, and died in an asylum for the insane.*

If this was the fate of the assimilated and estranged, one may guess the effect of the reaction on the religious. If the students of the universities sacrificed their careers, their daily bread, for the austere satisfaction of discharging their moral obligation to the best of their knowledge, the students of the Law, always loyal to the heritage of their people, became more zealous than ever. Lilienblum who, in 1877, believed that life without a university education was not worth living, became a repentant sinner. Russian Jewry seethed with

279

religious enthusiasm. Moses Isaac Darshan, " the Khelmer Maggid," preached for six hours at a time to crowded synagogues. Asher Israelit, less trenchant, but equally effective, exhorted crowds to repentance. Zebi Hirsh Masliansky, a finished orator, went from town to town, and aroused a love for whatever was connected with the history and religion of the Jewish people. In Kovno those who were preparing themselves for the rabbinate formed something like a new sect, the Mussarnikes (Moralists), which practiced asceticism and self-abnegation to an extraordinary degree.[1]

Those, however, were most affected who had been misled by dreams of assimilation. They suffered most, for they lost most. Their hopes were blighted, their hearts broken. The leading-strings proved to be a halter. They saw they had little to expect at the hands of those they had believed to have become fully civilized, and they were embittered toward civilization, which had showed them flowers, but had given them no fruit. In a work, *Sinat 'Olam le-'Am 'Olam (Eternal Hatred for the Eternal People,* Warsaw, 1882), Nahum Sokolov proved, like Smolenskin before him, that anti-Semitism was ineradicable, that the fight against the Jews was a fight to the death, that even emancipation

**MOSES LÖB LILIENBLUM**
1843-1910

helps little to remove the animosity innate in one people against another, and until the " end of days " foretold by the prophets of yore there will never cease the eternal hatred to the eternal people. This became the dominant opinion. It dawned upon many that the only salvation for the Jews lay in becoming a nation once more. A yearning for a new fatherland and a new country seized young and old. The times were auspicious. Cosmopolitanism was everywhere giving place to nationalism. The little Balkan States had broken the yoke of Ottoman rule, and become self-governing nations since 1878. In Poland, Hungary, and Ireland, home rule was advocated with fervor that threatened a revolution. Italy and Germany became united under their own king or emperor. And the Russian Jews, tired of the constant conflicts with the surrounding peoples, experienced the desire which had prompted their ancestors to be like all the other nations.

Sokolov's sentiments were reinforced in an anonymous pamphlet written by Doctor Leo Pinsker (1821-1891), one of the foremost physicians of Odessa. His *Auto-Emancipation* (Berlin, 1882) is now recognized as the forerunner of Herzl's *Judenstaat*, which appeared fifteen years later. Pinsker accepts as an axiom what Sokolov had tried to demonstrate as a proposition. Jew-hatred, he claims, like Lombroso in his work on anti-Semitism, is a " platonic hatred," a hereditary mental disease, which two thousand years' duration has so aggravated as to render it incurable. As the Jewish problem is international, it can be solved only by nationalism. He admits some of the charges brought against the Jews by anti-Semites, but Jewish failings result from Christian intolerance. In a land of their own they will develop into a Musternation, a model people.

The wretches—cries he—they mock the eagle that once soared sky-high, and saw divinity itself, because he can no longer fly after his wings are broken! Give us but our independence, allow us to take care of ourselves, grant us but a little strip of land like that of the Servians and Rumanians, give us a chance to lead a national existence, and then prate about our lacking manly virtues. What we lack is not genius (Genialität) but self-consciousness (Selbstgefühl) and appreciation of our value as men (Bewusstsein der Menschenwürde), of which we were deprived by you!

Of course, it requires many years and a great expenditure of money to establish a nation on a firm basis. But in Pinsker's dictionary the word " impossible " does not exist. " Far, very far," says he, " is the haven of rest towards which our souls are turning. We know not even whether it be East

or West. But be the road never so long, it cannot
seem too long to the wanderers of two thousand
years."

Pinsker's impassioned appeal made a deep impression. It was obvious that colonization would
be the shortest road to renationalization. But as
to the place in which the colonies should be established, no agreement could be reached. Pinsker,
like Herzl after him, left the problem unsolved.
Some preferred America or even Spain. In southern Russia a society, 'Am 'Olam (The Eternal Nation), was organized on communistic principles. It
sent an advance guard to the United States, where,
as the Sons of the Free, they established several settlements, the best-known of which was New Odessa,
in Oregon.* The majority, however, preferred Palestine, the land which, in weal or woe, in pain or
pleasure, remains ever dear to the Jewish heart; the
land to which the ancient exiles by the waters of
Babylon had vowed that sooner than forget her
would their right hands forget their cunning and
their tongues cleave to the roofs of their mouths;
the possession whereof had been held out as the
most alluring promise, and to be deprived of which
the prophets had regarded as the severest punishment.

Zionism, even Territorialism, among the Russian Jews is by no means solely the result of modern anti-Semitism. At the same time that Mordecai Manuel Noah was planning his Jewish state Ararat in western New York (1825), Gregori Peretz, who, as a child, had been converted, with his father, to the dominant religion, and had been advanced to the rank of an officer in his Majesty's army, was dreaming of the renationalization of his alienated brethren. As a leading figure in the councils of the Dekabrists, he never ceased his efforts until his comrades accepted the restoration of Israel to his pristine place among the nations of the earth as part of their revolutionary programme. But with the suppression of the Dekabrists by Nicholas I the scheme died " a-borning," and sank into oblivion. Later, David Gordon revived the yearnings of Judah Halevi by his articles in the weekly Ha-Maggid (1863), which he edited in Lyck, Prussia. Smolenskin's writings resound with a love for Zion from the very beginning of his literary career. And a rising young Hebraist, Eliezer ben Yehudah, while still a student of medicine, wrote, in 1878, and again in 1880, stirring letters to the editor of Ha-Shahar, in which he advocated the return to the Holy Land and the revival of the holy tongue as a *conditio sine qua non* for the realization of the Jewish mission. These views, at first advocated by the Hebrew-writing and Hebrew-reading Maskilim, gradually filtered into the various strata of Russo-Jewish society, and when the clouds began to gather fast in Russia's sky, and the change in the monarch's policy augured the approach of evil times, Zionism rapidly made enthusiastic converts even among the most Russified of the Jewish youth. On November 6, 1884, for the first time in history, a Jewish international assembly was held at Kattowitz, near the Russian frontier, where representatives from all classes and different countries met and decided to colonize Palestine with Jewish farmers.

Since then Haskalah in Russia has become nationalistic and Palestinian. Even those who were at first opposed to it gradually grew friendly, and finally became " lovers of Zion " (Hobebe Zion). Among the Russo-Jewish students in Vienna, Smolenskin, the militant Zionist, organized an academic society, Kadimah, a name which, meaning Eastward and Forward, contains the philosophy of Zionism in a nutshell. Seeing that the Alliance Israélite Universelle encouraged emigration to America, both he and Ben Yehudah published violent attacks on the French society, and endeavored to thwart its plans as far as possible.° The Hebrew weekly Ha-Meliz, published in St. Petersburg, was a staunch supporter of the movement, and a little later Ha-Zefirah, published in Warsaw, which was at first indifferent, if not antagonistic, joined the ranks. In Russian, too, the Razsvyet and especially the Buduchnost spread Zionism among their readers, while books, pamphlets, and poems were published in Yiddish for circulation among the masses. In addition to the Hobebe Zion societies formed in many cities, secret societies were organized, such as the famous Bene Mosheh (Sons of Moses), which had for its object the moral and intellectual improvement of the future citizens of the Jewish Republic; the Bilu (initials of Bet Ya'akob leku we-nelekah, " O House of Jacob, come and let us go "), formed by Israel Belkind, who went to Palestine with his fellow-students of the University of Kharkov, and founded the colony of Gederah; and the Hillul (Hereb la-Adonaï u-le-Arzenu, " A sword for God and our land "), the members of which pledged themselves to remove any obstacle to the cause of nationalism, even at the cost of their lives. The Bone Zion (Builders of Zion), a sort of Masonic fraternity, was a very potent secret society, which undertook to constitute itself a provisional Jewish Government, and assiduously watched the Zionistic societies and their leaders in every portion of the globe.[10]

These dreamy youths, however, heartbroken and disgusted with a civilization which had failed to redeem its promises, proved but poor material for laying the foundations for a future nation. It was as with the Darien Company organized by William Paterson when Scotland was sorely distressed, and the Champ d'Asile, by the remnant of Napoleon's grand army—a fine idea, but the men and the means were wanting to execute it. The colonies in Palestine fared no better than those in America. They were opposed by the Government from without and by many of the orthodox Jews from within. The former, though claiming to be glad to see the Jews emigrate, though declaring to the Jewish delegation that pleaded for mercy, *Zapadnaya graniza dlya vas otkrita* (" the Western frontier is open to you "), was still, Pharaoh-like, reluctant to see so many " undesirable citizens " leave, and prohibited the formation of organizations to accomplish the end. The orthodox were against the movement on religious grounds, because it was " forcing the end " of Israel's trouble before

the destined day of God arrived." But with the
" nineties " the movement received a strong impetus. Alexander Zederbaum, the publisher of
Ha-Meliz, succeeded in obtaining a charter (February 9, 1890) for the Association for the Aid of
Colonization in Palestine and Syria. Such eminent
rabbis as Mordecai Eliasberg, his son Jonathan,
Samuel Mohilever, N. Z. Y. Berlin, and Mordecai
Joffe espoused the cause, and set the example for
their less prominent colleagues. When the question
arose whether Jewish argiculturists in Palestine are
obliged to observe the Biblical injunction not to till
the ground in the seventh year (shemittah), Rabbi
Isaac Elhanan Spector of Kovno, the leading rabbi
and Talmudist of his time, decided, in opposition
to the Jerusalem rabbinate, that the law had ceased
to be effective with the destruction of the Temple.
Baron Edmond de Rothschild of Paris also came
to the rescue of the colonists, and, more important
still, there began an immigration of Russo-Jewish
farmers into Palestine, of the class, numbering
about ninety-five thousand souls, whom Arnold
White described as " an active, well set-up, sun-
burnt, muscular, agricultural people, marked by all
the characteristics of a peasantry of the highest
character." With them the colonies began to flour-

ish, the debts were paid off, and a better regime set in. " There was no crime or drunkenness," says Bentwich, " in those settlements, and the only usurer was a Russian peasant, who charged the Jewish borrowers thirty-six per cent for loans. If ever I saw practical religion carried into daily life, it was among those brave and sober Hebrew ploughmen." [12]

Whatever may be one's views on Zionism, there can be no doubt that it has proved a power for good in Russia. It introduced new ideals and revived old expectations. It has accomplished, in a measure, the fond hope of the Maskilim and awakened within the Russian Jew a feeling of self-respect and a " consciousness of human worth." Different and contending elements it has coalesced into one. It has, above all, brought back to the fold the doubting Thomases and careless Gallios, even the avowed scoffers, among the Jewish youth, and imbued them with courage and pride,[13] and given them a new shibboleth, *Meine Kunst der Welt, mein Leben meinem Volke* (" My art for the world, my life for my people ").

" We have seen our youths return to us," writes Lilienblum,[14] " and our hearts were filled with joy. In their restoration we found balm for our wounds, and with rapturous wonderment we asked ' who has borne us these? ' " The poets welcomed them with songs. Gordon, whose sorrow had silenced his muse, was inspired once more and called:

> Behold our sons, of whom we despaired,
> Return to us, the great and the small;
> God's grace is not ended, our power's unimpaired,
> Again we shall live, and rise after the fall!

Frug sang in Russian:

> My own Nation,
> Thou art not alone; thy sons behold
> Coming back in crowds as in days of old!

And Zunser represented Rachel as soliloquizing in Yiddish:

> Through the windows what am I seeing,
> Like turtle-doves hitherward fleeing?
> Are my Joseph and Benjamin knocking at my door?
> O Heavens, O mighty wonder!
> Those are my children yonder!
> Yes, my dearest and my truest coming home once more!

But Zionism is not exclusively either a political or a religious movement. It is both plus something else; it is eminently educational. It has produced novelists and poets, whose writings are full of the virility and beauty of a rejuvenated nation. In

Jaffa it established a high school (Bet ha-Sefer), it inspired Doctor Chazanowicz to establish a national library, and ways and means are being considered to establish a national university in Palestine. Even among the devotees of the arts it has given rise to a new romantic school, young painters and sculptors who are depicting their Judenschmerz.

Their cunning hands—says Mr. Leo Mielziner—have mastered the technique of their art, be it in Moscow or Munich, or Berlin, or Paris, but the heart which inspires their brush or mallet pulsates in Palestine. The wandering Jew in them pauses, not to portray the impression of the foreign lands and stranger customs, but to depict his own suffering, his own Heimweh, his own aspirations.

Struck, Ashkenasi, Maimon, Hirszenberg, Gottlieb, Epstein, Löbschütz, and Schatz are the leaders of this new movement. The last-named, together with Ephraim Moses Lilien of Galicia, perhaps the greatest Jewish illustrator of our time, has founded a national school, Bezalel, to propagate Jewish art in Palestine, on the same principles on which the great national art schools of other countries are based. The language of instruction is Hebrew.

Meanwhile the Society for the Promotion of Haskalah continued its work of Russification and general civilization. After 1880 its activity was greatly enhanced, and its members worked with renewed zeal. It opened elementary schools, and expended large sums on stipends for students, and the publication of useful and scholarly books. The branch in Odessa secured two hundred and thirty-one new members in one year (1900), making the total in that city alone nine hundred and sixty-eight. It organized a bureau of information on pedagogic subjects, and through the liberality of Kalonymos Wissotzky instituted prizes for original works in Hebrew or Russian. Individual philanthropists did their utmost to counterbalance the restrictions on education.[15]

Trade schools were opened by the Committee for the Promotion of a Knowledge of Trade and Agriculture among the Jews of Russia, in Minsk, Vilna, and Vitebsk, besides fifteen manual training schools for boys and twenty for girls, in which the indigent pupils are provided with food, clothes, and books. In 1900 thirteen new schools were opened in Kherson and Yekaterinoslav, to supply the educational demand of the thirty-eight colonies existing in those Governments. In the vicinity of Minsk a Junior Republic was organized, and in many cities art and choral societies were formed.[16]

The desire for self-help and the tendency towards organization, to which Zionism gave an impetus, was rapidly reflected in every sphere of Russo-Jewish activity. In a series of works and articles, Jacob Wolf Mendlin, who studied under Lassalle, pointed out the importance of the co-operative system. Accordingly, a union was organized by the Jewish salesmen in Warsaw. In 1897 a conference of Jewish workingmen was held in that city and Der allgemeine jüdische Arbeiterbund in Littauen, Polen, und Russland (Federation of Jewish Labor Unions in Lithuania, Poland, and Russia) was perfected. It published three papers as its organs, Die Arbeiterstimme, Der jüdischer Arbeiter, and, in Switzerland, Letzte Nachrichten. Soon workmen's associations and artisans' clubs appeared wherever there was a sufficient number of Jewish tailors, hatters, bookbinders, etc., for the purpose of increasing and improving the value of their production, and to do away with middlemen and money-lenders. They organized a tailors', dyers', and shoemakers' union in Kharkov, and a carpenters' union in Minsk, for mutual support in the struggle for existence, and for the construction of sanitary workingmen's houses. The cultural desire of the handicraftsmen, constituting twelve per cent of the Russo-Jewish population and occasionally fifty-two per cent (Odessa), seventy-three per cent (Kovno), and even ninety per cent (Byelostok), is phenomenal. Their object is not only physical improvement. Their highest aim is that their members be enabled, by means of efficient night schools and private instruction, to acquire elementary and higher education; in the words of the constitution of the carpenters' union of Minsk, " to protect their material interests, raise their moral and intellectual status, and foster efforts of self-help." [17]

The Hebrew teachers, a class which, though more respected, underwent as hard a struggle as the workingmen, banded themselves together in 1899 in the Society for Aiding Hebrew Teachers of the Province of Vilna. Their president was Michael Wolper, the inspector of the Hebrew Institute and successor to Wohl as censor of Hebrew publications. Similar attempts were made in Bessarabia. Rabbi Shachor, chairman of the Hebrew Teachers' Association of Yekaterinoslav, was instrumental in opening a normal school conducted on Chautauqua principles, and so advanced the cause of education considerably. [18]

With the establishment of the rabbinical seminaries and the ukase (May 3, 1855) that only such may officiate as rabbis as have completed a prescribed course of study, Russian Jewry was placed in a sore predicament. It was a very difficult task to find men who united secular knowledge with that thorough mastery of Talmudic literature which the Jews of Russia exact from their rabbis. Every community was compelled to appoint two rabbis: an orthodox rabbi (dukhovny rabbin) and a "crown," or Government, rabbi (kazyony rabbin). The people recognized only the authority of the former, the Government that of the latter. The consequence was that a man with a mere high-school education would apply for, and would often receive, the position of crown-rabbi. His duties consisted in merely keeping a register of marriages, births, and deaths, administering the oath, and the like. The many lawyers and physicians who were debarred from practicing their professions sought to become candidates for the rabbinate. To avoid the unpleasant results which followed, Rabbi Chernovich of Odessa and Rabbi I. J. Reines of Lyda established seminaries in Odessa and Lyda, to take the place and to continue the teaching of the Vilna and the Volozhin yeshibot, which had been closed, and to furnish proper rabbis for the various congregations.[19]

The century-long struggle for enlightenment had a telling effect. What the early Maskilim had only dreamed of finally came to be. The metamorphosis was so great and so general as to be hardly credible. It was shown by Mr. Landman, in a paper read before the Russo-Jewish Historical Society of Odessa, that while among the Gentiles of that city the reading public constituted seven per cent of the population, among Jews it was no less than thirty-three per cent, and twenty-five per cent of all readers were Jewish women.[20] By 1905 there were two Yiddish and three Hebrew dailies, besides several weekly, monthly, and quarterly periodicals and annuals in Yiddish, Hebrew, and Russian, notwithstanding the fact that a numerous class depended on the general Russian literary output for their mental pabulum.

As the number of those who read Hebrew was still considerable, Abraham Löb Shalkovich (Ben Avigdor) began, with the assistance of a number of Maskilim, the publication of " penny literature " (Sifre Agorah, Warsaw, 1893). Shortly afterwards the Ahiasaf Society and, a little later, the Tushiyah Society were founded. The object was to edit and publish " good and useful books in the Hebrew language for the spread of knowledge and the teaching of morality and culture among the Hebrew youth, also scientific books in all departments of learning." Both these associations have done admirable work. They have published many good text-books for teaching Hebrew and Jewish history, an illustrated periodical for children, 'Olam Katan (The Little World), and numerous works of interest to the adult. Among their publications were, besides the original writings of Peretz, Taviov, Frischman, Berdichevsky, Chernikhovsky, and others, also translations from Bogrov, Byron, Frug, Hugo, Nordau, Shakespeare, Spencer, Zangwill, Zola, critical biographies of Aristotle, Copernicus, George Eliot, Heine, Lassalle, Nietzsche, Rousseau, and a great many equally famous men of letters, which followed each other in promiscuous but uninterrupted succession, all handsomely printed and prettily bound, and sold at a moderate price.

One evil, however, remained, in the face of which both the Maskilim and the financiers found themselves utterly helpless, the evil of the exclusion of Jews from the universities. They could found elementary and high schools for the young, night schools and Sabbath Schools for the adult workingmen, but to establish a university was an absolute impossibility. Jewish youths were again compelled, as in the days of Tobias Cohn and Solomon Maimon, to seek in foreign lands the education denied them in their own. Austria, Switzerland, France, and chiefly Germany, became once more the Meccas whither Russo-Jewish graduates repaired to finish their studies, and where they formed a sort of Latin Quarters of their own, and led almost a communal life. Their numbers in the German universities grew to such proportions, and their material condition became so wretched, that a society was organized in Berlin for the express purpose of helping them. On the other hand, the authorities protested (1906) against expending the funds granted each year for German educational institutions on the education of non-Germans, and the Akademischer Club of Berlin passed resolutions demanding a regulation against their admission. In Leipsic alone, of the six hundred and sixty-two foreign students who attended the university, three hundred and forty, or over one-half, are Russian Jews (1906). Of the five hundred and eighty-six students enrolled in the Commercial University, three hundred and twenty-two are foreigners, among whom Russians predominate, and of the

eight hundred students who attend the Royal Con-
servatory of Music, three hundred are foreigners,
also mostly Russians. Russians constitute two hundred and two of the three hundred and forty-seven
pupils in the Dresden Polytechnicum, and sixty out
of one hundred and thirty-seven in the Dresden
Veterinary College, while in the Freiberg School
of Mines and in the Tharand Forestry Academy
they are in a majority, though they pay twice, and
in some places three times, the amount of tuition
fee required from the native students. The proportion is still greater in the Swiss universities of
Basle, Berne, Geneva, Lausanne, and Zurich, where
they sometimes constitute three-fourths of the entire
student body in the medical schools (Geneva,
1907).

And as for the progress made by the Russo-Jewish woman, it is wonderful, indeed. It is hardly
a quarter of a century since attention began to be
given to her mental development, and yet she has
seldom lagged behind her sisters in more enlightened lands, and has lately attained to a proud
height. Vilna, with her "many well-educated
wives," attracted the attention of Montefiore in the
early " forties "; Tarnopol speaks in terms of high
praise of the Jewish women of Odessa in the " six-

ties "; they " charm by their culture, by the ease and precision with which they speak several European languages, by the correctness of their judgment, and the beauty of their conversation." [21] The memoirs of Madame Pauline Wengeroff throw a sidelight also on the accomplishments of her sisters in the less enlightened districts of Russian Jewry. But in the last quarter of the nineteenth and the early part of the twentieth century, their advance was prodigious.[22] When decent Jewish women were prohibited to reside in St. Petersburg, some of the Jewish female students, at the risk of their reputation, secured the yellow ticket of the prostitute rather than sacrifice their education. But the majority went to other countries. The press has lately been interested in what these seekers for light in foreign lands have accomplished, and reported the successes of Fanny Berlin, who graduated from the University of Berne as doctor of law *summa cum laude,* and of Miss Kanyevsky of Zinkoff (Poltava), who was the first woman to take her degree as engineer at the Ecole des Pontes et Chaussées, in Paris

It is a curious fact—remarks a correspondent in the Pall Mall Gazette—the majority [of lady doctors practicing in Paris] are Russian Jewesses, just as are the greatest number of young women medical students. At a rough calculation there are three hundred ladies pursuing medical studies at the various schools, and working side by side with the male students. The reason of the invasion of the Jewess is, of course, the disabilities that exist in Russia for those of the faith of Israel . . . disabilities that are hardly lessened in Germany. Moreover, there exists only one university in Russia, and that is in St. Petersburg. Some of the women who graduate in medicine do extremely well afterwards in practice, and are greatly in vogue in the highest society in Paris. . . . The lady doctor who is also a Russian subject has likewise found a field for her energies in China, where Russian influence is so dominant at the present moment.

Another writer, in Harper's Bazaar, speaking of girl-students in Paris, has this to say:

The Russian students are an interesting class in Paris. There are some one hundred and thirty of them in all, nearly all Hebrews, as the Russian universities admit only about four Jews to every hundred students. Their monthly allowance from their families is often no more than twenty dollars, and out of that they must pay board, room-rent, and all outside expenses. These Russian "new women" are extraordinary students. Mlle. Lepinska, one of the first to graduate in medicine, presented a thesis six hundred and sixty pages long to her astonished professors.

With pitying admiration the world looks on the struggle for enlightenment of these brave sons and daughters of Judah. Their trials and tribulations, their heart-burnings and disappointments, have inspired poets and painters, novelists and playwrights. From Chamisso's *Abba Glusk Leczeka* to Korolenko's *Skazanye o Florye Rimlyaninye,* czars have died or have been assassinated, statesmen have risen and fallen, but the Russian Jew, like the heroes of the poem or novel, did not wait to conquer by submitting. Thanks to his indomitable spirit he has made unexampled progress. Within the last twenty-five years he has not only emancipated himself, but he is now the most potent factor in the struggle for the emancipation of his countrymen. Within these years he has become the recognized torch-bearer of liberty and enlightenment in darkest Russia. Uvarov justified his inhuman treatment of the Jews by the plea that they are " orthodox and believers in the Talmud." The latest excuse (1904) of von Plehve was that " if we admitted Jews to our universities without restriction, they would surpass our Russian students and dominate our intellectual life." But neither the former prevails, nor the latter, nor their henchmen who fill the columns of the Grazhdanin, Kievlyanin, Novoye Vremya, and the like. The words and writings of such noble and world-famous Russians as Popoff, Demidov, Strogonoff, Bershadsky, Shchedrin, Tolstoi, and the cream of the Russian " intelligentia," as well as such foreigners as Mommsen, Gladstone, Leroy-Beaulieu, and Michael Davitt, will have their salutary effect. The consciousness of the Russian people will awaken. The attitude lately manifested both in St. Petersburg and the provinces against the *Kontrabandisti*, a libellous play written by an apostate Jew, Levin, will become more and more general. Then the heroic effort and the unexampled progress of the Russian Jews will be more fully appreciated, and a patriotic nation will gratefully acknowledge its indebtedness to that smallest but most energetic and self-sacrificing portion of its heterogeneous population, the Jews, who have done so much, not only for Jewish Russians, but for Christian Russians as well, to hasten the time when " many shall run to and fro, and knowledge shall be increased."

[Notes, pp. 327-330.]

# NOTES

## ABBREVIATIONS USED IN THE NOTES

AZJ   = Allgemeine Zeitung des Judenthums, Leipsic, 1837—.
FKI   = Fünn, Keneset Yisraël, Warsaw, 1860.
FKN   = Fünn, Kiryah Ne'emanah, Vilna, 1860.
FSL   = Fünn, Safah le-Ne'emanim, Vilna, 1881.
GMC   = Ginzberg and Marek, Yevreyskiya Narodniya Pyesni,
           St. Petersburg, 1901.
HUH   = Harkavy, Ha-Yehudim u-Sefat ha-Selavim, Vilna, 1867.
JE   = Jewish Encyclopedia, 12 vols., New York, 1901-1906.
LBJ   = Levinsohn, Bet Yehudah, Warsaw, 1901.
LTI   = Levinsohn, Te'udah be-Yisraël, Warsaw, 1901.
WMG = Wengeroff, Memoiren einer Grossmutter, i., Berlin, 1908.

## CHAPTER I

### THE PRE-HASKALAH PERIOD

#### ?-1648

#### (pp. 17-52)

[1] Mention might, indeed, be made of Dr. Zunz's pioneer work in his Aelteste Nachrichten über Juden und jüdische Gelehrte in Polen, Slavonien, Russland (Gesammelte Schriften, Berlin, 1875, iii. 82-87), and Firkovich, who, in his Abne Zikkaron (Vilna, 1872), threw much light on the history of the Crimean Jews. The best contributions to the subject, however, are those of Harkavy, Russ i Russkiye v Sred. Yevr. Lit. (Voskhod, 1881), and Malishevsky, Yevreyi v Yuzhnoy Rossii i Kieve, v. x-xii. Vyekakh, St. Petersburg, 1878.

[2] LTI, p. 33, n. 2; LBJ, ii. 94, n. 2.

[3] See JE, s. v. Azov, and Kertch. See also Fishberg, The Jews: A Study of Race and Environment, New York, 1911, pp. 150, 192-194.

[4] See Judah Halevi's Kuzari, Introduction.

[5] Minor, Rukovodstvo, Moscow, 1881, iv; Ha-Pardes, St. Petersburg, 1902, p. 155.

[6] HUH, pp. 31-32, 69-76.

[7] Yevrey Minister, Voskhod, 1885, v. 105 f.

[8] JE, i. 112, 119, 223; viii. 652.

[9] The synagogue in Brest-Litovsk, which Saul Wahl built in memory of his wife Deborah, was demolished in 1836. WMG, p. 84.

[10] HUH, pp. 77-134.

[11] JE, x. 569.

[12] The story of Zacharias de Guizolfi deserves to be given at greater length. He was a prince and ruler of the Taman peninsula near the Black Sea (1419). After he had been unsuccessful in a war against the Turks, Czar Ivan III sent him a message sealed with the gold seal (March 14, 1484) as follows:

"By the grace of God, the great ruler of the Russian land, the Grand Duke Ivan Vassilyevich, czar of all the Russias, to Skariya the Hebrew.

"You have written to us through Gabriel Patrov, our guest, that you desire to come to us. It is our wish that you do so. When you are with us, we shall give you evidence of our favorable disposition toward you. Should you wish to serve us, we will confer honors upon you. But should you not wish to remain with us, and prefer to return to your country, you shall be free to go."

For some reason or other, Zacharias never accomplished his contemplated trip, notwithstanding the many inducements repeatedly offered by the czar during a period of eighteen years. Perhaps it was because of the disturbances which rendered transportation dangerous; possibly because he preferred to serve the khan rather than the czar, for we find him, in 1500, a resident of Circassia. See JE, vi. 107-108; vi. 12.

[13] E. g. Barakha, the hero (1601), Ilyash Karaimovich, the starosta (1637), and Motve Borokhovich, the colonel (1647). See JE, ii. 128; iv. 283; ix. 40.

[14] See Czacki, Rosprava o Zhydakh, Vilna, 1807, p. 93; Buchholtz, Geschichte der Juden in Riga, Riga, 1899, p. 3; Mann, Sheërit Yisraël, Vilna, 1818, ch. 30; Virga, Shebet Yehudah, Hanover, 1856, pp. 147 f., and Graetz, Geschichte der Juden, ix. 480.

[15] The Subbotniki, Dukhobortzi, and the other dissenting, but non-Jewish, sects are not referred to here, though they may have received their inspiration from Jews or through Judaism.

[16] Voskhod, 1881, i. 73-75; JE, vii. 487-488; ix. 570; Bramson, K Istorii Pervonachalnaho Obrazovaniya Russkikh Yevreyev, St. Petersburg, 1896, pp. 4-6.

[17] Sternberg, Die Proselyten im xvi. und xvii. Jahrhundert, AZJ, 1863, pp. 67-68 (ibid. in L'univers israélite, 1863, pp. 272 f.); Mandelkern, Dibre Yeme Russyah, Warsaw, 1875, pp. 231 f.; Yevreyskaya Enziklopedya, s. v. Zhidostvuyushchikh; Bedrzhidsky in Zhurnal Ministerstva Narodnaho Prosvyeshchanya, St. Petersburg, 1912, pp. 106-122; Jewish Ledger, Jan., 1902, p. 3; Emden, Megillat Sefer, ed. Cohan, p. 207, Warsaw, 1896. On Count Pototzki, see Ger Zedek, in Yevreyskaya Biblyotyeka, St. Petersburg, 1892; Gershuni, Sketches of Jewish Life and History, New York, 1873, pp. 158-224 (also Introduction), and S. L. Gordon's ballad in Ha-Shiloah (Ger Zedek), i. 431. On Pototzki and Zaremba, see Gere Zedek (Anon.), Johannisberg, 1862. On modern Russian Gerim, see Die Welt, July 5, 1907, pp. 16-17 (Palestine), B'nai B'rith News, May 13, 1913 (United States), and Leroy-Beaulieu, Israel among the Nations, Engl. transl., New York, 1900, p. 110, n. 1; Yiddishes Tageblatt, July 16 and 23, 1913, Gerim in Russland, and Vieder vegen Gerim; JE, i. 336; vii. 369-370, 489.

[18] HUH, pp. 3, 21 f.; Minor, op. cit., p. 4; Yevreyskiya Nadpisi, St. Petersburg, 1884, p. 217; Sefer ha-Yashar, no. 522; Eben ha-'Ezer, no. 118. On הרוגי ארץ כנען, see Monatsschrift, xxii. 514.

[19] Catalogue de Rossi, iii. 200; Ha-Maggid, 1860, pp. 299-302; HUH, pp. 33, 40.

[20] Autobiography, p. 39.

[21] LBJ, ii. 95, n.; Ha-'Ibri, New York, viii., no. 33; Lehem ha-Panim, Hil. Nedarim, no. 228.

[22] Nishmat Hayyim, Lemberg, 1858, p. 83a; Azulaï, Shem ha-Gedolim, s. v. Horowitz; FKN, p. 74, and Ha-Maggid, iii. 159. Cf. Sheërit Yisraël, ch. 32, and Edelman, Gedulat Shaül, London, 1854. Reifman, in Ha-Maggid, claims that to Luria belongs the honor of being the first-known Jewish author.

[23] See Zikronot, ed. Cohan, pp. 62-66, 90, 313, 336, 380, passim; Schechter, Studies in Judaism, Philadelphia, 1908, ii. 132.

[24] Margoliuth, Hibbure Likkutim, Venice, 1715, Introduction.

[25] Horowitz, Frankfurter Rabbinen, Frankfort-on-the-Main, 1883, pp. 30-35; FKN, pp. 73-91; Emden, op. cit., p. 125; and biographies.

[26] LTI, ii. 81, n.; Hannover, Yeven Mezulah, Warsaw, 1872, p. 7b.

[27] Zunz, Literaturgeschichte, pp. 433-435, 442; Buber, Anshe Shem, Cracow, 1895, pp. 307-309; Benjacob, Ozar ha-Sefarim, p. 396; JE, xi. 217; Bikkure ha-'Ittim, 1830, p. 43. Jacob of Gnesen, I suspect, must have lived in Russia.

[28] Steinschneider, Jewish Literature, pp. 235, 240; Benjacob, op. cit., p. 396.

[29] JE, xii. 265-266: "Enfin les incrédules les plus déterminés n'ont presque rien allégué qui ne soit dans le Rampart de la Foi du Rabbin Isaac."

[30] Nusbaum, Historya Zhidóv, i. p. 180; Edelman, op. cit., attributes the coming of Saul Wahl to this cause.

[31] The Elim (Amsterdam, 1629), if not, as the Karaites maintain, actually the work of Zerah Troki, was surely the result of the problems submitted by him to Delmedigo.

[32] JE, iv. 504; vii. 264; xii. 266; Ha-Eshkol, iii. and iv. (R. M. Jaffe); LTI, ii. 80; Benjacob, op. cit., no. 1428.

[33] Zunz, Ritus, Berlin, 1859, p. 73, and Gottesdienstliche Vorträge, Frankfort-on-the-Main, 1892, p. 452, n. a.; Wessely, Dibre Shalom we-Emet, ii. 7; Benjacob, op. cit., no. 1187.

[34] Voskhod, 1893, i. 79; New Era Illustrated Magazine, v.; FNI, p. 28 f.; JE, i. 113; ii. 22, 622; xii. 265.

[35] JE, vii. 454.

[36] JE, i. 372; iv. 140; Ha-Yekeb, 1894, p. 68.

[37] Bersohn, Tobiasz Cohn, Warsaw, 1872.

[38] Cf. FKN, pp. 38-42 (Vilna constitution); Hannover, op. cit., p. 23a; Ha-Modia' la-Ḥadashim, II. i. 11, and JE, s. vv. Council, Kahal, Lithuania, etc.

[39] See GMC, pp. 59 f., and compare with this Lermontoff's Cossack Cradle-Song, which may be taken as a type:

Sleep, my child, my little darling, sleep, I sing to thee;
Silently the soft white moonbeams fall on thee and me.
I will tell thee fairy stories in my lullaby;
Sleep, my child, my pretty darling, sleep, I sing to thee.
Lo, I see the day approaching when the warriors meet;
Then wilt thou grasp thy rifle and mount thy charger fleet.
I will broider in thy saddle colors fair to see,
Sleep, my child, my little darling, sleep, I sing to thee.
Then my Cossack boy, my hero brave and proud and gay,
Waves one farewell to his mother and rides far away.
Oh, what sorrow, pain and anguish then my soul shall fill,
As I pray by day and night that God will keep thee still!
Thou shalt take a saint's pure image to the battlefield,
Look upon it when thou prayest, may it be thy shield.
And when battles fierce are raging, give one thought to me;
Sleep, my darling, calmly, sweetly, sleep, I sing to thee.

—Westminster Gazette.

See Güdemann, Quellen zur Geschichte des Unterrichts, Berlin, 1891, pp. 285-286; Ha-Boker Or, i. 315 (on Dubno); Ha-Meliz, 1894, no. 254 (on Mohilev); Zunz, Gottesdienstliche Vorträge, pp. 122g and 470a; cf. Weiss, Zikronotaï, Warsaw, 1895, pp. 53-83.

[41] Cf. Güdemann, Geschichte des Erziehungswesens, iii. 94, n., and see Dembitzer, Kelilat Yofi, Introduction, and Meassef, St. Petersburg, 1902, p. 205, n.

## CHAPTER II

### DAYS OF TRANSITION

1648-1794

(pp. 53-109)

[1] JE, s. v. Bratzlav.

[2] In the diary of a Polish squire we find the following item: "Jan. 5. As the lessee Herszka had not yet paid me the rental of 91 gulden, I went to his house to get my debt. According to the contract, I can arrest him and his wife for as long as I wish, until he settles the bill, and so I ordered him locked up in the pig-sty and left his wife and his sons in the inn. The youngest son, however, I took with me to the palace to be instructed in the rudiments of our religion. The boy is unusually bright and shall be baptized. I already wrote to our priest concerning it, and he promised to come to prepare him. Leisza at first stubbornly refused to make the sign of the cross and repeat our prayers, but Strelicki administered a sound whipping, and to-day he even ate ham. Our venerable priest Bonapari . . . is inventing all manner of means to break his stiff-neckedness." Meassef, St. Petersburg, 1902, pp. 192-193.

[3] See Wolkonsky, Pictures of Russian History and Literature, Boston, 1897, p. 136.

[4] Orshansky, in Yevreyskaya Biblyoteka, ii. 207.

[5] Meassef, St. Petersburg, 1902, p. 195; Beck and Brann, Yevreyskaya Istoriya, p. 326; JE, iv. 155; xi. 113.

[6] Meassef, p. 200. On Russia at the time of Peter the Great, see Macaulay, History of England, ch. xxiii., where he describes the "savage ignorance and the squalid poverty of the barbarous country." In that country "there was neither literature nor science, neither school nor college. It was not till more than a

hundred years after the invention of printing that a single printing-press had been introduced into the Russian empire, and that
printing-press speedily perished in a fire, which was supposed to
have been kindled by priests." When Pyoter Vyeliki (Peter the
Great), while in London, saw the archiepiscopal library, he
declared that "he had never imagined that there were so many
printed volumes in the world." See also Carlyle, History of
Frederick the Great, iv. 7.

[7] FKN, pp. 126-132; Voskhod, 1893; on the Hasidim and
Mitnaggedim see below.

[8] Ma'aseh Tobiah, p. 18; Meassef, pp. 206-209; Geiger (Melo
Hofnayim, Berlin, 1840, pp. 1-29) published Delmedigo's cor-
roboration of this statement.

[9] Rapoport, Etan ha-'Ezrahi, Ostrog, 1776, Introduction.

[10] Cf. Zederbaum, Keter Kehunnah, pp. 72-74, 84, 121, etc., and
Ha-Shiloah, xxi. 165; Schechter, Studies in Judaism, i., Philadelphia, 1896, i. 17 f., and Greenstone, The Messiah Idea in
Jewish History, pp. 237 f. According to some, Judah he-Hasid
and his followers went to Palestine in the expectation, not of the
Messiah, but of Shabbataï Zebi, who was believed to have been in
hiding for forty years, in imitation of the retirement of Moses in
Midian for a similar period of years. "The ruins of Rabbi Judah
he-Hasid's synagogue" and Yeshibah in Jerusalem still keep the
memory of the event fresh in the minds of Palestinian Jews.

[11] Among the many wonderful episodes in the life of the master,
his biographer mentions also that he could swallow down the
largest gobletful in a single gulp (Shibhe ha-Besht, Berdichev,
1815, pp. 7-8). The best, though not an impartial work on Hasidism is Zweifel's Shalom 'al Yisraël, 4 vols., Zhitomir, 1868-1872.

[12] Ha-Boker Or, iv. 103-105: הנגון מעלה נשמות מן האפקורסות.

[13] Cf. Emden, op. cit., p. 185, and Shimush, Amsterdam, 1785, pp.
78-80, with Pardes, ii. 204-214.

[14] See Schechter, op. cit., pp. 73-93; Silber, Elijah Gaon, 1906;
Levin, 'Aliyat Eliyahu, Vilna, 1856, and FKN, pp. 133-155.

[15] Levin, op. cit., pp. 28-30.

[16] See Ha-Bikkurim, i. 1-26; ii. 1-20; Ha-Zeman (monthly), 1903, ii. 6; Plungian, Ben Porat, Vilna, 1858, p. 33; Keneset Yisraël, iii. 152 seq.

[17] Sirkes (Bayit Hadash, Cracow, 1631, p. 40) decides that Jews may employ in their synagogue melodies used in the church, since "music is neither Jewish nor Christian, but is governed by universal laws." See also Hayyim ben Bezalel's Wikkuah Mayim Hayyim, Introduction, and passim.

[18] See J. S. Raisin, Sect, Creed and Custom in Judaism, Philadelphia, 1907, p. 9, and ch. viii.; Ha-Meliz, x. 186, 192-194.

[19] See Ha-Zeman (monthly), 1903, ii. 7.; Shklov, Euclidus, Introduction; Keneset Yisraël, 1887, and Hagra on Orah Hayyim, Shklov, 1803, Introduction.

[20] See Graetz, op. cit., xi. 590, 604, 606. The Gaon, who as a rule was very mild, lost patience with the Hasidim and wielded the weapons of the kuni (or stocks and exposures) and excommunication without mercy. The Hasidim were also accused of being not only religious dissenters but revolutionaries. Zeitlin, quoted in Yiddishes Tageblatt, from the Moment, March, 1913.

[21] See Karpeles, Time of Mendelssohn, p. 297; Kayserling, Mendelssohn, p. 12; Ha-Meliz, 1900, nos. 194-196.

[22] Epstein, Geburat ha-Ari, Vilna, 1870, p. 29; Rabinovich, Zunz, Warsaw, 1896; Wessely, op. cit., ii.; Linda, Reshit Limmudim, Berlin, 1789, and Ha-Zeman (monthly), ii. 28.

[23] Delitzsch, Zur Geschichte der jüdischen Poesie, Leipsic, 1836, p. 118; Bernfeld, Dor Tahapukot, Warsaw, 1897, pp. 88 f. Dubno also edited Luzzatto's La-Yesharim Tehillah, which, according to Slouschz, marks the beginning of the renaissance in Hebrew belles-lettres.

[24] Published in Berlin in 1793. It was translated into English by Murray (Solomon Maimon, Boston, 1888) and into Hebrew by Taviov (Warsaw, 1899).

[25] Bernfeld, op. cit., ii. 66 f. JE, s. v. Maimon; and Autobiography (Engl. transl.), p. 217. For Maimon's system of philosophy and also for a complete bibliography of his writings, see

Kunz, Die Philosophie Salomon Maimons, Heidelberg, 1912, pp. xxv, 531.

[26] Wolff, Maimoniana, Berlin, 1813, p. 177.

[27] How touching and suggestive is the word שבי in an acrostic at the end of his Introduction to his Gibe'at ha-Moreh, a commentary on the Moreh Nebukim:

קורא יקר אהובי
תדע שמי ושם אבי
בהתבוננך במלת שב"י

[28] See Murray's Introduction to the Autobiography; Auerbach, Dichter und Kaufmann; Zangwill, Nathan the Wise and Solomon the Fool.

[29] FKI, p. 196.

[30] Maggid, Toledot Mishpehot Ginzberg, pp. 52-53; Emden, Sheëlat Ya'abez, Altona, 1739, p. 65 a.

[31] FKN, pp. 109-114, 269; FKI, p. 300.

[32] FKI, p. 394; Delitzsch, op. cit., p. 84.

[33] L'univers israélite, liii. 831-841: " C'est, vous le voyez, un juif polonais qui contribua puissamment à l'émancipation des juifs de France.   Et je me demande si le Judaisme du monde entier ne doit pas rendre hommage à notre coreligionnaire polonais autant peut-être qu' à Menasse ben Israël." FKI, p. 333; Ha-Meliz, ii. no. 50; Shulammit, iii. 425; Graetz, op. cit. (Engl. transl.), v. 443.

[34] See Berliner, Festschrift, 1903, pp. 1-4.

[35] See Ha-Meliz, viii. nos. 11, 22, 23; FSL, p. 139; Monatsschrift, xxiv, 348-357.

[36] Delitzsch, op. cit., pp. 115-118; Ha-Zeman (monthly), ii. 23 f.

[37] See Meassef, 1788, p. 32, and Levin's ed. of Moreh Nebukim, Zolkiev, 1829, Introduction.

[38] Ha-Meassef, 1809, pp. 68-75, 136-171.

[39] See Sefer ha-Berit, Introduction, and Weissberg, Aufklärungsliteratur, Vienna, 1898, p. 83.

[40] FKI, p. 428.

[41] See Emden, Torat ha-Kenaot, pp. 123-127, and Hitabkut (Pinczov's letters) ; Voskhod, 1882, nos. viii-ix; FSL, pp. 136-137; Friedrichsfeld, Zeker Zaddik, p. 12.

[42] Maimon, Autobiography, pp. 106-107; FSL, p. 135.

[43] See LTI, ii. 96, n. 1, and Yellin and Abrahams, Maimonides, p. 160, and reference on p. 330, n. 72; Ha-Zeman (monthly), i. 102-103; Margolioth, Bet Middot, p. 20. Heine's admiration for these idealists or those who succeeded them is well worth quoting. In his essay on Poland, he says: " In spite of the barbaric fur cap which covers his head and the even more barbaric ideas which fill it, I value the Polish Jew much more than many a German Jew with his Bolivar on his head and his Jean Paul inside of it . . . . The Polish Jew in his unclean furred coat, with his populous beard and his smell of garlic and his Jewish jargon, is nevertheless dearer to me than many a Westerner in all the glory of his stocks and bonds."

[44] Op. cit. Letter ii.

[45] Likkute Kadmoniot, Vilna, 1860, Introduction.

CHAPTER III

THE DAWN OF HASKALAH

1794-1840

(pp. 110-161)

[1] See Orshansky, in Yevreyskaya Biblyotyeka, ii. 240; Drabkin, in Monatsschrift, xix-xx.

[2] FKN, pp. 27, 303.

[2] JE, iv. 301; Plungian, op. cit., p. 59.

[4] FKN, p. 193.

[5] JE, iv. 407.

[0] FKN, p. 193; Jellinek, Kuntres ha-Rambam, pp. 39 f.

[7] Occident, v. 360.

[8] Jost, Culturgeschichte, Berlin, 1847, p. 302.

[9] Steinschneider, 'Ir Vilna, 1900, p. 146.

[10] Voskhod, 1881, ii. 29-30; 1900, p. 55.

[11] FKN, pp. 277-279.

[12] See Rabinovitz, Ma'amar 'al ha-Defosat ha-Talmud, Munich, 1876, p. 112. Cf. Zweifel, op. cit., iv. 7.

[13] FKN, pp. 277-279.

[14] Toledot Adam, pp. 14 b, 16 b, 24 b, 75 b, 84 a.

[15] See Plungian, op cit., pp. 46-47, 91; Voskhod, 1900, ix. 77; Ha-Zeman (monthly), 1903, iii. 22-30; see also Die Zukunft, New York, July, 1913, pp. 713 f.

[16] Voskhod, Dec., 1890, pp. 142 f.; Ha-Boker Or, Jan., 1881.

[17] Voskhod, 1888, iii. 37 f; Rodkinson, Toledot 'Ammude Ha-BaD.

[18] Cohan, Rabbi Yisraël Ba'al Shem Tob, 1900, p. 67.

[19] 'Ammude Bet Yehudah, xxvii., and see Ha-Zeman (monthly), ii. 8-15.

[20] Buchholtz, op. cit., Beilage 14, pp. 137-138.

[21] See Weissberg, op. cit., p. 53; Talmud Leshon Russiah, Vilna, 1825; Moda' li-Bene Binah, ibid., 1826; cf. Baër Heteb, Introduction.

[22] Helel ben Shahar, Warsaw, 1804, Introduction, and p. 81. See Peri ha-Arez Yashan, Letter 2, quoted by Dubnow, Pardes, ii. 210-211.

[23] Keneset Yisraël, i. 138; Morgulis, Voprosi Yevreyskoy Zhizni, pp. 7-10.

[24] Enziklopedichesky Slovar, St. Petersburg, 1895, xvii. 642.

[25] Ha-Shahar, x. 44-52; FKN, p. 33; Ha-Boker Or, i. 145-146.

[26] FSL, p. 164.

[27] See Günzburg, Ha-Debir, Warsaw, 1883, ii. 55; Israelitische Annalen, 1840, p. 263.

[28] Ha-Zeman (monthly), iii. 10.

[29] Minor, op. cit., p. 46; Lerner, Yevreyi v Novorossiskom Kraye, Odessa, 1901, p. 234; Monatsschrift, xviii. 234 f., 477 f., 551 f.

[30] Voskhod, 1881, i-iii; Ha-Zeman (monthly), iii. 11-14.

[31] Op. cit., pp. 208-209.

[32] Cf. Graetz, xi. 50; Kayserling, op. cit., p. 288; Fünn, Sofre Yisraël, Vilna, 1891, pp. 138-143; WMG, p. 135.

[33] Graetz, xi. 590, 604, 606; Annalen, xx. 467; Kayserling, op. cit., p. 307; Landshut, Toledot Anshe Shem, p. 85.

[34] בספרי רמ"ד אל תשלחו יד. Weiss, Zikronotaï, p. 58, n.; Ha-Zeman (monthly), i. and iii. 18-19.

[35] Zweifel, op. cit., pp. 35-40, and Ha-Hasidut we-ha-Musar in Ha-Meliz, 1897; Toledot Mishpehot Shneersohn, in Ha-Asif, v. 35-40, and Nefesh Hayyim, iii. 3.

[36] Mandelkern, Dibre Yeme Russyah, iii. 98; American Israelite, nos. 15, 18, etc. (My Travels in Russia); Gordon, Ha-Azamot ha-Yebashot, Odessa, 1899; AZJ, 1854, p. 22; Zunser, Biography, New York, 1905, pp. 15-19 (Engl. transl., pp. 14-18); Shenot Ra'inu Ra'ah, in Ha-Meliz, 1860; Sefer ha-Shanah, iii. 82-101, and GMC, nos. 43-50. One of these songs runs as follows:

On the streets in tears we're wading,
In our bairns' blood we might be bathing;
What a misfortune, ah, wellaway—
Will never dawn the better day?

Little infants from heder are torn,
And forced to wear the soldier's uniform;
What a misfortune, etc.

Our leaders, rabbis, and honored elders,
E'en help to impress them for the czar's soldiers;
What a misfortune, etc.

Seven sons has Zushe Rakover,
Yet not a one for the army is over;
What a misfortune, etc.

Leah, the widow, has an only son,
And for the kahal's sins he's gone;
What a misfortune, etc.

[37] GMC, no. 42. On similar enthusiasm among the Galician Maskilim, see Erter, Kol Kore, in Ha-Zofeh le-Bet Yisraël, Warsaw, 1890, pp. 131-133.

[38] Elk, Die jüdischen Kolonien in Russland, Frankfort-on-the-Main, 1886, pp. 28-53, 60-80, 119-140, 153-160, 205-208; Jastrow, Beleuchtungen, etc., Hamburg, 1859, pp. 109-113.

[39] See Zunz, Gesammelte Schriften, Berlin, 1875, pp. 279-290; Jost, Freimüthige Beleuchtung, Berlin, 1830; and Culturgeschichte, pp. 302-303.

[40] Rabinovitz, op. cit., pp. 11-18.

[41] On Volozhin, see Ha-Kerem, 1887, pp. 67-77; Bikkurim, 1865, pp. 6-45; Ozar ha-Sifrut, iii.; Ha-Asif, iii.; Ha-Meliz, 1900, nos. 16-18; Schechter, op. cit., i. 93-98; Horowitz, Derek 'Ez ha-Hayyim, Cracow, 1895. The yeshibah was reopened under the deanship of Rabbi Raphael Shapira of Bobruisk, and still exists, though in a rather precarious condition.

[42] Read the vivid description in WMG, p. 147.

[43] Occident, ii. 563-564.

[44] Uvarov's opinion of the Talmud was "razvrashchal i razvrashchayet" ("it has been degrading and is degrading"). Nicholas granted special privileges to the Karaites, and claimed they were the genuine Israelites, chiefly because they did not follow the precepts of the Talmud.

[45] Occident, ii. 562-563.

[46] See Loewe, Diaries of Sir Moses and Lady Montefiore, London, 1890, i. 100, 231, 311-312, passim; Günzburg, Debir, ii. 99-108; [Dick], Ha-Oreah, Königsberg, 1860.

[47] Günzburg, op. cit., pp. 115-117, 122-125; Leket Amarim (suppl. to Ha-Meliz), St. Petersburg, 1887, pp. 81-86; AZJ, ix. nos. 46-50; x. nos. 5, 49, etc.; Jastrow, op. cit., p. 12, Lubliner, De la condition politique . . . . dans le royaume de Pologne, Brussels, 1860 (especially pp. 44-45).

[48] GMC, no. 255.

CHAPTER IV

## CONFLICTS AND CONQUESTS

1840-1855

(pp. 162-221)

[1] Diakov states that " when the population degenerated in West Russia, business and industry declined, and the number of the rich greatly diminished, while the nobles, embittered against the Government, did absolutely nothing for their country, the Jews formed an exception . . . . There is no doubt that they are doing their utmost for the regeneration of our land, despite the restrictions heaped upon them without any cause " (Elk, op. cit., p. 41 seq.). Surovyetsky likewise maintains that " after the devastation of Poland because of the numerous wars, the ruining of so many cities, and the almost total extermination of their inhabitants . . . . the Jews alone effected the regeneration of our trade. They alone upheld our tottering industries . . . . We may safely affirm that without them, without their characteristic mobility, we should never have recovered our commerce and wealth " (Jastrow, op. cit., p. 12).

[2] See AZJ, April 29, 1844, and Orient, 1844, p. 224, in which the correspondent adds: " It is a touching sight to see these laborers [as longshoremen], for the most part aged, perform their fatiguing duties in the streets during the hottest seasons, endeavoring to lighten their heavy burdens by the repetition of Biblical and Talmudic passages."

[3] Ozar ha-Sifrut, 1877; Annalen, 1839, pp. 345-346, and 1841, no. 31. Bikkure ha-'Ittim, 1821, pp. 168-172; FSL, p. 150; Paperna, Ha-Derammah (Eichenbaum's letter) ; Ha-Boker Or, 1879, pp. 691-698; Occident, v. 255; Pirhe Zafon, ii. 216-217; Ha-Maggid, 1863, p. 348; Orient, 1841, p. 266; Lapin, Keset ha-Sofer, Berlin, 1857, p. 8, and Morgulis, op. cit., p. 48.

[4] Jost, Culturgeschichte, pp. 308-309; Morgulis, op. cit., p. 27; Atlas, Mah Lefanim u-mah Leaher, Warsaw, 1898, pp. 44 f.

[5] Sbornik of the Minister of Education, iii. 140; Ha-Shahar, iv. 569.

[6] See An die Verehrer, Freunde und Schüler, etc., Leipsic, 1823, pp. 122-125.

[7] Ueber die Verbesserung der Israeliten im Königreich Polen, Berlin, 1819.

[8] Zunz, Gesammelte Schriften, pp. 296-297; Jost, op. cit., p. 304; Jastrow, op. cit., pp. 41 f.; and Zederbaum, Kohelet, St. Petersburg, 1881, p. 6.

[9] Occident, v. 493.

[10] Maggid Yeshu'ah, Vilna, September, 1842. It is reproduced, together with many Haskalah reminiscences, by Gottlober in Ha-Boker Or, iv. (Ha-Gizrah we-ha-Binyah). According to Gottlober the Hebrew is Fünn's translation from the original German. Yet Hebrew letters (Leket Amarim, St. Petersburg, 1888) were published in Lilienthal's name.

[11] See AZJ, 1842, no. 41; Mandelstamm, Hazon la-Moëd, Vienna, 1877, pp. 19, 21, 25-27; Leket Amarim, pp. 86-89; Kohelet, p. 12; Morgulis, op. cit., p. 55; Ha-Pardes, pp. 186-199; Nathanson, Sefer ha-Zikronot, Warsaw, 1878, p. 70; Lilienthal, in American Israelite, 1854 (My Travels in Russia), and Jüdisches Volksblatt, 1856 (Meine Reisen in Russland), and Der Zeitgeist, 1882, p. 149.

[12] Occident, v. 252, 296.

[13] WMG, pp. 185-200; AZJ, 1844, pp. 75, 247; 1845, pp. 304-305; 1846, p. 18; American Israelite, i. 156.

[14] Rede, etc., Riga, 1840, p. 5.

[15] Ha-Pardes, i. 202-203. See Bramson, op. cit., pp. 26-27; WMG, p. 118.

[16] Ha-Kokabim, 1868, pp. 61-78; Ha-Kerem, 1887, pp. 41-62; Zweifel, op. cit., pp. 55-56.

[17] Ha-Mizpah, 1882, p. 17; Kohelet, p. 16; Sbornik of the Minister of Education, 1840, pp. 340, 436-437, and Supplement, pp. 35-38; Prelooker, Under the Czar and Queen Victoria, London, pp. 4-5; cf. AZJ, 1846, p. 86.

[18] Elk, op. cit., ch. iii.

[19] Occident, v. 493; Nathanson, Sefat Emet, p. 92; Mandel-stamm, op. cit., pp. 31-32, and Morgulis, op. cit., pp. 102-147. On tax collectors, cf. the English ballad quoted by Macaulay (History of England, ch. iii.):

> Like plundering soldiers they'd enter the door,
> And made a distress on the goods of the poor,
> While frightened poor children distractedly cried;
> This nothing abated their insolent pride.

And the Yiddish folk song (GMC, no. 55):

> The excise young fellows,
> They are tremendously wild:
> They shave their beards,
> And ride on horses,
> Wear overshoes,
> And eat with unwashed hands.

Their lack of confidence in the permanence of the schools is expressed in the following song (GMC, no. 53):
May we soon be released from the Jewish Goless,
When we shall be expelled from the Gentile Shcoless (schools).

On the struggle to retain the so-called Jewish mode of dress, see I. M. D[ick], Die Yiddishe Kleider Umwechslung, Vilna, 1844.

[20] Op. cit., pp. 12-13; cf. Letteris, in Moreh Nebuke ha-Zeman, Introduction, pp. xv-xvi; Bramson, op. cit., pp. 34-35, 43-44, and Levanda, Ocherki Proshlaho, St. Petersburg, 1876.

[21] Cf. Buckle, History of Civilization, New York, 1880, ii. 529-538.

[22] "Fifty years ago," says Mr. Rubinow (Bulletin of the Bureau of Labor, no. 72, Washington, Sept., 1907, p. 578), "the educational standard of the [Russian] Jews was higher than that of the Russian people at large is at present."

[23] Mandelkern, op. cit., iii. 33.

[24] Buckle, op. cit., pp. 140-142, notes 33-37.

[25] The same phenomenon was witnessed to a certain extent also in Galicia, where for a while Haskalah flourished in great splendor. There, too, the charm and fecundity of German literature, the similarity of Yiddish to German, and the privileges the Austrian Government accorded them, proved too strong a temptation for the Jews, and many of those who became enlightened were rapidly assimilated with their Gentile countrymen. While, therefore, in Galicia the Haskalah movement lasted longer than in Germany, it had ceased long before it reached its fullest development in Russia. Austrian civilization accelerated the assimilation of the educated, Polish prejudice retarded the progress of the masses. So that though Erter, Letteris, Krochmal, Goldenberg, Mieses, Rapoport, Perl, and Schorr exerted a great influence in Russia, their own country remained unaffected. Many of them, like A. Peretz, Eichenbaum, Feder, Pinsker, Werbel, and Rosenfeld emigrated to Russia, where they found a wider field for their activities, while others, like Professor Ludwig Gumplowicz, the sociologist, Marmorek, the physician, and Scheps, the litterateur, became alienated from their former coreligionists.

[26] Keneset Yisraël, iii. 84; Gottlober, Za'ar Ba'ale Hayyim, Zhitomir, 1868: כי אליד נפשי תערוג (comp. Ps. xlii, and Shir ha-Kabod, last verse).

[27] Occident, v. 243. Cf. Buchholtz, op. cit., pp. 82-116.

[28] Occident, v. 255; Yevreyskaya Biblyotyeka, ii. 207-210.

[29] 1840, no. 9.

[30] Emden, Megillat Sefer, p. 5; Günzburg, Debir, ii. 105-106; Mandelstamm, op. cit., i. 3-4, 11; Annalen, 1841, no. 31.

[31] FKN, pp. 246-247; Günzburg, op. cit., i. 48. Moses Reines also points out the fact that the prominent rabbis did not withhold their approval of the most typical Haskalah works when their authors were not suspected of heresy, as shown by Abele's haskamah on Levinsohn's Te'udah be-Yisraël, Tiktin's on Günzburg's Toledot ha-Arez, and Malbim's on Zweifel's Sanegor (Ozar ha-Sifrut, 1888, p. 61).

[32] Ha-Boker Or, 1879, no. 4; FKI, pp. 537-538, 1132; Ha-Lebanon, 1872, no. 35; Ha-Zefirah, 1879, no. 9; Jewish Chronicle, May 4, 1877; Keneset Yisraël, 1887, pp. 157-162; Ha-Meliz, ix. (1889), nos. 198-199, 201, 232; Jost, op. cit., p. 305. Da'at Kedoshim, St. Petersburg, 1897, pp. 19, 22, 27.

[33] These biographical sketches, first published respectively in the New Era Illustrated Magazine (1905, pp. 387-396) and the American Israelite (April 25, 1907), are drawn from the following sources; Houzner, I. B. Levinsohn (Russian), Odessa, 1862; Nathanson, Sefer ha-Zikronot (Heb.), Warsaw, 1878; Yiddishe Bibliotek (Yid.), Kiev, 1888; also Annalen, 1839, no. 17; Ha-Maggid, 1863, p. 381; Ha-Zefirah, 1900, p. 197; Maggid, op. cit., pp. 86-115; Günzburg, Debir, i. and ii., Warsaw, 1883; Kiryat Sefer, Vilna, 1835 (esp. Letters 85-93, 101-102); Abi'ezer, Vilna, 1863; Lebensohn, Kiryat Soferim, Vilna, 1847; Pardes, i. 192; Recke und Napyersky, Allgemeines Schriftsteller und Gelehrten Lexicon der Provinzen Livland, Esthland und Kurland, Mitau, 1829, pp. 147-148; and the works referred to in the text.

CHAPTER V

RUSSIFICATION, REFORMATION, AND ASSIMILATION

1856-1881

(pp. 222-267)

[1] San Donato, The Jewish Question, St. Petersburg, 1883, p. 36.
[2] Ha-Meliz, 1888, nos. 95, 163; Gordon, Iggerot, Warsaw, 1894, ii., and Russky Vyestnik, 1858, i. 126.
[3] Scholz, Die Juden in Russland, Berlin, 1900, pp. 102-107; Hessen, Galeriya, p. 23; Voskhod, 1881, v. 1893; viii; Russky Yevrey, 1882, i.
[4] Second Complete Russian Code, xxv, nos. 24, 768; xxvii. nos. 26, 508.
[5] Voskhod, October, 1881; Chwolson, Die Blutanklage, Frankfort-on-the-Main, 1901, p. 117.
[6] Zunser, Biography, p. 28.

[7] Kol Shire Mahallalel, i. 79-91.

[8] Kol Shire YeLeG, i. 43.

[9] Bramson, op. cit., pp. 52-54; Russky Yevrey, 1879, nos. 16-17.

[10] Rosenthal, Toledot Hebrat Marbe Haskalah, i. 3, 19, 103, 158-159; ii. Introduction.

[11] How happy the Maskilim of that time were to save their fellows from the darkness of ignorance can be seen from the following anecdote told by a Maskil in a retrospective mood (Ha-Shiloah, xvii., 257-258): "Among the first of our young men to enter the gymnasium of my native town of Mohilev were Ackselrod and the Leventhal brothers. The former began to give instruction while he was still in the third grade . . . . One morning he suddenly disappeared. After several days of anxious search it was discovered that he had left on foot for Shklov, a distance of about thirty vyersts, and while there he succeeded in persuading fifteen boys to leave the yeshibah and come with him to Mohilev, where, like a puissant warrior returning in triumph, he went with his little army to the different homes to secure board and lodging for them while they were being prepared for admission into the gymnasium."

[12] Op. cit., p. 35 (Engl. transl., p. 26).

[13] Op. cit., p. 9.

[14] Max Raisin, The Reform Movement, etc. (reprint from the Year Book of the Central Conference of American Rabbis, xvi.), Introduction.

[15] Odessky Yevrey, 1847 (Novaya Yevreyskaya Synagoga v Odessa).

[16] Hessen, op. cit., p. 68; Voskhod, 1881, p. 132.

[17] Rosenthal, op. cit., p. 70; Gordon, Iggerot, nos. 60-62; Ha-Meliz, xx, nos. 8, 11, 13.

[18] Voskhod, 1900, v.; Sefer ha-Shanah, ii. 288-290.

[19] Ha-Meliz, 1899, no. 39.

[20] Ben Sion, Yevrey Reformatory, St. Petersburg, 1882. In his manifesto (Ha-Meliz, April 21, 1881) Gordon declared: "We have discarded the dusty Talmud. We cannot rest satisfied, in questions of religion, with the worm-eaten carcass, with the ob-

servances of rabbinical Judaism." See Ha-Shiloah, ii. 53. See
also Kahan, Meahore ha-Pargud (reprint from Ha-Meliz, 1885),
St. Petersburg, 1886.

[21] Prelooker, op. cit., pp. 24 f.; Voskhod, Feb. 3, 1886; Razsvyet,
1881, no. 25.

[22] Duprey, Great Masters of Russian Literature (Engl. transl.
Dole, New York, 1886), p. 151.

[23] Rosenthal, op. cit., i. 66, 103, 158-159; Ha-Maggid, 1868, p.
18. Cf. McClintock and Strong, Biblical, Theological and Ecclesi-
astical Cyclopedia, New York, 1891, ii. 805. The beautiful synagogue which the Jews began to erect in Moscow at the cost of half
a million rubles was declared by Pobyednostsev to be " too high
and imposing," and they were compelled to destroy the cupola
and deform the interior. Nevertheless it had to remain a " dead "
synagogue, until Nicholas II was pleased to give permission to
open it.

[24] Shereshevsky, O Knigie Kahala, St. Petersburg, 1872; Seiberling, Gegen Brafmann's Buch des Kahals, Vienna, 1881; Ha-
Shahar, iv. 621; xi. 242.

[25] Prelooker, Heroes and Heroines of Russia, London, p. 120;
Ha-Shiloah, xvii. 257-263.

[26] Zederbaum, 'Ayin Zofiyah, Warsaw, 1877, pp. 7-8; Prelooker,
Under the Czar, etc., pp. 8-21.

[27] It may not be superfluous to quote here the vivid picture given
of the period I am now describing by Eliakum Zunser in his
interesting autobiography; the more, as it is depicted very much
in the style of the Maskilim of to-day:

"It is an accepted law in hygiene that the digestive system
must not be overburdened at any one time by too much food, that
eating must not be done hastily, and, above all, great care must be
taken to choose wholesome and digestible food. These principles
are still more important to one who is hungry, who has abstained
from food for any length of time. He should select the healthy
and light foods, and partake of little at first until the powers of
digestion are fully restored. Should he neglect to observe these
simple rules, he will ruin his digestive system, the food will

turn into poison, and he may contract a stubborn disease which no physician will be able to cure.

"This is exactly what happened to our Russian Jews from 1860 to 1880. For many long centuries they had endured an intellectual fast. The Government had debarred them from the world's culture. They were closely packed together in the narrow and dark ghettos. They knew of their synagogues, yeshibot, and prayer-houses (Kloisen) on the one hand, and of their little stores on the other. That there was a great world beyond and without, a world of culture, education, and civilization, of this they had only heard. A great many of them strove to break through the bounds that confined them and step into the world of light and life; but the Cossack, lead-laden whip in hand, stood there ready to drive them back.

"The thirst for education and civilization became daily more intense, and reached the utmost limits of endurance. Five million Russian Jews raised their hands to the Government and pleaded for mercy: 'Release us from this ghetto! We, too, are human beings! Give us breathing space! Give us light! We are faint and starving!' And the Cossack promptly answered 'Nazad ('Back!') Here you are and here you remain—not a step further!'

"And all at once, lo! there came a light! Alexander II, as soon as he ascended the throne, opened wide the doors of the ghetto, and the Russian Jews, young and old, men and women, rushed to the new culture. All crowded to the dainty dish, and no time was lost in making up for the intellectual fast.

"But here happened what usually occurs after a long fast. The wiser partook of food with discretion. They selected the ingredients which were wholesome, and which their system could digest. All unripe, objectionable food they rejected; their main object was to select the food which the Jewish system could assimilate. The governing principle was to unite Jewish learning with the new culture. They knew that among the new delicacies there were many that were injurious and unhealthy, though the defects were disguised by alluring spices; but those who had not lost the innate, unerring Jewish scent found no difficulty in distinguishing that which was sound from the injurious, and they remain strong and faithful Jews to this day.

" Others, and they formed the greater part of the Russian Jews, seized things as they came. Nay, the more dangerous the delicacy, the more the relish with which it was devoured. And these delicacies were gorged at such a rate as to cause constitutional disorder. They who were a little wiser somehow shook off the objectionable matter, and became ' whole ' again ; and a great number ' died,' and a still greater number are dangerously ' sick ' to this very day.

" The sick among our Russian brethren, those who partook in dangerous quantities of the unwholesome delicacies, believed that they would solve all difficulties by ' Russification,' that is, by abandoning the old Jewish culture and adopting Russian manner-isms and customs—by ceasing to lead Jewish lives and by leading the lives of Russians. A great number of Jewish literary men of those times believed that if the Russian Jews would become ' Russified,' and would adopt modern civilization, they would receive full and equal rights, on the same terms as the other nationalities. These literary men were dazzled by the little liberty Alexander II granted the Russian Jews, and they did not understand that he pursued the same object as his father, Nicholas I. In the days of Alexander II, many more Jews were converted to Christianity than in the bitter days of Nicholas I; and many who were not converted remained but caricatures of real Jews.

" The so-called ' Jewish Aristocracy ' in Russia, and especially the wealthy Jews of North Russia, of St. Petersburg, Moscow, and Kharkov, Russified at top speed. They removed from their homes and their home-life anything that was in the least degree Jewish. They shattered all that for thousands of years had been holy and dear to the Jew. Like apes they imitated the manners and customs of the Christians. The younger children did not even know that they were descended from Jews, as was the case in the first

326

' pogroms,' when the children asked their parents: ' Why do they beat us? Are we, too, Jews (Razve vy tozhe Yevrey)?' "

[28] For a full biography see Brainin, Perez ben Mosheh Smolenskin, Warsaw, 1896; Keneset Yisraël, i. 249-286; Ha-Shiloah, i. 82-92, and his works, especially Ha-Toëh be-Darke ha-Hayyim, Vienna, 1876.

CHAPTER VI

THE AWAKENING

1881-1905

(pp. 268-303)

[1] Most of this is based on Persecution of the Jews in Russia, Philadelphia, 1891, pp. 8-18, 22, 35, 51-82, 184-185; Frederick, The New Exodus, London, 1892, pp. 192-208; Errera, Les juifs russes, Brussels, 1893, pp. 29, 43 f., 89-90, 188-189. Between 1883 and 1885, the Mining Institute and Engineering Institute for Public Roads adopted the five per cent limit, the Kharkov Technical Institute a ten per cent limit, and the Veterinary Institute, of the same city, the only one of the sort in Russia, excluded Jews altogether.

" My zemlyakes " (countrymen), says a reminiscent writer, " soon after they had finished their course in engineering, had taken each a different road. One became a crown-rabbi, one a flour merchant, a third a bookkeeper, but none of them could, on account of his religion, legally pursue his chosen vocation " (Yiddishes Tageblatt, New York, May 13, 1908).

[2] Urussov, Memoirs of a Russian Governor (Engl. transl., New York, 1908), pp. 70, 90-91. " Out of 266 students admitted to the Kharkov University in 1901, only 8 were Jews, though at least 12 had ' finished the gymnasium,' not only with the ' highest possible ' marks, but with gold medals. At the Technological Institute of the same city, 7 were Jews in a total of 240, though 12 applying for admission had received the ' highest possible ' marks. At the Kiev University, of 580 new students, 32, all of them medal-

327

lists, were Jews. How many applied for admission, the daily and weekly press, from which these figures are taken, did not report."

² Ner ha-Ma'arabi, vii, 27.

⁴ "He who claims that a spirit of reaction has affected our people as a whole," says Moses Reines (Ozar ha-Sifrut, ii. 45), "is greatly mistaken. That the children of the poor from whom learning cometh forth still forsake their city and country and acquire knowledge, . . . . that societies for the spread of Haskalah are formed every day, . . . . that strict and pious Jews send their sons and daughters to where they can obtain enlightenment, that rabbis, dayyanim, and maggidim urge their children to become proficient in the requirements of the times . . . . write for the press . . . . and deplore the gezerot (restrictions) regarding admission to schools—all this proves convincingly that they do not see right who complain that our entire nation is going backward."

⁵ See Ha-Maggid, 1899, no. 160. While in 1848 there were 2446 and in 1854, 4439 converts, in 1860-1880 there were from 350 to 450 per annum, in 1881, 572, in 1882, 610, and in 1883, 461 converts. With the spread of Zionism conversions continued to diminish, and, while there were relapses during the renewed pogroms of 1891 and 1901, they decreased materially, though the Jewish population is constantly on the increase.

⁶ Autobiography, pp. 42-51. See also Kahan, Meahore ha-Pargud, pp. 15-17.

⁷ Ha-Meliz, 1900, no. 123; Luah Ahiasaf, 5696, p. 312; Zablotzky and Massel, Ha-Yizhari, Manchester, 1895, Introduction; Ha-Meliz, xxxvii, no. 36; The Menorah, April, 1904.

⁸ Yalkut Ma'arabi, 1904, pp. 46 f.

⁹ Ha-Shahar, x. 511, 30; Habazelet, 1882, no. 2.

¹⁰ Ha-Le'om, 1906, nos. 21-22; Belkind, in Ha-Zefirah, no. 46, 1913; Lubarsky and Lewin-Epstein, Derek Hayyim, New York, 1905.

¹¹ Greenstone, The Messiah Idea in Jewish History, ch. viii.

¹² The Progress of Zionism, pp. 3-4; cf. Voskhod, 1895, iv.

[12] Zamenhof's new universal language was primarily intended to be the international language of his people, " who are speechless, and therefore without hope, scattered over the world, and hence unable to understand one another, obliged to take their culture from strange and hostile sources."

[14] Ahiasaf, iv.; Gordon, op. cit., i. xxi; Razsvyet, 1882, i.; Magil's Kobez (Collection), no. 3, p. 45.

[15] Ha-Meliz, 1899, no. 256; 1901, no. 2; weekly Voskhod, 1893, no. 40; monthly Voskhod, 1894, iv. Some Jewish financiers erected gymnasia in Vilna and Warsaw, improved the condition of the hadarim, and turned many Talmud Torahs into technical schools. Of the Lodz Talmud Torah a writer says that " no Jewish community, even outside of Russia, possesses such an institution, not excepting the Hirsch schools in Galicia."

[16] London, Unter jüdischen Proletariern, 1898, pp. 81-83; Bramson, K Istorii, etc., pp. 63-69, 71-74; Ha-Meliz, xli., no. 246 (1901, no. 35); Ha-Zefirah, xxix., no. 285; and the Jewish Gazette, July 16, 1909 (Kunst und Nationalismus). The Ha-Zamir (a choral society), founded in Lodz by Nissan Schapira, counts its members by the thousands.

[17] London, op. cit., pp. 64-74; Ha-Meliz, 1900, nos. 192-193; Rubinow, op. cit., pp. 530-532, 548-553, 561-566.

[18] Ha-Meliz, 1901, nos. 20, 27, 36, 54, 95.

[19] Atlas, Mah Lefanim u-mah Leaher, pp. 53 f.; Ha-Meliz, 1900, no. 47; 1901, no. 27.

[20] Ha-Meliz, 1901, no. 87.

[21] Réflexions sur l'état des israélites russes, Odessa, 1871, pp. 121-122.

[22] Kayserling, Die jüdischen Frauen, Leipsic, 1879, pp. 306-313; Rubinow, op. cit., p. 581. The Russian Jewess has already produced several writers above the average (Einhorn, Mosessohn, Ben Yehudah, Sarah and Eva Schapira) in Hebrew, has given Russian literature at least one novelist of note (Rachel Khin), has furnished leaders in the movement for the emancipation of women (Maria Saker), and especially for the liberation of Russia

(Finger, Helfman, Levinsohn, Novinsky, Rabinovich). According to Mr. Rabinow, the Russo-Jewish "women and girls use every available means" to obtain an education, and at least fifty per cent of them possess a knowledge of Russian in addition to their vernacular Yiddish.

# BIBLIOGRAPHY

An asterisk (*) marks a book or periodical of especial importance.

Antin, The Promised Land, Boston and New York, 1912.
Atlas, Mah Lefanim u-mah Leaher, Warsaw, 1898.

Baskerville, The Polish Jew, New York, 1906.
Ben Sion, Yevreyi Reformatory, St. Petersburg, 1882.
Bentwich, The Progress of Zionism, New York, 1899.
Bernfeld, Dor Tahapukot, Warsaw, 1897.
Bershadsky, Zhurnal Ministerstva Narodnaho Prosvyeshchaniya, St. Petersburg, 1912.
Bersohn, Tobiasz Cohn, Warsaw, 1872.
Blaustein, Memoirs, New York, 1813, pt. I.
*Brafmann, Kniga Kahala, Vilna, 1869.
*Brainin, Perez ben Moses Smolenskin, Warsaw, 1896.
*Bramson, K Istorii Pervonachalnaho Obrazovaniya Russkikh Yevreyev, St. Petersburg, 1896.
*Buchholtz, Geschichte der Juden in Riga, Riga, 1899.

Chwolson, Die Blutanklage, Frankfort-on-the-Main, 1901.
Cohan, Rabbi Yisraël Ba'al Shem Tob, 1900.
Cohn, Ma'aseh Tobiah, Venice, 1707.
*Czacki, Rosprava o Zhydakh, Vilna, 1807.

Delitzsch, Zur Geschichte der jüdischen Poesie, Leipsic, 1836.
*[Dick], Ha-Oreah, Königsberg, 1860.
*D[ick], Yiddishe Kleider Umwechslung, Vilna, 1844.
*Dob Bär, Shibhe ha-Besht, Berdichev, 1815.
Duprey, Great Masters of Russian Literature (Engl. transl.), New York, 1886.

# BIBLIOGRAPHY

Edelman, Gedulat Shaül, London, 1854.
*Elk, Die jüdischen Kolonien in Russland, Frankfort on-the-Main, 1886.
Emden, Megillat Sefer, ed. Cohan, Warsaw, 1896.
Epstein, Geburat ha-Ari, Vilna, 1870.
*Errera, Les juifs russes, Brussels, 1893.
Erter, Ha-Zofeh le-Bet Yisraël, Warsaw, 1890.
Ezekiel Feivel, Toledot Adam, Warsaw, 1854.

Firkovich, Abne Zikkaron, Vilna, 1872.
Fishberg, The Jews: A Study of Race and Environment, New York, 1911.
*Frederick, The New Exodus, London, 1892.
Friedländer, An die Verehrer, Freunde, und Schüler, etc., Leipsic, 1823.
*Friedländer, Ueber die Verbesserung der Israeliten im Königreich Polen, Berlin, 1819.
Friedrichsfeld, Zeker Zaddik, Amsterdam, 1809.
*Fünn, Keneset Yisraël, Warsaw, 1860.
*Fünn, Kiryah Ne'emanah, Vilna, 1860.
Fünn, Safah le-Ne'emanim, Vilna, 1881.
Fünn, Sofre Yisraël, Vilna, 1891.

Geiger, Melo Hofnayim, Berlin, 1840.
Gershuni, Mein Entrinung vun Katorga, New York, 1907.
Gershuni, Sketches of Jewish Life and History, New York, 1873.
Ger Zedek, Yevreyskaya Biblyotyeka, St. Petersburg, 1892.
*Ginzberg and Marek, Yevreyskiya Narodniya Pyesni, St. Petersburg, 1901.
*Glückel von Hameln, Zikronot, ed. Cohan, 1896.
Gordon, Ha-Azamot ha-Yebashot, Odessa, 1899.
*Gordon, Iggerot, Warsaw, 1894.
Gordon, Kol Shire YeLeG, Vilna, 1898.
*Gottlober, Ha-Gizrah we-ha-Binyah, in Ha-Boker Or, iv.
Gottlober, Za'ar Ba'ale Hayyim, Zhitomir, 1868.
Gottlober, Zikronot mi-Yeme Ne'uraï, Warsaw, 1800.

# BIBLIOGRAPHY

Graetz, Geschichte der Juden, Leipsic, 1866-1882, 11 vols. (also in Hebrew, Dibre Yeme Yisraël, Warsaw, 1905).

Greenstone, The Messiah Idea in Jewish History, Philadelphia, 1906.

*Güdemann, Geschichte des Erziehunghswesens und der Cultur der abendländischen Juden, Vienna, 1880 and 1884.

Güdemann, Quellen zur Geschichte des Unterrichts, Berlin, 1891.

*Günzburg, Abi'ezer, Vilna, 1863.

*Günzburg, Ha-Debir, Warsaw, 1883.

Günzburg, Ha-Moriah, Warsaw, 1878 (" Kikayon Yonah ").

Günzburg, Kiryat Sefer, Vilna, 1835.

Günzburg, Maggid Emet, Leipsic, 1843.

*Halevi, Kuzari, Introduction.

*Hannover, Yeven Mezulah, Warsaw, 1872.

*Harkavy, Ha-Yehudim u-Sefat ha-Selavim, Vilna, 1867.

*Harkavy, Russ i Russkiye v Srednikh Yevropeyskaya Literatura, Voskhod, 1881.

Horowitz, Derek 'Ez ha-Hayyim, Cracow, 1895.

*Houzner, I. B. Levinsohn (Russian), Odessa, 1862.

Hurwitz, 'Ammude Bet Yehudah, 1765.

Hurwitz, Hekal 'Oneg, Grodno, 1797.

Hurwitz (Phinehas Elijah), Sefer ha-Berit, Brünn, 1897.

Ilye, Alfe Menasheh, Vilna, 1827.

Ilye, Pesher Dabar, Vilna, 1807.

Izgur, Shalosh Tekufot, Niezhin, 1898.

*Jastrow, Beleuchtungen, etc., Hamburg, 1859.

*Jewish Encyclopedia, 12 vols., New York, 1901-1906.

Jost, Culturgeschichte, Berlin, 1847.

Jost, Freimüthige Beleuchtung, Berlin, 1830.

Kahan, Beërot Nishbarim, St. Petersburg, 1879.

Kahan, Meahore ha-Pargud, St. Petersburg, 1886.

# BIBLIOGRAPHY

Katz, Le-Korot ha-Yehudim be-Russyah, Polin, we-Lita, Berlin, 1889.

Katz, Toledot Haskalat ha-Yehudim be-Russyah, Ha-Zeman, St. Petersburg, 1903.

Klausner, Novo Yevreyskaya Literatura, Warsaw, 1900.

Kohen, Megillah 'Afah, in Aben Virga, Shebet Yehudah, ed. Wiener, Hanover, 1856.

Kohn, Hut ha-Meshullash, Odessa, 1874.

Kovner, Heker Dabar, Warsaw, 1865.

Kovner, Zevov Perahim, Odessa, 1868.

Kunz, Die Philosophie Salomon Maimons, Heidelberg, 1912.

Lapin, Keset ha-Sofer, Berlin, 1857.

Lebensohn, Emet we-Emunah, Vilna, 1867, 1870.

Lebensohn, Kiryat Soferim, Vilna, 1847.

Leket Amarim, supplement to Ha-Meliz, St. Petersburg, 1887.

*Lerner, Yevreyi v Novorossiskom Kraye, Odessa, 1901.

Levanda, Ocherki Proshlaho, St. Petersburg, 1876.

*Levin, Aliyat Eliyahu, Vilna, 1856.

*Levinsohn, Bet Yehudah, Warsaw, 1901.

*Levinsohn, Te'udah be-Yisraël, Warsaw, 1901.

Lilienblum, Derek La'abor Golim, Warsaw, 1899.

Lilienblum, Derek Teshubah, Warsaw, 1899.

*Lilienblum, Hattot Ne'urim, Vienna, 1876.

*Lilienblum, Kehal Refaïm, Odessa, 1870.

*Lilienblum, 'Olam ha-Tohu, in Ha-Shahar, 1873.

Lilienblum, Orhot ha-Talmud, in Ha-Meliz, 1868.

*Lilienthal, Maggid Yeshu'ah, Vilna, 1842.

Lilienthal, Meine Reisen in Russland, Jüdisches Volksblatt, 1856.

*Lilienthal, My Travels in Russia, American Israelite, 1854.

Lilienthal, Rede, Riga, 1840.

Lilienthal, Sketches of Jewish Life in Russia, The Occident, v.

Linetzky, Dos Polische Yingel, Lemberg, 1880.

*Loewe, Diaries of Sir Moses and Lady Montefiore, London, 1890.

*London, Unter jüdischen Proletariern, 1898.

Lubarsky and Lewin-Epstein, Derek Hayyim, New York, 1905.

# BIBLIOGRAPHY

*Lubliner, De la condition politique . . . dans le royaume de Pologne, Brussels, 1860.

*Maggid, Toledot Mishpehot Ginzberg, St. Petersburg, 1899.
*Maimon, Autobiographie, Berlin, 1793; Engl. transl., Boston, 1888; Heb. transl., Warsaw, 1899.
*Malishevsky, Yevreyi v Yuzhnoy Rossii i Kieve v. x-xii. Vyekakh, St. Petersburg, 1878.
Mandelkern, Dibre Yeme Russyah, Warsaw, 1875.
*Mandelstamm, Hazon la-Moëd, Vienna, 1877.
Mann, Sheërit Yisraël, Vilna, 1818.
*Mapu, 'Ayit Zabua' Warsaw, 1873.
Margolioth, Bet Middot, Prague, 1786.
Minor, Rukovodstvo, Moscow, 1881.
*Morgulis, Voprosi Yevreyskoy Zhizni, St. Petersburg, 1889.

Nathanson, Sefat Emet, Warsaw, 1887.
*Nathanson, Sefer ha-Zikronot, Warsaw, 1878.
Nusbaum, Historiya Zhidóv, Warsaw, 1888-1890, 5 vols.

Orshansky, Yevreyskaya Biblyotyeka, ii.

Paperna, Ha-Derammah, Odessa, 1867.
*Persecution of the Jews in Russia, Philadelphia, 1891.
Pinsker, Auto-Emancipation, Berlin, 1882.
Pinsker, Likkute Kadmoniot, Vilna, 1860.
Plungian, Ben Porat, Vilna, 1858.
*Polonnoy, Toledot Ya'akob Yosef, Lemberg, 1856.
Prelooker, Heroes and Heroines of Russia, London.
*Prelooker, Under the Czar and Queen Victoria, London.

Rabinovitz, Ma'amar 'al ha-Defosat ha-Talmud, Munich, 1876.
Rhine, Leon Gordon. An Appreciation, Philadelphia, 1910.
Rodkinson, Toledot 'Ammude HaBaD, Königsberg, 1876.
Rosensohn, 'Ezah we-Tushiah, Vilna, 1870.
Rosensohn, Shelom Ahim, Vilna, 1870.

# BIBLIOGRAPHY

*Rosenthal, Toledot Hebrat Marbe Haskalah, i., St. Petersburg, 1885; ii., ibid., 1890.
*Rubinow, Bulletin of the Bureau of Labor, No. 72, Washington, Sept., 1907.
*San Donato, The Jewish Question, St. Petersburg, 1883.
Sbornik of the Ministry of Education, iii., St. Petersburg.
Schechter, Studies in Judaism, i., Philadelphia, 1896; ii., ibid., 1908.
*Scholz, Die Juden in Russland, Berlin, 1900.
*Seiberling, Gegen Brafmann's Buch des Kahals, Vienna, 1881.
Shatzkes, Ha-Mafteah, Warsaw, 1866-1869.
*Shereshevsky, O Knigie Kahala, St. Petersburg, 1872.
Silber, Elijah Gaon, New York, 1906.
Slouschz, La renaissance de la littérature hébraïque, Paris, 1903. Heb., Warsaw, 1906; Engl. transl., Philadelphia, 1909.
*Smolenskin, Ha-Toëh be-Darke ha-Hayyim, Vienna, 1876, 4 vols.
Smolenskin, Keburat Hamor, ibid., 1874.
Sokolov, Sinat 'Olam le-'Am 'Olam, Warsaw, 1882.
*Steinschneider, 'Ir Vilna, Vilna, 1900.
Sternberg, Die Proselyten in Polen im xvi und xvii Jahrhundert, AZJ, 1863, pp. 67-68; L'univers israélite, 1863, pp. 272-273.

*Tarnopol, Réflexions sur l'état des israélites russes, Odessa, 1871.
Troki, Hizzuk Emunah, Leipsic, 1857.

*Urussov, Memoirs of a Russian Governor, Engl. transl., New York, 1908.

Weiss, Zikronotaï, Warsaw, 1895.
Weissberg, Aufklärungsliteratur, Vienna, 1898.
Weissberg, Le-Toledot ha-Sifrut ha-'Ibrit ha-Hadashah be-Polin we-Russyah, Mi-Mizrah u-mi-Ma'arab, Berlin, 1895.
*Wengeroff, Memoiren einer Grossmutter, i., Berlin, 1908.
Wessely, Dibre Shalom we-Emet, Berlin, 1782.

# BIBLIOGRAPHY

Wiener, The History of Yiddish Literature, New York, 1899.
*Wolf, Maimoniana, Berlin, 1813.
Wolkonsky, Pictures of Russian Life and Literature, Boston, 1897.

Yevrey Minister, Voskhod, 1885, v.
Yevreyskaya Enziklopedya, St. Petersburg, 14 vols.

Zablotzky and Massel, Ha-Yizhari, Manchester, 1895.
*Zederbaum, 'Ayin Zofiyah, Warsaw, 1877.
Zederbaum, Keter Kehunnah, Odessa, 1868.
Zederbaum, Kohelet, St. Petersburg, 1881.
*Zunser, Biography, Yiddish (and Engl. transl.), New York, 1905.
*Zunz, Aelteste Nachrichten über Juden und jüdische Gelehrte in Polen, Slavonien, Russland. Gesammelte Schriften, Berlin, 1875, iii. 82-87.
Zweifel, Sanegor, Warsaw, 1894.
*Zweifel, Shalom 'al Yisraël, Zhitomir, 1868-1872, 4 vols.

# INDEX

Abele, Abraham, Talmudist, 164, 199.

*Abi'ezer*, by Günzburg, 220.

Abraham, son of Elijah Gaon, 119,

Abramovich, Andrey, statesman, 22.

Abramovitsch, Solomon Jacob, novelist, 203.

Adelsohn, Wolf, " the Hebrew Diogenes," 200.

Aguilar, Grace, on Russo-Jewish misery, 154.

Ahiasaf Society, 296-297.

Aleksey (Abraham), proselyte-priest, 25.

Alexander I, during his period of tolerance, 111-113; during his period of intolerance, 127-138, 140, 144, 163, 170, 192, 201, 249, 251, 253.

Alexander II, referred to, 11, 79, 261; reign of reforms, 222-226; favorable attitude towards Jews, 224-225, 229-231; the Narodniki, 236; change of policy, 248-255; plotted against and assassinated, 255-258.

Alexander III, referred to, 80, 255; restrictions, 268-270; pogroms, 269; " May Laws," 270-273; Jews excluded from schools by, 273-275.

Alexander Jagellon and the Jews, 21.

Allgemeine jüdische Arbeiterbund, Der, in Littauen, Polen, und Russland, 293.

Alliance Israélite Universelle, programme of, 236; criticism of, 285-286.

Altaras, Jacques Isaac, philanthropist, 157.

America. See United States, the.

'Am 'Olam Society, 283.

Amsterdam, referred to, 22; a place of refuge for Russo-Polish proselytes, 27; elects Russo-Jewish rabbis, 33-34; place of study, 81, 93, 109, 126, 165.

Antokolsky, Mark, sculptor, 241.

Anton, Carl, author, 64.

Apostol, Cossack hetman, 57.

Apotheker, Abraham Ashkenazi, author, 40.

Arbeiterstimme, Die, 293.

Aristotle, 50, 216, 297.

*Ascension of Elijah*, 134.

Ashkenazi, Meïr, envoy of the Khan of the Tatars, 23.

Ashkenazi, Meïr, rabbinical author, quoted, 31, 33.

Ashkenazi, Solomon, statesman, 23.

Assemblies, Jewish, under Alexander I, 117, 128; under Nicholas I, 151, 173, 174-176; in Vilna, 165; under Alexander II, 230; at Kattowitz, 285.

Auerbach, Berthold, on Maimon, 88.

Austria, Haskalah in, 12, 188; influence on Russian Maskilim, 195; place of study for Russian Jews, 285, 298. See also Galicia.

*Auto-Emancipation*, 281-283.

*'Ayit Zabua'*, 244-245.

339

Baku, antiquity of, 20.
Barit, Jacob (" Yankele Kovner "),
    scholar, 200, 255, 259.
Bathòry, Stephen, 59, 253.
Beer, Michel, champion of Jewish
    rights, 114.
Behalot, 63, 161.
Behr, Issachar Falkensohn, poet,
    90-91, 108.
Belkind, Israel, Zionist, 286.
Belzyc, Jacob Nahman, author, 36.
Bene Mosheh Society, 286.
Bennett, Solomon, of Polotzk, en-
    graver, champion of Jewish
    rights in England, 95-96.
Bentwich, on Jewish colonists in
    Palestine, 289.
Ben Yehudah, Eliezer, Hebraist,
    284-285.
Beobachter, Der, an der Weichsel,
    124, 196.
Berdichev, 123, 175, 200, 206, 239.
Berek, Joselovich, colonel, 115.
Berlin, 37, 78, 80, 81, 84, 85, 90,
    91, 93, 120, 126, 132, 192, 245,
    251, 257, 291, 298.
Berlin, Moses, uchony Yevrey,
    230.
Berlin, Naphtali Zebi Judah, dean
    of Yeshibah, 152, 254, 288.
Bernfeld, on Maimon, 86.
Besht, Israel Baal Shem [Tob],
    referred to, 65, 122, 123; his
    life, 66-69; opposition to rab-
    binism, 67, 70, 71, 75; his in-
    fluence, 76; his biography, 134.
Bet ha-Midrash, description of the,
    50-51.
Bet ha-Sefer, in Jaffa, 290-291.
Bet Yehudah, by Levinsohn, 209-
    210.
Bezalel, school of art, 291.
Bibikov, on Russian Jews, 162.

Bible, the, ancient Russo-Jewish
    commentaries on, 28; customs
    of (according to Elijah Vil-
    na), 74; the Biur on, 81, 82;
    Mendelssohn's translation, 105,
    131, 193, 203; translated into
    Russian, 239, 252.
Bibleitsy (Dukhovnoye Bibleyskoye
    Bratstvo), 247-248.
Bielski, on Jewish proselytes, 27.
Bilu Society, 286.
Biur, commentary, collaborators
    on, 81; welcomed, 82; banned,
    132; studied, 193; referred to,
    265.
Blood-accusation, 59, 115, 145, 155,
    208, 213, 229, 253, 275-276.
Bogdanovich, Judah, merchant, 22.
Bokhara, 127, 271.
Bolingbroke, quoted, 215.
Bompi, Issachar, bibliophile, 166-
    167, 200.
Bone Zion Society, 286-287.
Book of Common Prayer, old
    translation of, 30; suggested
    changes in, 175; new Russian
    translation, 239, 252.
Brafmann, Jacob, delator, 254.
Bratzlav, 53-54.
Brest-Litovsk, Jewish community
    in, 20; granted privileges, 21;
    Talmudists of, 34; persecution
    of Hasidim in, 76; Haskalah
    in, 105, 166, 200.
Brody, 195.
Buchner's Der Talmud in seiner
    Nichtigkeit, 146.
Buckle, on Russian civilization,
    190; referred to, 245.
Buduchnost, 286.
Byelostok, 113, 199, 201, 294.

Calvinism, in Poland, 56.
Cantonists, 138-139, 142, 171, 225.
Carlyle, quoted, 88, 109.

# INDEX

Caro, Joseph Hayyim, rabbi, 200.
Casal, Jonas, physician, 39.
Casimir IV, Jews under, 26, 253.
Catherine II, favors the Jews, 110-111, 112, 147, 249.
Chamisso, on "the Glusker Maggid," 132, 302.
Chaucer on "beggar students," 48.
Chazanowicz, Joseph, Zionist, 291.
Chernichevsky's *What to Do*, 257.
Chernigov, Isaac of, Talmudist, 29.
Chernyshev, Governor - General, proclaims religious liberty, 110.
Chiarini, Abbé Luigi, anti-Talmudist, 145, 146.
Chmielnicki, Cossack hetman, 48, 52, 53, 54, 58, 64, 77, 149.
Chozi Kokos, statesman, 23, 55.
Chufut-Kale (Rock of the Jews), 19.
Clement VIII, pope, 72.
Clement XIV, pope, 253.
Clermont-Tonnerre, on Zalkind Hurwitz, 93.
Coën, Moses, court physician and statesman, 40-41.
Cohen, Shalom, litterateur, 99.
Cohn, Tobias, physician, 41-42; on Polish Jews, 64; referred to, 101, 298.
Coins, with Hebrew inscriptions, 21.
Colonists, under Nicholas I, 140-144, 160; under Alexander II, 228; in America, 283; in Palestine, 283, 286-289.
Commendoni, on Lithuanian Jews, 24.
Converts to Christianity, 25, 26, 64, 130, 136, 139, 146, 168, 177-178, 248, 254, 260, 270-273, 278-279, 303.
Cossacks, Jews as, 23-24.

Costume, Jewish, origin of, 115; opposition of Maskilim to, 166, 175; Friedländer opposes, 170; enforced change of, by Government, 179; in Courland, 194.
Council of the Four Countries, 44, 208.
Courland, Jews admitted into, 111; annexed to Russia, 113; taxes in, 129; colonists from, 140; stronghold of Haskalah, 193-194.
Cracow, 27, 78.
Crémieux, Adolphe, statesman, 154, 175.
Crimea, the, 19, 23.
Crusades, the, 18, 52.
Cyril, apostle to Slavonians, 28.
Czacki, Tadeusz, Polish historian, defends Jews, 114; praises them, 115.
Czartorisky, Prince, and the Polish Jews, 94, 116.
Czatzskes, Baruch, translator, 124.
Dainov, Zebi Hirsh, "the Slutsker Maggid," 246.
Damascus Affair, the, 155, 208.
Danzig's *Hayye Adam*, 147.
Darshan, Moses Isaac, "the Khelmer Maggid," 280.
*Dead Souls*, by Gogol, 257.
Delacrut, philosopher, 37.
Delitzsch, on Dubno, 81; on Hebrew poetry, 98; on Satanov, 99.
Delmedigo, Joseph, physician, 24.
*Derek Selulah*, by Temkin, 146.
Diakov, on Russian Jews, 162, 318 (n. 1).
Dillon, Eliezer, financier, 118, 125.
Dob Bär, biographer of Besht, 123.
Dolitzky, Menahem Mendel, poet, 98, 243.

# INDEX

*Dos Polische Yingel*, by Linetzky, 242, 244.

Dostrzegacz Nadvisyansky, 196.

Dubno, 65, 200.

Dubno, Solomon, grammarian, 81-82, 98, 105.

Dubnow, Simon, historian, 17.

Dyerzhavin's *Mnyenie*, 118.

Edels, Samuel (Maharsha), Talmudist, 72.

*Efes Dammim*, by Levinsohn, 208, 213.

Efrusi, Hayyim, communal worker, 165.

Eger, Akiba, rabbi, 149.

Eisenmenger's *Entdecktes Judenthum*, 146.

Eishishki, antiquity of, 20.

Eliasberg, Jonathan, rabbi, 288.

Eliasberg, Mordecai, rabbi, 288.

Elijah Gaon, 70-76; his curriculum of study, 73, 74; his appreciation of science and influence on Haskalah, 74, 75; reputed to be the author of *Sefer ha-Berit*, 102; his disciples, 119-121, 126, 150; his biography, *Ascension of Elijah*, 134; referred to, 164, 197, 201, 212, 220.

Eliot, George, on Maimon's Autobiography, 88; referred to, 297.

Elizabeta Petrovna, 57, 135, 195.

Emden, Jacob, Talmudist, 78, 91, 94, 197.

England, Russian Jews in, 29, 93-96, 109; sympathy of, 154-157, 270.

*Entdecktes Judenthum*, by Eisenmenger, 146.

Erter, Isaac, satirist, 205, 217.

Esterka, Polish Jewish queen (?), 22.

Euclid, in Hebrew, 105.

Exportation Law of 1843, 152-154, 179.

Eybeschütz, Jonathan, Talmudist, 64, 78.

Falk, Hayyim Samuel Jacob, Baal Shem, 93-94.

*Fathers and Sons*, by Turgenief, 257.

Finkel, Elijah, educator, 164.

Folk Songs, 137-138, 141, 161, 232, 316 (n. 36), 320 (n. 19). See also Lullabies.

France, Russian Jews in, 29, 92-93, 96, 109, 298, 300-301.

Franco-Russian war, 116-117, 204.

Frank, physician, 91, 127.

Frank, Jacob (Yankev Leibovich), founder of the Frankists, 64-65, 66, 69, 104, 131.

" Freitisch," 47, 151.

Friedländer, David, scholar and philanthropist, referred to, 105, 237; on the improvement of Jews in Poland, 169-170.

Frug, Simon, poet, 290, 297.

Fünn, Joseph, historian, 106, 203.

Gaden, Stephen von, court physician and statesman, 40.

Galicia, Haskalah in, 12, 321 (n. 25); Hasidism in, 69; referred to, 163, 195, 205, 291. See also Austria.

Germany, Haskalah in, 12; emigration from, 30; Russo-Polish rabbis in, 33-34; Russo-Jewish Maskilim in, 77-91, 104, 106; Hebrew poetry of, 97-98; object of Maskilim in, 99-100, 107; Haskalah encouraged by the Government, 102; by Jewish financiers, 237; opposition to Haskalah in, 105-106, 131-

133, 188; state of Judaism in,
168-169; reason for speedy
Germanization of Jews in,
191; Jewish science in, 219;
influence of, on Russian Maskilim, 192-198; a place of refuge, 252; restrictions against
refugees in, 298-299, 301.
Gibbon, Edward, referred to, 24.
Ginzberg, Asher (Ahad Ha-'Am),
and Haskalah, 13.
Glückel von Hameln's *Memoirs,*
33.
"Glusker Maggid, the," 132, 302.
Goethe on Maimon, 89; on Behr,
90; referred to, 189, 192.
Gogol's Jewish traitor, 224; influence of his *Dead Souls,*
257.
Gordin, Jacob, ethical culturist,
247.
Gordon, David, litterateur, 284.
Gordon, J. L., and Haskalah, referred to, 13, 252, 261; poetry
of, 98; and Levinsohn, 212;
on the new era, 232; attacks
the Talmud, 243; laments the
effect of Haskalah, 260; on
Zionism, 290.
Gordon, Jekuthiel, scientist, 92.
Gottlober, Abraham Bär, on Hasidism, 69; on Luria, 168; and
Levinsohn, 212; on Russification, 231; defends Mendelssohn, 265.
Graetz, on Maimon, 83; on Slavonic Jews, 103.
Granovsky, on Jewish emancipation, 228.
Grazhdanin, 253, 302.
Gregory X, pope, 253.
Grodno, Jewish community in, 20;
a Talmudic centre, 32, 34;
scene of martyrdom, 57; per-

secution of Hasidim in, 76;
Talmud published in, 148-149;
Maskilim, 201.
Guizolfi, Zacharias de, statesman,
23, 55, 306 (n. 12).
Günzberg, Benjamin Wolf, stu-
dent, 91.
Günzburg, Horace, financier, 237.
Günzburg, Joseph Yosel, financier,
237.
Günzburg, Mordecai Aaron, 13,
204, 225; his life, 213-221;
on Minhagim, 215; his im-
press on Hebrew literature,
217-219; his *Abi'ezer,* 220.
Gurovich, Marcus, educator, 228.

HaBad, reform sect of Hasidim,
122.
Ha-Boker Or, 265.
Ha-Emet, 256.
Haggadah shel Pesah, Russian
translation of, 239.
Haidamacks, 59, 269.
Hakohen, Ephraim, rabbi, 34.
Hakohen, Joseph, rabbi, 19, 195.
Hakohen, Raphael, rabbi, 78.
Ha-Maggid, 284.
Ha-Meliz, 242, 286, 288.
Hannover, Nathan, his *Safah Berurah,* 39; his *Yeven Mezulah,*
quotation from, 48-49.
Harkavy, Abraham, Orientalist,
17, 29, 203.
Ha-Shahar, 242, 261-262, 265, 267.
Hasidim, 65; their teachings, 66,
67, 150; spread, 69; persecuted by the Mitnaggedim, 76,
131; efforts at reconciliation
with Mitnaggedim, 120-121,
260; reformed, 122; united
with Mitnaggedim against Haskalah, 134; fought by Maskilim, 168.

# INDEX

Haskalah, definitions of, 12-13; writers on, 14; regarded differently in Germany and Russia, 103-108, 131; opposition to, 132-150, 185-188; in the "forties," 164-197; influence of Germany on, 191-199; in Galicia, 205; Levinsohn's advice on, 212; Günzburg's opinion of, 216; spreads under Alexander II, 230-248; disappointments of, 232-234; and Reform Judaism, 242-248; cosmopolitan, 255-257; romantic and pessimistic, 278-281; Zionistic, 283-291.

Ha-Toëh be-Darke ha-Hayyim, 266, 267.

Hattot Ne'urim, 232-234.

Hayye Adam, by Danzig, 147.

Ha-Zefirah, 286.

Hebrew literature: style, 96, 97, 217-218; poetry, 98; Reform Judaism in, 242-248; necessity of (Smolenskin), 264.

Heder, 46, 184.

Hegel, 86, 192.

Heilprin, Joseph, financier, 175.

Heine, referred to, 297; on Polish Jews, 314 (n. 43).

Helena, Princess, proselyte, 26.

Heller, Yom-Tob Lipman, rabbi, 37.

Herz, Marcus, disciple of Kant, 85.

Herzl, Theodore, Zionist, 263, 281, 283.

Hillul Society, 286.

Hirsch, Baron de, 277.

Hizzuk Emunah, Voltaire's opinion on, 37.

Hobebe Zion, 285, 286.

Horn, Meïr, educator, 164.

Horowitz, Isaiah, Cabbalist, 33.

Horowitz, Phinehas, rabbi, 78.

Horowitz, Shabbataï, rabbi, 34.

Horowitz, Shmelke, rabbi, 78.

Horwitz, Aaron Halevi, rabbi, 78.

Hurwitz, Hirsh, educator, 164.

Hurwitz, Hyman, professor, 95.

Hurwitz, Judah Halevi, translator, 92, 105, 121, 123, 125, 134.

[Hurwitz], Phinehas Elijah, encyclopedist, 101-103, 214.

Hurwitz, Zalkind, champion of Jewish rights in France, 92-93.

Huss, influence of, in Poland, 26.

Hut ha-Meshullash, by Kohn, 244.

Ibn Ezra, Abraham, commentaries on his works, 30, 106.

Ignatiev, Nicholas, 268.

'Illuyim, 47.

Ilye, Manasseh of, Talmudist, 120-121, 125, 132, 134.

Information about the Killing of Christians, etc., by Skripitzyn, 229.

Innocent IV, pope, 253.

Inventions, 201-202.

Israelit, Asher, Maggid, 280.

Israelita, Polish weekly, 247.

Isserles, Moses, rabbi, 50, 78.

Italy, a place of attraction for Russian Jews, 37, 40, 91-92, 126, 165.

Ivan the Terrible, 55-56, 152.

Jacob Isaac, court physician, 39.

Jaffe, Daniel, scholar, 90.

Jaffe, Mordecai (Lebushim), Talmudist, 37, 61, 105.

Jastrow, Marcus, rabbi, 159, 246.

Jekuthiel, Solomon, financier, 204.

Jerusalem, by Mendelssohn, 209.

Jerusalem, pilgrimage to, 65.

Jesuits, in Poland, 54, 58.

Joffe, Mordecai, rabbi, 288.

Joseph ben Isaac Levi, philosopher, 38.
Josephovich, Abraham, statesman, 21-22.
Josephovich, Michael, nobleman, 21-22.
Judah Halevi, poet and philosopher, 28, 98, 106, 284.
Judah Hasid, mystic, founder of the original Hasidim, 65.
Judaizing heresy. See Proselytism.
*Judex Judaeorum*, 44.
Jüdischer Arbeiter, Der, 293.

*Kab ha-Yashar*, referred to, 63.
Kadimah Society, 285.
Kahal, 44; oppression by, 61; denunciation of, 254.
Kalisz, antiquity of, 20.
Kamenetz-Podolsk, antiquity of, 41.
Kant, favorite with Maskilim, 79, 192; on Maimon, 85, 88, 89; referred to, 189.
Kant, the Hebrew, 106.
Kaplan, Wolf, educator, 225.
Karaites, discussions with Rabbanites, 36; with Christians, 37; Nicholas I on, 136.
Katkoff, defends Jews under Alexander II, 225; becomes a reactionary under Alexander III, 269.
Kattowitz, conference of, 285.
Katz, Meïr, Talmudist, 61.
Katzenellenbogen, Hayyim, Talmudist, 40.
Katzenellenbogen, Moses, 40.
Kaufman, Governor-General, convokes conference, 255.
Kertch, Archbishop of, tries to convert Jews, 25.
Kharkov, 286.
Khazars, 18, 20, 25.
Khelm, antiquity of, 20.

Khelm, Ephraim of, liturgist, 35.
Kherson, 28, 142, 144, 160, 292.
Kiev, early settlement of Jews in, 19-20; their influence, 23; proselytism in, 25; Talmudists of, 29, 31; University of, 126; expulsions from, 153; referred to, 200, 226, 227, 275.
Kishinev, 154, 164, 185, 248, 276.
Kissilyef, on emigration, 158.
Klaczke, G., educator, 166.
*Kniga Kahala*, 254-255.
Kobrin, Joseph of, liturgist, 35.
Kohen, Naphtali, rabbi, 34.
Kohen, Shabbataï, rabbi and historian, 35-36.
Kohn's *Hut ha-Meshullash*, 244.
Kol Mebasser, 242.
Königsberg, 33, 79, 90, 120, 126, 132.
*Kontrabandisti*, by Levin, 303.
Körner, on Maimon, 89.
Korobka, 129.
Korolenko's *Skazanye O Florye Rimlyaninye*, 302.
Kovno, Government of, 20; city of, 21; Talmudists of, 34; Maskilim in, 201, 246; Mussarnikes in, 280; referred to, 288, 294.
Kramsztyk, Isaac, rabbi, 247.
Krochmal, Nahman, philosopher, 205.
Krüdener, Baroness, 127, 129, 251.
Kruzhevan, 276.
Kryloff, 175, 189.
Kuritzin, Theodore, proselyte, 26.
Kusselyevsky, physician, 127.

Ladi, Shneor Zalman of, 116, 122-123.
Landau, Ezekiel, rabbi, 78, 133.
Landau, Moses, educator, 164.
Lassalle, 257, 293, 297.

Lebensohn, Abraham Dob Bär, poet, 98, 212, 244.
Leczeka, Abba, " the Glusker Maggid," 132, 302.
Leibnitz, 79, 88.
Leibov, Baruch, martyr, 57.
Lemberg, court of, 44; fair at, 49.
Leo, the court physician, 23, 39, 55.
Lermontoff's spy, 224.
Leroy-Beaulieu, Anatole, on Maimon, 130; on university restrictions, 276-277; referred to, 303.
Lessing, Ephraim, on Israel Zamoscz, 77; on Behr, 90; referred to, 192.
Letteris, Meïr Halevi, poet, 205.
Letzte Nachrichten, 293.
Levanda, Lyev, novelist, 203, 279.
Levin, Judah, merchant, 204.
Levin, Mendel, Hebrew and Yiddish author, 99-101, 116, 119, 195, 217.
Levin's Kontrabandisti, 303.
Levinsohn, I. B., and Haskalah, 13; on the settlement of Jews in Russia, 18; on the effect of Chmielnicki's massacres, 52; his life, 204-213; Te'udah be-Yisraël, 205-207, 209, 210, 221; Efes Dammim, 208, 213; Bet Yehudah, 209-210; Zerubbabel, 210-211, 213; referred to, 219-220.
Liboschüts, Jacob, physician and philanthropist, 91.
Liboschüts, Osip Yakovlevich, court physician, 126.
Lichtenstadt, Moses, communal worker, 165.
Lieberman, Aaron (" Arthur Freeman "), socialist, 256.
Lieven, Prince Emanuel, 209.
Lilien, Ephraim Moses, artist, 291.

Lilienblum, Moses Löb, skeptic, 232-234; attacks the Talmud, 242; repentant, 279; Zionist, 289-290.
Lilienthal, Max, referred to, 14, 117, 151, 164, 183, 277; opens school in Riga, 165, 170; his personality, 171-172; his Maggid Yeshu'ah and his efforts in behalf of Russian Jews, 174-176; his disillusionment, 177-180; his opinion on Russia, 179; how regarded by Maskilim, 172-173, 180-181; on the Jews of Courland, 194; on the Jews of Odessa, 196; his supporters, 198-199, 200; Günzburg on, 216.
Linetzky's Dos Polische Yingel, 242, 244.
" Lishmah " ideal, 107.
Lithuania, Magna Charta of, 21; Jewish merchants of, 22; description by Cardinal Commendoni and by Delmedigo, 24; Talmudic centre, 31-35; status of Jews of, under Ivan the Terrible, 55; after the massacres, 60; opposition to Hasidism in, 65, 69; method of study in, 71-72; inclination to Haskalah in, 105-109; annexed to Russia, 113; Russified, 124-125; colonization in, 143-144, 159; Talmud published in, 148-149; referred to, 195.
Litvack, Judah, deputy, 93.
Livonia, Jewish merchants of, 22; Gentiles remonstrate on behalf of Jews of, 57; stronghold of Haskalah, 193-194.
Loewe, Louis, Orientalist, quoted, 155, 199.
London, 94, 126, 129.

Louis XIV, and the Treaty of Ryswick, 22.
Lover of Enlightenment societies, 165.
Lublin, 31, 34, 40; fair at, 49; Haskalah in, 105.
Lublin, Meïr (Maharam), Talmudist, 72.
Lukas, "the little Jew," 25.
Lullabies, Russo-Jewish, quoted, 46, 309 (n. 39). See also Folk Songs.
Luria, David, philanthropist, 166, 168, 203.
Luria, Solomon, Talmudist, 40; censures the liberality of Isserles, 50; opposes the kahal, 61; his method of study, 72.
Luther's doctrines in Poland, 26.
Luzzatto, Moses Hayyim, poet, 92.
Lyons, Israel, grammarian, 95.

Ma'aseh Tobiah, 42.
Macaulay, on Russian civilization, 310 (n. 6).
McCaul's Old Paths, 146, 211.
Maggid Yeshu'ah, by Lilienthal, 174-176.
Maimon, Solomon, 81-89; quoted, 31, 60, 106; Autobiography, 83, 88; his philosophy, 84-87; his contributions to the Meassef, 98; referred to, 108, 130, 132, 192, 298.
Maimuni, commentators on his Moreh Nebukim, 38, 84, 89; retranslated by Levin, 100; his Mishneh Torah, translated, 186, 200; his Hebrew style, 97.
Malak, Abraham, Hasid, 122.
Malak, Hayyim, Hasid, 65.
Manasseh ben Israel, 32; his Nishmat Hayyim, 63; his activity, 96.

Mandelkern, Solomon, rabbi, 203, 246.
Mandelstamm, Benjamin, on Lilienthal, 173; quoted, 186; on Vilna, 198; and Levinsohn, 212.
Mandelstamm, Leon, graduate from University of St. Petersburg, 186, 200, 252.
Mane, Mordecai Zebi, poet, 98.
Mann, Eliezer, "the Hebrew Socrates," 38.
Mann, Menahem, martyr, 27.
Manoah, Handel, mathematician, 38.
Mapu, Abraham, novelist, 244-245.
Margolioth, Judah Löb, rabbi, 105, 125.
Markusevich, Isaac, physician, 127.
Marx, Karl, his teachings promulgated, 256; his name assumed, 257.
Masliansky, Zebi Hirsh, Maggid, 280.
May laws, 270-275.
Meassef, contributors to, 98-100; condemned, 132; referred to, 265.
Megillah 'Afah, 36.
Meisels, Berish, rabbi, 246.
Melammedim, in Germany, 35, 78, 80; in Russia, 47, 294.
Memorbuch of Mayence, 29.
Mendelssohn, Meyer, communal worker, 140.
Mendelssohn, Moses (Rambman, "Dessauer"), appealed to by Mitnaggedim, 75; his contact with Russiam Jews, 76-78; his friends and followers, 81-90, 135; his philosophy, 88; referred to, 92; presumed to be author of Sefer ha-Berit, 102; his translation of the Pentateuch, 78, 81, 105, 132, 133,

203; post-Mendelssohnian period in Germany, 168; in Russia, 192, 193; his *Jerusalem*, 209; his *Phaedon*, 214; Alexander I's ideal Jew, 128; the " Russian Mendelssohn," 213; Smolenskin and Gottlober on, 265.
Mendlin, Jacob Wolf, socialist, 293.
Meseritz, Bär of, promoter of Hasidism, 65.
*Midrash Talpiyot*, 63.
Mielziner, Leo, on Zionist artists, 291.
Mikhailovich, Czar Aleksey, 40.
Milman, on Maimon's Autobiography, 88.
Minhagim, according to Elijah Vilna, 73-74; according to M. A. Günzburg, 215.
Minor, Solomon Zalkind, " the Russian Jellinek," 235, 236.
Minsk, 21; Talmudists of, 34, persecution of Hasidim in, 76; schools in, 166-167, 292; reception of Lilienthal in, 172, 173; Maskilim of, 200, 201-235, 246; referred to, 292, 293.
Mirabeau's reference to Hurwitz, 92.
Mitau, 123, 216.
Mitauer, Elias, communal worker, 140.
Mitnaggedim, opposition to Hasidism, 70, 131; efforts of, at reconciliation with Hasidim, 120-121; make common cause with Hasidim against Maskilim, 134, 260.
*Mnyenie*, by Dyerzhavin, 118.
Mohilev, 31, 104, 119, 128, 202.
Moldavia, 40-41.
Molo, Francisco, economist, 22.

Montefiore, Sir Moses, visits Russia, 155-157; invited to Russia, 175; entertained, 200; visit of 1872 to Russia, 230; on the pogroms, 270; on Russo-Jewish women, 299.
Morgulis, Manasseh, litterateur, 14, 187-188.
Morschtyn, George, proselyte (?), 26.
*Mosaïde*, by Wessely, 98.
Moscow, proselytism in, 25, 26; expulsions from, 56, 153, 271; Jews admitted to, 111; converts in, 177; Russification in, 240; restrictions in the University of, 274, 276; referred to, 291.
Moses, martyr, 57.
Mussarnikes, 280.
Muzhiks, emancipation of, 222-223; education of, 236-237; restlessness of, 249-250; socialism among, 257.
Mylich, George Gottfried, Lutheran champion of Jewish rights, 113-114.

Nachlass, Wolf, Cantonist, 139.
Napoleon, convokes the Sanhedrin, 93; his invasion of Russia, 112, 113; his defeat, 115-117, 128; on Vilna, 197.
Narodnaya Volya Society, 257, 278.
Narodniki, 236-237.
Nazimov, Governor-General, champion of Jews, 201, 225.
Nebakhovich, Alexander, theatrical director, 201.
Nebakhovich, Leon (Löb), first defender of Russian Jews in Russian, 114, 125, 130; dramatist, 189.

Nebakhovich, Michael, editor of comic paper, 201.
Nemirov, 59.
Nemirov, Jehiel Michael of, scholar, 35.
Nestor's Chronicles, 20.
Nicholas I, referred to, 104, 202, 222, 229, 246, 249, 253, 260, 268, 284; his policy, 135-160; his recruiting, 135-139; his colonization scheme, 140-143; attempts at conversion of Jews, 144-147, 188; his Exportation Law, 152-154; his accusations refuted, 162-164; investigates number of learned Jews, 167, 168, 198; outwitted, 184; on Jews of Odessa, 196.
Nicholas II, referred to, 80, 192; persecution of Jews under, 275-277.
Nieszvicz, 82, 114, 118, 127, 197.
Nisanovich, Itshe, physician, 39.
Nishmat Hayyim, by Manasseh ben Israel, 63.
Noah, Mordecai Manuel, statesman, 284.
Nomenclature, Russo-Jewish, 30.
Notkin, Nathan, diplomat and philanthropist, 118, 125.
Novgorod, 25, 139, 271.
Novy Israil Society, 248.

Odessa, schools in, 164, 185; Lilienthal in, 176; Jewish influences in, 194-197; Talmud Torah of, 226; Haskalah in, 233-235; Russification of, 240, 246, 255; assimilation in, 248; pogromy in, 253; referred to, 251, 292, 294, 295, 296; Jewish women of, 299-300.
'Olam Katan, 297.
Old Paths, by McCaul, 146, 211.
Ostrog, 44, 206.

Pale, the Jewish, 188, 199, 271, 274.
Palestine, rehabilitation of, 13; settlers from, in Russia, 18, 27; longing for, 153, 283; Smolenskin on, 263-264.
Parlovich, Arthur, physician, 126.
Patapov, Governor-General, convokes a conference, 259.
Paul I, 62, 111, 112.
Paul III, pope, 253.
Pechersky, St. Feodosi, 25.
Peretz, Abraham, diplomat, 118, 125, 130.
Peretz, Gregori, Dekabrist, 192, 249, 284.
Perl, Joseph, educator, 163, 164, 205.
Perl, S., educator, 166.
Persia, immigrants from, 19.
Peter the Great, conquers the Tatars, 54; his attempts to civilize Russia, 56; surrender of Riga to, 123.
Phaedon, by Mendelssohn, 214.
Philippson, Ludwig, rabbi, 154, 158, 175.
Phillips, Phinehas, founder of the Anglo-Jewish family, 94.
Pinczows, the, scholars, 104-105.
Pinner, Ephraim Moses, Talmudist, 145.
Pinsk, 76, 197, 202, 242.
Pinsker, Leo, nationalist, 263, 281-283.
Pinsker, Simhah, scholar, 108-109, 164, 195.
Pirogov, Nikolai Ivanovich, liberal school superintendent, 226-228.
Plehve, von, on restrictions, 302.
Plungian, Ezekiel Feivel, Talmudist, 119, 203.

Pobyedonostsev, influences Alexander II, 250-251; procurator of the Holy Synod, 269; his policy regarding Jews, 270; on Jewish superiority, 273.

Podolia, 60, 64, 69, 162, 195, 277.

Pogodin, on early Russian Jews, 19.

Pogromy, 253, 269-270.

Poimaniki, 136-138, 152, 162, 184.

Poimshchiki, 137.

Polack, Jacob, Talmudist, 72, 104.

Poland, early settlement of Jews in, 20; political eminence of, 22-23; proselytism in, 26; after Chmielnicki's massacres, 53-55; influence of Calvinism in, 56-57; during the rozbior, 58; after the annexation, 113; Jewish loyalty to, 115-116; under Nicholas I, 158-159; use of Polish in, 196; sympathy with, and adoption of language of, 246-247.

Polonnoy, Jacob Joseph of, follower of Besht, 65; his *Toledot Ya'akob Yosef* burnt in Vilna, 76; mentioned, 122, 132.

Polotsk, 55, 95.

Poltava, 200, 239, 300.

Popes, 72, 253.

Posner, Solomon, philanthropist, 143-144.

Pototzki, Count Valentine, proselyte, 27.

Prayer book. See Book of Common Prayer.

Prelooker, Jacob, 241-242, 248.

Printing-press, permission to establish, 110; first publications from, 124; restrictions removed from use of, 230.

Prochovnik, Abraham, Jewish king of Poland (?), 22.

Proselytism, 18, 20, 24-28.

Public schools, admission of Jews to, 111, 118, 125; exclusion of Jews from, 273-275.

Pumpyansky, Aaron Elijah, rabbi, 203, 246.

Pushkin's prisoner, 224.

Querido, Jacob, mystic, 64.

Rabbinical seminaries, 144-145, 165, 170, 173, 182, 196, 202-203.

Rabbis, position of, in Russo-Poland, 44-45; required to know Russian, German, or Polish, 125; opposed by Maskilim, 173; Lilienthal on, 174, 181; Günzburg on, 216-217, dukhovny and kazyony, 295-296.

Rabinovich, Osip, litterateur, 201, 238, 243.

Rabinowitz, Joseph, assimilationist, 248.

Rachmailovich, Affras, merchant, 22.

Radziwill, Prince, 24, 39, 62.

Rapoport, Solomon Löb, rabbi, 205.

Rasiner, Israel, zaddik, 211.

Raskolniki, 248.

Rathaus, Abraham, merchant, 200.

Razsvyet, 238, 243-244, 286.

Reform Judaism, and the Haskalah, 242-248; sermons in Russian, 246; Smolenskin on, 264-265.

Reform synagogues, in Odessa, 196; in Warsaw, 197; in Vilna, 198.

Reines, Isaac Jacob, rabbi, 295.

Reis, Joseph, grandfather of Wessely, 77.

Revolutionaries, 192, 248-251, 255-258.

Riesser, Gabriel, champion of Jewish emancipation, 78.

Riga, 123, 164, 170, 180, 185, 195, 197, 225, 246, 271.

Risenci, Jonathan of, rabbi, 104.

Rivkes, Moses, commentator, 34.

Romm, Menahem Mann, publisher, 148-149.

Rosensohn, Joseph, rabbi, 127.

Rosensohn, Moses, reformer, 247.

Rosenthal, Leon, financier, 200, 237-238.

Rothschild, Baron Edmund de, 288.

Rurik, Varangian prince, 19.

Russia, Haskalah in, contrasted with Haskalah in Galicia and Germany, 12; arrival of German Jews in, 18; antiquity of Jews in, 19; privileges of Jews in, 21; Jewish envoys to, 22; mentioned by medieval scholars, 28-29; Sefardim and Ashkenazim resort to, 33-34; scientists in, 37-39; physicians in, 39-42; status of Jews of, before Chmielnicki's uprising, 42-45; Jewish self-government, school system, and mode of living in, 45-52; under Ivan the Terrible, 55-56; under Peter the Great, 56; under Elizabeta Petrovna, 57; state of civilization of, 60, 107; favorable conditions in, under Catherine II, Paul I, and Alexander I, 110-128; Jewish patriotism toward, under Alexander I, 117; Russification of Jews of, 124-125; opposition to Haskalah in, 133 f.; Jewish colonization in, 140-144; crusade against the Talmud in, 145-147; opinions of prominent Gentiles on Jews of, 162, 224-225; literature and civilization of, under Nicholas I, 189-190; under Alexander II, 222-226; Jewish contribution to civilization of, 201-202, 255; sermons in, 246; defenders of Jews in, 302-303; Macaulay on civilization of. 310 (n. 6).

Sack, Hayyim, financier, 200.

Sackheim, Joseph, merchant, 200.

Safah Berurah, by Hannover, 39.

St. Petersburg, Imperial Hermitage in, 19; scene of martyrdom, 57; referred to, 91, 104, 267, 276, 286, 300; Jews permitted in, 111, 117, 126; expelled from, 128, 153, 271; deputation to, 129; rabbinical conferences, 151, 173, 174-176, 230; converts in, 177; first graduate of University of, 200; restriction of students in, 274; Russification in, 240; revolutionaries at, 258.

Salanter, Israel, rabbi, 241.

Samuel ben Avigdor, rabbi, 79.

Samuel ben Mattathias, Talmudist, 40.

Sanchez, Antonio Ribeiro, physician, 57.

Sanhedrin, the, and French Russian Jews, 93.

Satanov, Isaac Halevi, litterateur, 99, 217.

Schapira, Moses, publisher, 148.

Schapiro, Constantin, poet, 98.

Schechter, Solomon, on Hasidism, 69.

Schick, Baruch (Shklover), scientist, 94, 96, 105-106, 119, 125.

# INDEX

Schiller, on Maimon, 89; referred to, 192.
Schools, secular, 163-165, 182-185, 195-196, 227-228, 229, 235, 239, 253, 273-274, 276-277, 290-292, 297.
*Sefer ha-Berit*, 102.
Seiberling, Joseph, censor of Hebrew books, 200.
Shabbataï Zebi, pseudo-Messiah, 64, 69.
Shalkovich, Abraham Löb (Ben Avigdor), 296.
Shatzkes' *Ha-Mafteah*, 244.
Shavli, Moses of, writer of polemics, 36.
*Shibhe ha-Besht*, 123, 134.
Shklov, 105, 124.
Shkud, Mikel of, rabbi, 61.
Shneersohn, Menahem Mendel, zaddik, 175, 176.
Shmoilovich, Abraham, merchant, 22.
*Shulhan 'Aruk*, commentators on, 34, 36; its effect on Jewish life, 73; Elijah Vilna on, 74; criticism of, 123; annotations to, 127; referred to, 215.
Siberia, 140-143, 160.
*Sin'at 'Olam le-'Am 'Olam*, 280-281.
Sixtus V, pope, 72.
*Skazanye O Florye Rimlyaninye*, by Korolenko, 302.
Skripitzyn's *Information about the Killing of Christians*, etc., 229.
Slonim, Samson of, rabbi, 106.
Slonimsky, Hayyim Selig, inventor and editor, 199, 200, 201-202, 203.
Slutsk, 76, 105, 202.
" Slutsker Maggid, the," 246.
Smolensk, 21, 162.

Smolenskin, Perez, and Haskalah, 13; his descriptions of the heder and yeshibah, 50, 266; his life, 261-267; his conception of Haskalah, 261; on nationalism, 262-263, 284; on reformers, 264-265; attacks Mendelssohn, 265; on the prophetic consciousness of the Jewish masses, 266-267; his popularity, 267; organizes the Kadimah, 285; opposes the Alliance Israélite Universelle, 285.
Sobieski, John, 39.
Society for the Promotion of Haskalah among the Russian Jews, 237-239, 246, 252, 291-292.
Sofer, Moses, rabbi, 133.
Sofer, Shabbataï, rabbi, 36.
Sokolov, Nahum, publicist, 280.
Sosima, monkish proselyte, 26.
Spector, Isaac Elhanan, rabbi, 288.
Speir, Bima, of Mohilev, opponent of Frank, 104.
Spinoza and Maimon compared, 86, 88.
Stern, Abraham Jacob, inventor, 201.
Stern, Bezalel (Basilius), pedagogue, 164, 165, 175, 176.
Strashun, Mattathias, Talmudist, 203.
Surovyetsky, on Russian Jews, 162, 318 (n. 1).
Switzerland, 257, 298, 299, 300.
*Talmud, Der, in seiner Nichtigkeit*, by Buchner, 146.
Talmud, the, the study of, 31, 71-72; burnt in public, 70; customs of, according to Elijah Gaon, 74; attacks on, 145-

147, 170, 242-248; published in Russia, 147-149; neglected in Germany, 168.

Talmud Torah, the, 47, 184.

Talmudists, ancient Russo-Jewish, 28-30; opposed by Hasidism, 66; in Vilna, 197-198.

Tarnopol, on Russo-Jewish women, 299-300.

Taz, David, rabbi, 34.

Temkin's *Derek Salulah*, 146.

*Te'udah be-Yisraël*, by Levinsohn, 205-207, 209, 210, 212.

*Toledot Ya'akob Yosef*, by Jacob Joseph Polonnoy, 65.

Tolstoi, 245, 250, 302.

Troki, city, 22.

Troki, Abraham, author and physician, 39.

Troki, Isaac ben Abraham, Karaite scholar, 36.

Turgenief, on Russia, 224; his *Zhid*, 224; referred to, 245, 250; on Alexander II, 251; his *Virgin Soil*, and *Fathers and Sons*, 257; his Lithuanian Jewish character, 259-260.

Tushiyah Society, 296-297.

Ukraine, the, Jewish community in, 20; famous for scholars, 35-36; Jewish self-government in, 44; expulsions from, 56-57; state of morality in, 64; Hasidism in, 69, 122; first school in, 164.

Uman, 59, 164.

United States, the, 158, 220, 270, 283.

Uvarov, on persecution, 155, 302; on "re-education," 171, 174, 175, 182.

Vassile Lupu, hospodar of Moldavia, 40.

Vassilyevich, Ivan, 23, 26.

Vernacular, the, 18, 29, 30-31, 38, 188, 194, 255.

Vilna, scene of martyrdom, 27; Talmudists of, 34; kahal of, 62; persecution of Hasidim, 76; the last rabbi of, 79; notables of, 91, 92, 124, 150; first graduates from University of, 126-127; opposition to Haskalah in, 133; first publication of the Talmud in, 148-149; first assembly of Maskilim in, 165; innovations in, 166; reception of Lilienthal in, 172, 173; rabbinical seminary at, 175, 186, 202; yeshibot of, 197; Haskalah in, 198, 200, 206, 246; champions of Jews in, 225; referred to, 230, 292, 295.

*Virgin Soil*, by Turgenief, 257.

Vital, Hayyim, Cabbalist, 103, 134.

Vitebsk, 128, 202, 292.

Vitebsk, Menahem Mendel of, zaddik, on Haskalah, 135.

Vladimir, grand duke, 20.

Volhynia, jurisdiction over, 44; massacres in, 60; Hasidism in, 69, 81, 104; first complete edition of the Talmud published in, 148; referred to, 162, 195; blood accusations in, 208.

Volozhin, Hayyim, dean, 135, 150-151, 175, 176.

Volozhin, Isaac of, dean, 151.

Volozhin, yeshibah of, 150-152, 245, 295.

Vosnitzin, Captain, martyr, 27, 57.

Wahl, Saul, Jewish Polish king (?), 22.

Warsaw, Jewish community in, 20; persecution in, 58; protest at, 62; defended by Jewish soldiers, 115; first Yiddish paper in, 124; rabbinic college of, 144-145, 170, 202; censor in, 148; condition of, 159; German influence in, 196; Maskilim of, 202, 206, 246; referred to, 286.

Way, Lewis, English missionary, 129-130, 144.

Weigel, Katharina, proselyte, 27.

Wengeroff's Memoirs, 163; on Russo-Jewish women, 300.

Wessely, Naphtali Hartwig, quoted, 38; course of study prescribed by, 75; his ancestry, 77; his opinion on Russo-Jewish students, 80, 92, 108; his Mosaïde, 98; his Yen Lebanon, 105; his Epistles and Yen Lebanon banned, 132, 133, 192.

What to Do, by Chernichevsky, 257.

White, on Jewish farmers, 288.

Wissotzky, Kalonymos, philanthropist, 292.

Wohl, censor of Hebrew books, 252, 294.

Wolf, Levy, jurist, 126.

Wolff's Metaphysics, 84-86; Mathematics, 90, 108.

Wolper, Michael, educator, 294.

Women's education, 45-46, 253, 258, 259, 276, 296, 299-301.

Words of Peace and Truth, by Wessely, 75.

Workingmen, Russo-Jewish, 163, 293-294, 318 (n. 2).

Yankele Kovner. See Barit, Jacob.

Yaroslav, fair of, 49.

Yaroslav, Aaron, friend of Mendelssohn, 81.

Yavan, Baruch, diplomat, 104.

Yelisavetgrad, 247, 269, 292.

Yen Lebanon, by Wessely, 105, 132, 133, 192.

Yeralash, 201.

Yeshibat 'Ez Hayyim, 150-152, 175, 184, 254.

Yeshibot, 32, 46-49, 168.

Yeven Mezulah, by Hannover, 48-49.

Yiddish, as spoken by Russian Jews, 38; first used for secular instruction, 100-101, 124; first weekly in, 123, 196; studied for missionary purposes, 145; employed by Maskilim, 167, 232; by Zionists, 286.

Zabludovsky, Jehiel Michael, Talmudist, 199.

Zacharias, monkish proselyte, 26.

Zacharias of Kiev, missionary, 25.

Zaddikim, 66, 122, 220.

Zamoscz, city, 90, 202.

Zamoscz, Israel Moses Halevi, instructor of Mendelssohn, 77, 90, 195.

Zamoscz, Reuben of, quoted, 80.

Zamoscz, Solomon of, liturgical poet, 35.

Zangwill, on Maimon, 88; referred to, 297.

Zaremba, proselyte, 27.

Zaslav, fair of, 49; blood accusation in, 208.

Zaslaver, Jacob, Massorite, 36.

Zbitkover, Samuel, financier, 116.

Zederbaum, Alexander, publisher, 288.

Zeitlin, Joshua, financier, 118-119.

Zeker Rab, 124.

Zelmele, Talmudist, 119-120.

# INDEX

*Zerubbabel*, by Levinsohn, 210-212, 213.

Zhagory, 200, 202.

Zhitomir, rabbinical seminary at, 175, 186, 197, 202, 248; printing-press in, 230; trade school in, 235; Evening and Sabbath schools in, 239.

Zionism, 267, 284-287; difficulties of, 287-288; effect of, 289-291.

*Zohar*, 63, 134.

Zunser, Eliakum, badhan, on Alexander II, 231; on Orthodoxy, 240-241; on the "intelligentia," 278; on Zionism, 290; on the awakening, 324-327 (n. 27).

The Lord Baltimore Press
BALTIMORE, MD., U. S. A.

Printed in the United States
70974LV00002B/56